How to Use
the Library

How to Use the Library

A Reference and Assignment Guide for Students

FRANK FERRO
NOLAN LUSHINGTON

GREENWOOD PRESS
Westport, Connecticut • London

√MAI 435·465𝑟

Library of Congress Cataloging-in-Publication Data

Ferro, Frank, 1948–
   How to use the library : a reference and assignment guide for
students / Frank Ferro, Nolan Lushington.
      p.   cm.
   Includes bibliographical references and indexes.
   ISBN 0–313–30107–7 (alk. paper)
   1. Reference books—Bibliography—Juvenile literature.
   2. Reference sources—United States—Catalogs—Juvenile literature.
   3. Library research—United States—Juvenile literature.
   I. Lushington, Nolan, 1929–   . II. Title.
   Z1035.1.F47   1998
   011'.02—DC21   97–48581

British Library Cataloguing in Publication Data is available.

Library of Congress Catalog Card Number: 97–48581
ISBN: 0–313–30107–7

First published in 1998

Greenwood Press, 88 Post Road West, Westport, CT 06881
An imprint of Greenwood Publishing Group, Inc.

Printed in the United States of America

The paper used in this book complies with the
Permanent Paper Standard issued by the National
Information Standards Organization (Z39.48–1984).

10 9 8 7 6 5 4 3 2

Contents

Acknowledgments

Many people have contributed to this book in a variety of ways.

Suzanne Bush, reference librarian at the Norwalk, Connecticut, Public Library, was invaluable in her assistance with the literature research chapter on Charlotte Brontë.

William Newport was extremely helpful with the annotations for the religious and history books.

Leatrice Fountain was very helpful in selecting and annotating computer books and books on sports.

Students in my reference and humanities resources courses at the Department of Library Science and Instructional Technology at Southern Connecticut State University contributed many suggestions on material to be included, and they clearly demonstrated the value of Thomas Mann's research methodology.

Thomas Mann's book, *Library Research Models,* was the inspiration for the multilayered research model used in the sample literature and history searches. This wonderful book clearly shows the variety of methods available for modern researchers and places these models in a timeless perspective for future use. It should be required reading for every library school student.

—Nolan Lushington

My wife, Susan, son, Alden, and daughter, Janine, graciously allowed me the time to work on this project, and then put up with my complaints.

My many coworkers at Norwalk Public Library, especially those in the Reference Department, and most significantly the library's director, Les Kozerowitz, supported and encouraged me.

Amy Terlaga's Internet and computer expertise is much appreciated. Amy is Internet Trainer for Bibliomation, Inc., Stratford, Connecticut.

Thanks to Emily Birch, a great, patient, and creative editor, and to the many members of the advisory panel who guided our efforts: Robert Birch, Mary Freedman, Kathy Golomb, Marlene Melcher, Vera Skop, Rachel Wheeler, and Linda Wilson.

—Frank Ferro

Introduction

This book was developed at the suggestion of Greenwood Press editor Emily Birch. Her research showed several things:

1. Many middle and high school students need to learn how to perform library book and computerized research. They need to learn how libraries are organized and how to use card catalogs or computerized catalogs. They need to learn how an atlas, an almanac, and an encyclopedia differ and the different functions these resources perform.

2. There is a core of reference resources common to most public and many school libraries.

3. Many grade-level homework and term paper assignments around the country are quite similar and cover the same basic body of knowledge.

4. No current book publication attempts to explain to students how a library is organized, how to find information resources in the library, or how to use its computerized resources. No current book publication attempts to list core resources that students will find helpful in completing homework and school assignments and annotates them with the students' needs in mind. No current book publication seeks to connect the student from the homework assignment subject or term paper topic to the resources most likely to help complete those assignments successfully.

At Birch's suggestion, we set out to write a book for student, parent, and librarian use that would improve student performance by teaching in an easy-to-use and -understand book the importance of library research in school careers, teach them how a library is organized and how to use its tools for successful completion of library research, list and annotate common core resources most likely to help students in successful completion of homework and term paper assignments, and connect the students directly to those resources through a unique keyword index in which they can recognize their own questions, topics, and homework and term paper assignments.

The book is organized into three parts. Part One explains the importance of library research and teaches how to use the library. Part Two lists and annotates core library reference resources by subject. It is organized alphabetically by subject, which aids in use of that section. Dewey Decimal numbers are provided within chapters, by subject, as another way of sending students to the correct subject area of the library. Part Three is the keyword index that connects the student via typical homework and term paper assignment questions to the resources most likely to help answer those questions.

We selected a reference source based on whether we thought it would help in the completion of common homework and term paper assignments. Other criteria included whether the resource was well reviewed, is commonly found in libraries, is on a list of librarians' favorite resources or on a list of "best resources" for a particular year or subject, or is listed in other library reference resource bibliographies (see the Bibliography at the end of this book).

Reference librarians often develop favorite resources for answering certain types of questions. A resource they use again and again because it always holds the answer they need, is well indexed or clearly written and easily understood, or well illustrated becomes a favorite. Over the years, they take a generation of students to the same resources. One reason is that teachers repeat their assignments, sometimes with small variations, for each new class each year. Reference librarians recognize the assignments as well as know the resources most likely to help students complete those assignments. We hope we have included most of these resources throughout Part Two of this book.

PART I

An Introduction to the Library

CHAPTER 1

Researching Class Assignments

Every teacher assigns research projects during the school year. Sometimes these are individual assignments, sometimes group assignments. Often teachers assign projects that make students pull in information from several different subject areas. These are called **interdisciplinary assignments**. They help students understand how knowledge can be used and that knowledge from one field can be applied to another. They may help the students broaden their understanding, learning, for example, that a specific event did not occur in a vacuum but within a broader historical context of time and place. Ultimately they help students learn by making the project more interesting and more of a challenge. Group projects also teach teamwork.

When students are trying to find information to complete a project, often one reference source is not enough. Most teachers want three at least. Some teachers will not accept encyclopedias as sources; others limit their use to one or two encyclopedias at most. Usually teachers require at least one book, a magazine article, and a newspaper article, and sometimes a **primary source** listed on the project's **bibliography.** More complex projects require more sources.

Here's an example of a project: Write a five-page paper describing the atom, its history, discovery, component parts, and role in science today.

Here's an interdisciplinary project: Write a five-page paper as above. Write a diary from the viewpoint of one of the scientists involved in discovering the atom. Build a model of an atom (a mobile, for example). List major events that occurred around the world at the time the atom was discovered. These can be political or social events, or events in the arts, sports, or sciences. Include some of each. List the rulers of at least one country on each continent at the time. Put on a brief skit dramatizing the effect of manipulating the atom on world culture.

How do you begin to research these assignments? Where do you go? Will someone help you? There's only one place to go: the library. You might start with your school library and will probably need to go to the public library in your area. You may need to go to other libraries too. Librarians will help you find the sources you need. They won't do the work for you, though. Here's why:

LEARNING TAKES WORK

Knowledge is an intellectual pursuit. It doesn't pop into your brain instantly. All knowledge, even physical knowledge, involves the intellect. Gaining knowledge of any kind takes time, effort, work, discipline, and practice. Research projects are mental exercises and skill developers.

When you find information in books or through a computer using a **CD-ROM** or **online database**, or through the **Internet**, you have to read, absorb, interpret, digest, understand, and then write it or speak it, or both, in your own words. This is how learning and understanding take place and become meaningful.

LIBRARIES ARE EXCITING

What's in a library? Everything! And, today, it is in every format possible. Libraries house all recorded history, all knowledge as we know it, from before humans to the present—all sciences, literature, philosophy, religion, anything and everything that is known, has been known, that you want to know. Information, education, and recreation are available in books, on audiotapes and videocassettes, audio compact disks (CDs), CD-ROM disks (used on computers), and online information services (used with computers) including what we're being told holds the answer to everything—what some people refer to as the Information Highway, the Internet.

CHAPTER 2

Navigating the Library

HOW IT'S ORGANIZED

When you walk into a **public library**, you will notice that it is arranged into several basic sections: the **children's department** (up to about age 12 or sixth grade) and the **adult department** (age 12 and up). Some libraries also have a **young adult section** or **department** with materials specifically for ages 12 to 18. Each of these has **circulating** (fiction and nonfiction) and **noncirculating** (reference and usually magazine and newspaper) sections. **Fiction** books tell stories. **Nonfiction** books state fact and opinion. *Circulating* means you may borrow the books with your library card, you may not borrow noncirculating books, but you may use them in the library to take notes or photocopy what you need. That way the books will be available for other library users when they need them. Different sections may sometimes be found on different floors.

New Books

If the book is brand new, it may be in another sequence with the other new books, often on display shelves near the entrance or the checkout desk. These books are usually marked with a spine sticker that clearly says "NEW."

Special Displays

Libraries often have special display areas. During Black History Month (February), for example, many of the library's materials on this topic are removed from their normal sequence and grouped together in a display area, often located at the entrance to the library or near the new materials.

Fiction

Adult fiction is usually organized according to the author's last name. Frequently libraries divide fiction into categories: general fiction, mysteries, science fiction, westerns, and romance novels, for example. These smaller groupings make it easier for people who like reading mysteries, for example, to find the authors and titles they're interested in. Each grouping is organized alphabetically by author's last name. **Children's fiction** is usually organized in a similar fashion, but frequently the subgroups are arranged by reading level: picture books, easy readers (for beginners), novels for children ages 6 to 12, and sometimes by type of novel (horse stories, for example).

THE DEWEY DECIMAL SYSTEM: NONFICTION AND REFERENCE

Most public libraries, except for the very largest, organize their nonfiction and reference collections according to the **Dewey Decimal system**. This system organizes books by subject, giving each book its own **call number**; by consulting a catalog or index, you can be directed to the precise spot on a shelf where the book you want is located. It's like an address for the book. The book lives in a "subject neighborhood" near other books on that subject, yet it has its own individual address. Usually no two books have the same address.

The **call number** is the number in the upper left corner of the **catalog card**, or the number given on the **online public access computer (OPAC)** catalog screen, which matches the number printed on the spine of the book. Reference books usually are designated by "R" or "REF" (a prefix) printed above or before the Dewey classification number. Circulating books usually have no prefix before the number, though some libraries use prefixes other than "R" or "REF" to designate separate collections.

There are other systems for organizing books by subject. The **Library of Congress System** is most common, especially in college and large libraries. The Dewey Decimal System is based on **numbers,** with each number corresponding to a subject. The Library of Congress system is based on **letters,** with each letter corresponding to a subject. There are other differences. Since most junior and high school students encounter the Dewey Decimal system in school and medium-sized public libraries, we'll concentrate on that. Here is the basic subject table for

Dewey, the "hundreds" table, with the Library of Congress (LC) letters in parentheses:

000 Generalities (A)
100 Philosophy, Psychology (B, BF)
200 Religion (BL-BX)
300 Social Science (H)
400 Language (PA-PG)

500 Science (Q)
600 Technology (T)
700 Arts, Sports (N, M, GV)
800 Literature (PQ-PT)
900 Countries, Travel, History (G, E, F)

NAVIGATING

Finding your way in a library is a skill that will open pathways to information power. There are three basic ways to search for materials in the library. One is to **browse** by walking up and down the book aisles looking for what you want or find interesting. The second is to go to the **card** or **public access (computerized) catalog** and look up specific authors, titles, or subjects. The third is to ask the **reference (information) librarian** for help.

To browse, it helps to know what you're browsing for and where that subject is most likely shelved. Say you have to write a report on atoms. You should know from your schoolwork, that the study of atoms is a scientific study. The basic number for science, as indicated in the list above, is 500. But *science* is a very broad term, a broad topic, and there are many smaller subdivisions of science. There are chemistry, physics, biology, and geology for starters. These really are large topics but fall within the general subject of science. So where in the 500s do you go for books on atoms? Each of the first ten divisions named above breaks down further. Here's the second breakdown, the "tens," indicated by the middle number, for the sciences (the 500s):

500 Science Generalities
510 Mathematics
520 Astronomy
530 Physics
540 Chemistry

550 Earth Science
560 Paleontology
570 Life Sciences
580 Botanical sciences
590 Zoology

You need to know a little about atoms to find in which division the study of atoms may fall. If you don't know, a quick look in an encyclopedia will tell you that physics includes the study of atoms, among other things. So you could browse in the 530s, which breaks down further into a third division, signified by the third number on the right, the "ones":

530 Physics Generalities	535 Light
531 Mechanics	536 Heat
532 Mechanics of Fluids	537 Electricity and Electronics
533 Mechanics of Gases	538 Magnetism
534 Sound	539 Modern Physics

If you think the study of atoms is, according to Dewey, a modern study, you're right. The number 539 is the place to browse.

The entire Dewey Decimal system works like this. Each general category is broken down further and more specifically with related topics. The **decimal point** is placed after the third number. There are charts and tables that add numbers after the decimal point breaking the subject down further and further, more and more specifically.

The larger the library is, the more books it will have in each category, so it helps to have an idea of what the most specific number is for your subject when you want to browse. Most libraries have Dewey Decimal guide cards, or signs, stack end labels, and shelf labels to help you find the subject area you want to browse in.

Understanding the Dewey Decimal system speeds your research. (See Appendixes A and B for listings of the Dewey and LC systems.) Nothing is perfect, however, and Dewey does contain some quirks, or at least some "arrangements" to understand. For instance, books on the science of electricity and electronics are located in 537. But books on the technology or applied science (600s) of electricity and electronics are located in Engineering (620s) at 621.3815. Repair of home wiring and electrical appliances is located at 643.6, electrical motors at 621.46.

You don't have to remember all this because every library indexes its collections—all its materials in all formats—in one or more card catalogs or electronically on computerized catalogs.

LIBRARY CATALOGS: INDEXES TO COLLECTIONS

Computerized catalogs were developed from card catalogs. Computerized catalogs are better in many ways because they can do things that can't be done with cards (more on this below). Cards can be flipped through faster than can electronic records, however, and they don't break down, though sometimes cards are filed in the wrong place or people pull them out instead of writing down the information.

For every book, several catalog cards are made. Each has the same information except the heading. The body of the card describes the book: author, title, place of publication, publisher, date of publication, number of pages, size in centimeters, whether illustrated or including photos, and subject headings assigned (ATOMS, for example). This is called the **bibliographic record**.

A **call number** is assigned to the book (539, for example), and an author code, often based on the first three letters of the author's last name, is added to it (539 ASI, for Isaac Asimov, for example). This number is printed on a label attached to the spine of the book, and the number is printed in the upper left corner of every catalog card made for the book.

A card is produced for the title; one for the author or authors (up to three); one for each subject heading (usually between one and five); and a control card for use of the librarians. The control card is filed in the librarian's work area. The remaining cards are filed alphabetically in a public catalog. Some libraries interfile all cards. Others file author and title cards in one file and subject cards in another catalog file. Some libraries interfile cards for all materials; others separate cards for books in one file and for audiovisual materials (audio and videotapes, LPs and CDs) in another.

In the computer, this same basic information is provided. The access points are the same. You can search by author, title, and subject. On most systems you can also search by call number—all the 539s, for example. On many systems you can search by **keyword** too, and by combining terms. For example, you could search for all the books written by anyone with the name "Asimov" and the word "atom" anywhere in the bibliographic record. This is a great advantage, especially when looking for materials with uncommon subject entries or when you can remember only part of a title, for example.

Whether you look up books in the card catalog or in the OPAC, whether you look them up by author, title, subject, or keyword, the information you find for each book will be the same: books on atoms are cataloged at 539.7. This is the number area to browse for more information on atoms. You should browse both the circulating and the reference sections.

When you're walking the shelves, looking for a specific address or call number, it helps to know the sequence in which the numbers are shelved. The number 539 would come after 538 and before 540, of course. Likewise 539.7 comes after 539 and before 540; 539.1026 would come after 539.1 and before 539.7 even though it seems, at first glance, like a bigger number than 539.7. Dewey numbers are treated just like decimals, where 539.7 is bigger than 539.1026, which is bigger than 539.1. Put another way, Dewey numbers are shelved number by number from left to right, both before and after the decimal point. The same is true for author and letter codes; for example, 539.7 ASI comes before 539.7 LET, but 539.1 LET comes before 539.7 ASI. Here's a sample sequence in order:

538.972 KRA
539.1 LET
539.1026 BRI
539.7 ASI
540 JAR

There are some other points about using the public library that you should know and understand before we take a brief look at the research options.

USE THE RIGHT LIBRARY

Not all libraries are the same. There are four basic types: **school, academic, public,** and **special.**

School and **academic (college and university) libraries** have the same general purpose: to support the coursework in the school or college. A library at a college that concentrates on business courses and degrees offers materials primarily on business topics. A library at a medical school offers materials primarily on health, medicine, nursing, biology, and related scientific topics. An engineering school offers materials that support coursework on mechanics, technology, engineering, mathematics, and related sciences. If you need to research property law, for example, a medical library won't yield the best results.

School libraries generally support classes taught in the high school, middle school, or elementary school. Unfortunately, many public school libraries are poorly supplied and contain outdated materials. Some public libraries are in this same, underfunded boat. Encyclopedias from the 1950s can still be found in some school libraries despite the fact that the information is out of date, biased, and/or inaccurate, not to mention missing 40 years of change in all fields.

Public libraries, being public, try to serve all people with all needs, from cradle to grave. They must provide materials that support the coursework in all public and private schools in their immediate geographic area. They must provide for the general reading interests of children and adults. They must meet the information needs of businesses and government. They must provide consumer product information, legal and health information, materials related to the daily lives of everyone: how to sew a dress, collect coins, repair a car, fix a doorbell, build a house, decorate a baby's room, cut hair, lessen stress, use a computer, and so on. A mechanic wants a shop manual, a secretary wants to improve stenography, a student investigates careers, a laid-off worker wants to produce a resumé, a Bible student is researching a fine point in the Old Testament. Public libraries do a pretty fair job of being all things to all people, but it is difficult, and librarians sometimes feel the impossibility of such a task and think they should concentrate on specific areas of strength.

Special libraries do concentrate on specific areas of interest. Special libraries come in all types. Corporate or business libraries concentrate on subjects related to their particular concerns. A pharmaceutical company's library supplies materials related to producing pharmaceutical products. A law library concentrates on law. Local history libraries concentrate on materials pertaining to that locale and the genealogy of the people who live there. Rare book libraries concentrate on their specific areas of interest—the books, papers, manuscripts, and other materials pertaining to Henry Wadsworth Longfellow, for example.

It is important that you recognize these differences among library types. You will be able to produce a successful five-page paper on atoms by using materials at your school and public library. If you're writing a college-level paper or thesis on atoms, you may need to research in a college library with a strong physics department. Ultimately you may need current research published in specialized journals held only in scientific libraries.

You may find information regarding significant Supreme Court decisions in your public library, but you may need to research specific points of state or federal law at a law library. Don't be disappointed if you don't find everything you need in your local public library. Reference librarians will refer you elsewhere if they feel their library has not satisfied your information needs. If they don't offer a referral, don't hesitate to ask them if they know of a library in the area that might better help you.

Some other points are important to keep in mind. Sometimes small or medium-sized libraries can often be easier to work in than libraries with large collections because it may be easier to find things in a smaller collection. In addition, staff are often more responsive to younger students than librarians used to dealing with serious researchers in a larger library. Librarians in a good medium-sized library can also easily search larger library collections electronically and obtain materials for you by **fax** or **interlibrary loan.** If the library is too small, say, fewer than 50,000 books, the collection may be too limited, and the staff may not be as well trained as librarians in medium-sized libraries. Libraries serving populations of 20,000 to 100,000 may be ideal for most high school and undergraduate students.

THE LIBRARIAN FACTOR

Information librarians have earned advanced degrees, commonly, the **master's degree in library science**. These librarians seldom work the circulation desk, which is commonly staffed by clerical support staff. You can find the trained and experienced degreed librarian at the **reference** or **information desk**. Information librarians in public libraries often have a bachelor's degree in liberal arts, which gives them a broad background knowledge of many areas of study. It enables them to help most people who come into the public library.

Information librarians are information athletes. Depending on the time of day, week, or year, the librarian may be trying to answer questions at a rate as high as 30 an hour. Instantly they have to know exactly in what part of the library collection, in what specific source, the needed information can be found. They may have to use a computerized catalog. They may have to use other computerized sources, each which may operate differently. They have to jump, question by question, from one part of the collection to another. The first question may seek current research on the particles of an atom; another wants information on the top commanders in Julius Caesar's army. A caller needs the address and telephone number of a business in Los Angeles. Librarians constantly run up and down the scale of of recorded history and knowledge from the beginning of time to the present. They must have knowledge of libraries, collections, sources, and computerized services. In the course of a day, a librarian may use 7 to 10 different computer systems and 10 to 20 software programs.

A librarian who can do all this is a tremendous resource, there to help you find the information you need. But librarians are human too. They wear down and tire out, as the day and the week grind on. They are overloaded with work with which they cannot keep up, they run and struggle from one end of the week to the other. In most libraries, librarians are helping users from the moment the library opens in the morning. Because they're so busy, some times are better than others to get the most help from them. A weekday morning, when you're not in school, may be better than three in the afternoon when every other student is there too. Ten o'clock on Saturday morning is usually better than two o'clock Saturday afternoon. When librarians have fewer people and fewer demands to deal with, they're more likely to spend more time with you and your specific research inquiry.

If you have already searched the catalog, you should explain how you have searched and what you have found. If you haven't found what you need, ask the information librarian for help. If you need help selecting a topic, the librarian may offer suggestions. The librarian can help you narrow the topic or make a selection from a variety of topics, at least partially based on materials and information available at the library. It's not much use selecting a topic for which the library has little or no information.

Your first question to the librarian should address the broad topic or alternative topics, not with a narrow topic or a single aspect. But you don't want your question to be too broad. Even the topic "atoms" can be broad, though already narrowed from "physics." "Physics," of course, has already been narrowed from "science." So to say to the librarian, "I need books on science," will only prompt the librarian to ask in turn, "Can you be more specific? Exactly what are you trying to find out about science?"

The question, "Can you help me find information about atoms?" is just about right and will encourage the librarian to show you reference books, circulating books, magazine and newspaper articles, vertical files (pamphlets and similar information), CD-ROM databases, and perhaps even videos and audiobooks.

REFERENCE SOURCES

Your question to the librarian should be a general one on the broad topic or alternative topics, not a narrow one on a particular library item. For example, don't ask the librarian about a specific book. Instead, ask about the topic. This will encourage the librarian to tell you how to use many other library resources, not just books. Libraries carry information in all these forms: books, magazines, electronic databases, vertical files, microform newspapers, audiobooks, videos, and CD-ROM workstations that allow you to interact with a variety of encyclopedias and multimedia reference sources.

ADVANCED RESEARCH METHODS

Students who desire to become skilled library researchers may want to use the following methodology to learn and demonstrate research competency. These are listed in sequence, but you may often find that a particular search requires an altogether different sequence. Become aware of the virtues and characteristics of each step and adopt a sequence appropriate to a specific search.

General articles and terminology—It is often useful to start with a general reference work that will familiarize you with the terminology and general information about the subject. Copy terms, names, and dates to aid in future searches.

General bibliography—Use a comprehensive bibliography to get an overview of the relevant reference sources in this area. *Guide to Reference Sources,* edited by Robert Balay, published by the American Library Association, 1996, is a comprehensive and authoritative source but is not complete in every subject area.

Special subject bibliography or special subject guide to research— These specific subject sources are complete in a narrow field but may not reveal sources in other related fields, so they may be misleading if you start here.

Classification number shelf search—Use the OPAC to obtain the relevant shelf number or letter for this particular subject. Then search the shelves nearby for other books on the same subject. Look inside the books for clues on where to search elsewhere. Use the table of contents, bibliography, index, and notes. The shelf search needs to be made in both the reference and circulating collections.

Catalog—precoordinated, controlled vocabulary search—Now use the OPAC again, this time to find the appropriate subject headings as well as related other terms that may be included in the catalog tracings for books on this subject. Some OPACs have an expert search option that may require a password or staff assistance. Be careful to include "see also" subjects. After you have discovered some subject headings, go to the LC subject heading volumes to find other related subject terms that may not have been used in the particular catalog you were searching. Use these terms in searching other remote catalogs such as OCLC, First-Search, and Internet. Invert terms in searching to see if the inverted term yields other information. For example, try English language and Language, English.

Type of literature search—Look at directories, almanacs, museum catalogs, serials, atlases, and other types of general reference resources that may not relate directly to the special subject.

Actual practice, principle of least effort—Ask your fellow students, colleagues at work, supervisors or friends. Especially librarians. Look at your home collection of books to see if you can find information.

Internet post-coordinated searches—Using Netscape, Microsoft Navigator, or other Internet search tool, search a variety of search engines: Open Text, Yahoo!, AltaVista, HotBot, Excite, Lycos, Web Crawler, Info Seek

CD-ROM multimedia searches—Use a multimedia resource such as a general encyclopedia (*Encarta*) or other specialized multimedia resource. Use several search terms, and look for audio, video, and picture resources. Evaluate the links as well as the hits, and compare with print resources.

Database searching on Dialog—Use a multidatabase resource, and identify several databases that might be useful on this topic. Look especially for recent information on the topic. Identify how recent the information is.

Special libraries—subject collections—Identify nearby libraries or other resources such as museums that might be helpful on this topic. Try to identify the world-class resource in this subject. In art, for example, *The Dictionary of Art* (see Chapter 7), is now *the* authoritative source.

LIBRARY RESEARCH MODELS

Thomas Mann, a reference librarian at the Library of Congress since 1981 and a former private investigator, wrote *Library Research Models* (Oxford University Press, 1993). He describes in detail the following methods:

1. **The specific subject or discipline** model emphasizes the in-depth resources directly related to the specific subject, such as bibliographies exclusively devoted to that particular subject, so that students researching business topics use *Business Periodicals Index* rather than more general sources, such as *The Reader's Guide to Periodical Literature.*

2. **The traditional library science model based on the classification scheme** relies on the subject shelf arrangement in most libraries that leads users to the particular shelf related to the subject of interest. Business researchers would thus go to the 330 section and look at the books on the shelf.

3. **The traditional library science model is also based on the vocabulary-controlled catalog,** which has been created to group together in a single alphabetical arrangement all materials the library owns pertaining to a given subject, author, or title. By looking in the catalog, you can find in one related sequence books by an author on a variety of subjects and books about that author, including biographies and critical works. For example, books on business in the business section are listed in the catalog together with business films, business bibliographies, and business histories.

4. **The traditional library science model is also based on published bibliographies and indexes** that group together all kinds of materials and often have the virtue of including materials too recent to be in books or library catalogs.

5. **The type of literature** model uses particular kinds of books that are found in many different disciplines to gain access to information—for example, almanacs for general statistical information, atlases for geographic information, directories for identifying knowledgeable organizations or experts, and yearbooks for information related to a particular year.

6. **The actual practice model** reveals that researchers often neglect the full area of research choices and focus on the **principle of least effort** by using the methods easily and readily available to them—seldom the most complete, seldom the fastest, and seldom the best methodology.

7. **The computer workstation model** incorporates many of the advantages of the earlier models by making it possible to include in one system a wide variety of searching alternatives and in being able to combine several terms in a single search.

Although this methodology is often very useful, it may not find specific material available in one of the earlier traditional models. An example may be found by contrasting **postcoordinated** and **precoordinated searching methodologies**. **Postcoordinated** searching, typically found in combined **Boolean** searching techniques employed in most computerized databases, allows the user to combine several terms, which are then used to search the database. For example, searching the combined terms, Hemingway and women, will result in sources that discuss anyone named Hemingway and anything about women. **Precoordinated** searching has existed for decades in subject headings that already combine terms for helping a user to find a subject. For example, "Minorities in medicine" is an existing subject heading that groups together all materials on this subject.

Very specific topics presented by users may be incapable of direct searching in a database. For example, a researcher trying to find out what life is like for people living along highways not near cities would find very few relevant hits combining the terms "life" and "highways," but a librarian familiar with the old Route 66 found four titles under that category and checking the catalog tracings under those titles came up with "automobiles," "road guides," and "United States" as combined terms useful in revealing many other titles.

Predictability allows librarians familiar with the formal, structured relationships in a traditional library catalog to find terms that would otherwise never be found. For example, research in "multinational corporations" as a database subject reveals very few hits, but in looking at the cross-references under that term, the more traditional library subject heading, "international business enterprises," is found, and that term yields many more references. Predictability is also a feature of subject shelf arrangement in a library and allows users to browse in a subject area and look inside the indexes, tables of contents, and full text of books to get clues to searches that would not be available in a database search.

Serendipity in a formal library context means the ability to find more material in the system than your initial search envisioned. Thus a researcher looking for capital punishment found 114 hits using those terms in a keyword search, and 361 hits by using the identical terms in a subject search. The keyword search related only to titles using those words; the subject search yielded all those books related to the topic whether or not the terms were in the title. The full display of tracings and other catalog information may yield more search topics than merely using the terms first chosen for the search.

If the full text of materials already available in digitized form were available for very fast searching, would the traditional techniques of formalized library structures be no longer relevant? Prohibitive cost of conversion, inputting and searching, and copyright law may make this a difficult objective to achieve. Archival preservation of electronic formats is still questionable. Psychological factors relating to the enormity of dealing with full-text searching relate to the limitations of human short-term memory, which make it difficult to deal with immense databases. Even medium-sized libraries yielding hundreds of hits in a database search can be discouraging to many users.

An expert library researcher would use many of these research models in combinations relevant to the particular subject being researched. The chart below summarizes some guides to search methods:

Subject	Shelf Location	OPAC catalog	Bibliography	Type of Literature	Computer
Ask experts	Find the right number	Precoordinated, predictable, find the right subject	Find a good list of materials	Use an index	Combine terms

CHAPTER 3

Where to Start

ENCYCLOPEDIAS

General Encyclopedias (030–039)

Your teacher has assigned you to write a five-page paper on atoms. You now know that in the Dewey Decimal system, the 500s area includes all science, the 530s physics, 539 modern physics, and 539.7 the study of atoms. What do you know about atoms? You should know something from your class work and your physics textbook, but let's assume you're just getting started and would like a little background. Start with a **general encyclopedia.**

Encyclopedias make excellent starting points. They summarize the important background and provide significant dates and names, giving you the basic knowledge you need to begin your research. They also lead you to other resources. A **bibliography**, usually at the end of the encyclopedia article, lists books that will expand on the topic well beyond the information the encyclopedia provides. This list of books is most useful, serving as recommendations for valuable resources. You can then check your library's catalog for these resources.

Encyclopedias are many and come in two main formats: book and CD-ROM. Most of the time, book encyclopedias are fine. They tell you what you need to know; they frequently offer illustrations, photos, charts, or maps; and they often give you leads to other information. They're arranged alphabetically, but they all include a comprehensive index as the last volume. Every library has them, and the nice thing is that while you're reading about atoms, someone else can be reading about the Civil War.

Academic American Encyclopedia

Danbury, CT: Grolier, 1997. 21 vols. Bibliographic references and indexes. Published annually with revisions. Available online via Prodigy, CompuServe, and others and on CD-ROM as *The Grolier Multimedia Encyclopedia* (see below).

Written for older students and adults, the *Academic American Encyclopedia* is one of the best of the medium-sized encyclopedias, according to Kenneth Kister, author of *Kister's Best Encyclopedias* (Phoenix, AZ: Oryx Press, 2d ed., 1994). Nearly every page includes a photograph, illustration, chart, or graph, most of them in color. It provides brief overviews that emphasize basic facts rather than in-depth analysis. It is strong on science and technology.

A four-and-a-half-page article in the 1997 edition begins with a definition of "atom," includes 11 illustrations and a five-item bibliography. It briefly outlines the history of atomic theory, discovery, and research, crediting the scientists important to the field.

Following "atom," there are several pages of articles describing "atomic bomb," "atomic constants," "atomic weight," and related items. Reading these articles reveals that the study of atoms falls under the science of physics but that the study of atoms and nuclear properties is a study unto itself. As you obtain this knowledge, you will find that you can write nearly as much as you want or as little. While science is a broad topic, physics less broad, and the atom less broad than physics, the atom turns out to be a large topic after all.

The bibliography at the end of the article lists one book that sounds interesting, Gerald Feinberg's *What Is the World Made Of?* (1977). It might be a good book to look into, and most public libraries should have it. If your library doesn't, it can probably tell you where to get it. If your library has it on the shelf, you will probably find other books about atoms near it.

The New Encyclopaedia Britannica

Chicago: Encyclopedia Britannica, 1994. 15th ed. 32 vols. Bibliographic references and index. Annual yearbook. Published annually with revisions. Available on CD-ROM and online.

Considered the granddaddy of English-language encyclopedias, the *Encyclopedia Britannica* was first published in 1768. It broke tradition in 1974 by altering the format from the 1–20 volume plus index formula to a 12-volume **Micropaedia** and a 16-volume **Macropaedia** plus a 2-volume index. The Micropaedia serves as an index to the Macropaedia while providing summary information beyond what an index would provide but less than the in-depth article which may be needed only some of the time. It also created a 1-volume **Propaedia**, which outlines knowledge and subdivides the broad categories such as science showing the relationships of subtopics within the broad subject. For example, it would help you determine in which branch of science the study of atoms falls.

Britannica renamed the work *The New Encyclopaedia Britannica* with the fifteenth edition in 1974. It further revised and reorganized this concept in 1985. Britannica enjoys using the English spelling of encyclopedia, "encyclopaedia," which also signals that its content and writing style (articles are submitted by experts from all over the world) are more scholarly than other general encyclopedias.

Start with the Propaedia. A glance through the table of contents reveals that Britannica has organized knowledge into 10 parts, each part divided and then subdivided. The parts are organized from the smallest component of matter, then progress to earth, life on earth, human life, society, art, technology, religion, human history, and finally the branches of knowledge. It's a logical progression, from the basic building blocks of all things living and nonliving to the most complex studies performed by the human mind. Part I, then is Matter and Energy. The first division discusses atoms, and on the first page we learn that this division "deals with subatomic and atomic physics." Physics is the science we're interested in.

Look in the Britannica Micropaedia and see what it says about atoms: "ATOM, smallest unit into which matter can be divided without charged particles being released. It is also the smallest unit of matter with the characteristic properties of an element. A brief treatment of atoms follows. For full treatment *see* MACROPAEDIA: Atoms: Their Structure, Properties and Component Particles."

In six paragraphs, the Micropaedia article briefly describes the discovery of and research into atoms. It briefly discusses the particles of an atom—the nucleus or core, the protons and neutrons (known together as nucleons), their properties and characteristics—and mentions that they are made up of even smaller particles known as quarks. It also mentions that the nucleus is surrounded by electrons. It describes an atom's atomic number or weight, which is its most significant characteristic. There's reference to a separate article on quarks. In eight paragraphs, this article fully, if briefly and in uncomplicated style, outlines the basics of what you need to know.

The Macropaedia article, by contrast, runs 50 pages and describes in considerable detail every aspect of atoms, atomic theory, research, energy, radioactivity, scientific use, and so on. It includes many scientific graphs, charts, and photographs.

Among general encyclopedias, *Britannica* is absolutely the best, most thorough, and comprehensive. It challenges readers to rise to its intellectual level.

Some libraries retain copies of the older editions of the *Britannica* published before 1914 since this encyclopedia was considered the best ever and includes some often useful historical perspectives on the state of knowledge at that time

World Book Encyclopedia
Chicago: World Book, 1996. 22 vols. Bibliographic references and indexes. Published annually with revisions. Annual yearbook.

Written with younger, elementary students in mind, *World Book* is surprisingly useful to older students and adults who are getting started on an unfamiliar topic. It's attractive in page layout and loaded with color photographs, charts, and graphs—you can often count on it to provide just the statistical chart, graph, or illustration you need. It summarizes the topic briefly and directly without taxing the child or insulting the intelligence of the adult. It succeeds at this difficult task by increasing the reading level after the second paragraph. This is called the **"pyramid" style**: beginning with the simple and becoming more complex. The first two paragraphs are meant to be sufficient for younger students, the entire article for older students. Vocabulary control also contributes to achieving this effect.

In seven pages, *World Book,* 1996, answers all the basic questions about atoms. The article describes each component part, the atomic number and weight, electric charge and chemical behavior, radioactivity, energy, and the history and development of atomic theory and includes color illustrations throughout. It concludes with an ten-item bibliography divided into Level I and Level II. Level I mentions Melvin Berger's *Our Atomic World* and Chris Cooper's *Matter.* Level II lists Isaac Asimov's *Atom: Journey Across the Subatomic Cosmos,* as well as Hans Von Baeyer's *Taming the Atom: The Emergence of the Visible Microworld.* You now have several book leads to follow up on in your library.

Other Encyclopedias

Collier's Encyclopedia with Bibliography and Index
New York: P. F. Collier. 24 vols. Published annually with revisions. Annual yearbook.

Kister calls Collier's "the best of the big sets." Collier's has the best revision program in the business that produces the most up-to-date set on the market. It aims at those of high school age and older; its clear and direct writing style requires good reading skills. Color graphics of all types have been improved considerably in the 1990s. Its large index makes specific topics easily accessible. The major difference from other sets is the bibliography in the front part of the index volume. Collier's does not publish bibliographic references at the end of articles The bibliography is arranged by subdivided broad subjects. The entries are not always up-to-date.

Columbia Encyclopedia

Columbia University Press. 5th ed. 1993. 1 vol. Revised editions published at 10- to 15-year intervals. Includes bibliographic references.

Kister calls *Columbia* "the best single volume general encyclopedia currently available in English." Large in size, exhaustive in content, biographical and geographical entries make *Columbia* useful for identifying people and places. Though strong on scientific and technologic topics, it lacks an index. Illustrations are few but valuable. Its readable prose is intended for serious students and adults. Entries contain excellent bibliographies.

Compton's Encyclopedia and Fact-Index

Chicago: Compton's Learning Co. 26 vols. Includes bibliographic references and index. Published annually with revisions. Annual yearbook. Available on CD-ROM and on America Online.

The chief competitor for *World Book, Compton's* employs the same pyramid style of writing, which succeeds so well for both younger students and the adults. Massive revisions and restyling, added illustrations, and use of color have improved the set immensely over the past 15 years. The writing is clear, and information is accessible. The overall organization can confuse, sometimes due to the use of the fact index as both an index and a quick reference with brief articles on specific topics not found in the first 25 volumes. Strong coverage of science and technology and geography is provided, with a bit more emphasis on the United States and Canada. Not as strong, though better than in the past, is coverage of the arts, humanities, and social sciences. The bibliographies need improving.

Encyclopedia Americana: International Edition

Danbury, CT: Grolier. 30 vols. Includes bibliographic references and index volume. Published annually with revisions.

Despite its subtitle, the main title is accurate: the *Americana* emphasizes information about North America, with coverage of U.S. and Canadian history, biography, and geography deserving special note. Coverage of science and technology and the behavioral and social sciences is also strong. The clear writing is intended for general readers of high school age and older. A large index provides valuable search assistance. Bibliographic references are not as up-to-date as desired. The illustrations need improvement.

Funk and Wagnall's New Encyclopedia
Mahwah, NJ: Funk and Wagnalls. 29 vols. Published twice a year with revisions. Annual yearbook.

Though sold only through supermarkets volume by volume, Funk and Wagnalls does not deserve disparagement based on its marketing method or its price. One of the cheapest options available, Funk and Wagnalls provides balanced subject coverage written in readable prose aimed at older students and adults with seventh-grade and above reading ability. Biographical and geographic topics are well represented, with science and social science topics well covered. Coverage of arts and humanities is weakest. Illustrations need improvement, as does typographical layout. A thorough index volume aids the user, and a separate bibliography at the end of the last volume lists books by subject. That *Microsoft's Encarta Multimedia Encyclopedia* (see below) is based on Funk and Wagnall's surprises at first but indicates the stature that Funk and Wagnall's has achieved.

CD-ROM Encyclopedias

CD-ROM stands for compact disk-read-only memory. The disk looks like a music CD but it holds information data instead of digitalized music. It won't work on a music CD player. You use it with a computer and CD drive that reads the contents. The operating software is built in. Read-only means you cannot change the contents of the disk. By contrast, you can both record on an audiotape, play back, and record again if you want. Encyclopedias, as well as other information **databases**, are available on CD-ROM. A database is any compilation of information that's manipulated by and accessible by computer. Some encyclopedias are also available **online.** That means you use a computer to dial in to the **database**. Online databases are updated more frequently (sometimes daily) than CDs, so you can be sure the online information is the latest available.

Computerized databases have many advantages. CD-ROM encyclopedias can be fun to use because most are **multimedia** products, which means they give you video clips and sound effects, as well as written material. CD-ROM encyclopedias are usually based on print encyclopedias and provide the same basic text as their printed counterparts.

One of the benefits of CD-ROM, especially if you have a computer at home, is that you can save the text and illustrations, load them into your word processor, and manipulate the text, rewrite it, insert the illustrations, and then print out the results. If you don't have a CD-ROM player attached to your computer at home, you can download to floppy disk the parts you need from the library's computer, bring the disk home, and load the file into your home computer. Of course, you can always print out your findings from the library's computer and take the information home with you in paper form. Another benefit of a CD-ROM encyclopedia, and of most CD-ROM databases, is **keyword searching**. The computer will find the word you're looking for anywhere it appears in the database. This technique can be useful for hard-to-find information.

Search speed is another benefit. Depending on the type of search, sometimes it can be quicker to search the computerized encyclopedia than to use the print index.

The Grolier Multimedia Encyclopedia
Danbury, CT: Grolier Electronic Publishing. Updated annually.

Based on the *Academic American Encyclopedia*, in 1983 this became the first electronic encyclopedia available online. Subscribers to CompuServe, Prodigy, and other services can access it today. In 1985 Grolier made history by releasing the entire 21-volume set on CD-ROM, a marvel at the time. In recent years, sound, pictures (both still and moving), and illustrations have been added. While the online and CD-ROM versions are about 1 million words larger than the print edition of *Academic American,* the print edition includes many more illustrations and photos than the CD-ROM while the online version contains none. As with the print version, the text is written for older students and adults.

A subject search of "atom" produced four or five pages of text exploring the development of the theory of atoms, the research and discovery, the significant scientists involved with some relevant illustrations, narration, and a bibliography, much the same information as discovered in print form.

With Grolier's, the computer hit 755 matches on the keyword "atom."

Microsoft Encarta Multimedia Encyclopedia
Redmond, WA: Microsoft Corp. Updated annually.

While it's a surprise to most that *Encarta* is based on *Funk and Wagnall's New Encyclopedia*, the subject coverage and writing in that publication are vastly improved and well rated in recent years. Authoritative, controlled vocabulary makes the text accessible to a fifth-grade reading level. Layout and illustrations leave much to be desired, however. *Encarta* remedies both complaints, so the marriage works well: *Encarta* is called simply the best, most exciting multimedia CD-ROM encyclopedia on the market according to most reviewers. Its publisher, the software giant Microsoft, has lent its talent and strength to its print partner to create an easy-to-use, fast computer product so loaded with pictures, illustrations, maps, charts, and video and sound clips that it far outpaces its competition. It is updated online.

BEYOND ENCYCLOPEDIAS

There are other general encyclopedias you may find in libraries. Some of the more common ones are listed here. Even if your teacher does not accept encyclopedias as a source, encyclopedias provide excellent background on your topic: they increase and improve your understanding of it, provide a good research starting point, and lead you to other materials. They do not write your paper for you, though. You need more sources and more information. Where else can you go for information? *Academic American* and *Grolier's Multimedia Encyclopedia* suggested Gerald Feinberg's *What Is the World Made Of?* (1977). To find it, along with the Asimov titles and Ardley's *World of the Atom* mentioned by *World Book*, use the catalog and browsing techniques described in Chapter 2, and you're well on your way to acquiring all the information you need for a 5-page or a 25-page paper.

ALMANACS, ATLASES, GAZETTEERS, STATISTICAL, AND OTHER GENERAL REFERENCE SOURCES

Almanacs are compendiums of information, commonly in one volume. They are amazing for the amount of information packed in a relatively small book.

Atlases contain collections of maps. These are usually maps of countries, but there are many different kinds of atlases. Some contain historical maps, such as maps of Europe before 1200, or military campaign maps, like an atlas of the Crusades. Sometimes atlases visually depict statistics. Census information, for example, might be depicted by color on a state map, showing population by ethnic group, general income level by town, or political affiliation by town.

Gazetteers provide descriptive written information to place names. They do not include maps except perhaps thumbnail drawings that provide brief visual locations. Organized alphabetically by place name, a gazetteer may provide in a short paragraph latitude and longitude, area, borders, geographic features, population, and maybe a brief history.

Statistical sources come in all sizes and varieties. General statistics sources are listed below, but there are subject specific sources, just as there are subject encyclopedias. There are books of health statistics, ethnic statistics, women's statistics, and manufacturing statistics, for example.

Each of these sources can be used to learn basic information quickly and to provide detail and depth to your research paper and support the main premise or argument of your paper. Statistics on drunk driving accidents involving teenage drivers combined with statistics on the numbers of teenagers who watch televised sports may support your premise that beer advertising should be banned from televised sports shows.

Almanacs (310)

Information Please Almanac
Boston: Houghton Mifflin. Annual. Incl. index.

Much of its content is similar to the *World Almanac*, but this title does include information on popular topics and on some different subjects that help distinguish it. There's a section on computers with suggestions for computer security, a section on the family with discussions of why marriages succeed or fail, a section on drug use, a list of the most important scientific discoveries and inventions, and a discussion of slavery in the United States.

The Universal Almanac
Wright, John W., ed. Kansas City, MO: Andrews & McMeel. Annual. Incl. index.

It has some repetition of information found in both the *World Almanac* and *Information Please Almanac*. Yet this title has some information the others do not, and it is supplemented by narrative text. The sections "Sex in America" and "U.S. Business," with its list of Fortune 500 companies and top companies by industry, are good examples.

Whitaker's Almanac
London: Whitaker. Annual. Incl. index.

The British cousin to the *World Almanac,* this compendium emphasizes Great Britain and its territories. It does not duplicate *World Almanac.* Its statistics and other information are distinctly of British origin. Of course, it contains a list of British royalty.

The World Almanac and Book of Facts
Mahwah, NJ: World Almanac Books. Annual. Incl. index.

An incredible book that opens with summary articles on the year's biggest issues and news stories and follows with a descriptive chronology of the year's major events. Obituaries of major world figures are listed. Government figures, statistics, agencies, and events are given. The book is organized in major categories, such as economics, employment, U.S. population, biographies of U.S. presidents, weights and measures, religion, nations of the world, and much more. In each category, all the major information, statistics, and description is provided for quick reference. There's an excellent index in the front of the book. It's worth leafing through the book for an hour to familiarize yourself with its contents. Reference librarians joke that with the *World Almanac* and the *World Book Encyclopedia*, they can answer most questions. That's not true, of course, but you get the idea: this is a valuable reference source. Many libraries keep it indefinitely, even though they buy each new edition, because it serves as a historical record of facts for the year. If you wanted to find the price of a dozen eggs in 1935, you might look in the *World Almanac* for that or the following year.

The World Almanac of the U.S.A.
Mahwah, NJ: World Almanac Books. Annual. Incl. index.

The source provides a profile of each state, including historical highlights, interesting facts, "superlatives," notable personalities, state facts (such as date admitted to union and state bird), and statistics by major category. Comparison charts and rankings are also included. A similar source is *Almanac of the Fifty States: Basic Data Profiles with Comparative Tables,* an annual published by Information Publications.

Atlases (912)

The main concern with world atlases, especially if you are researching Eastern Europe or Russia, is whether the atlas includes recent territorial boundary changes. Most major atlases were revised in 1992 to reflect changes in that part of the world, so be sure the publication date of the atlas you are using is 1992 or after. The publication date is sometimes printed on the title page but is most often on the reverse side of the title page. Look for the latest copyright (©) date and the latest edition date. The *World Almanac* includes maps, so you might compare maps from a current edition of the *World Almanac* with the same map from an atlas to be sure the atlas is up-to-date. Many libraries circulate older editions of atlases, so you need to be wary of these. Again check the publication date. If the map of Russia show it as the U.S.S.R., you know it's not current.

Most general atlases contain additional information to geographic maps. They may include maps on population, religions, natural resources, climate, agriculture, vegetation, water resources and aquatic life, politics, earthquakes, volcanoes and earth movement, flags. Some atlases follow country maps with regional or state maps. All have place indexes, locating specific places by map number and grid number (e.g., for K-21, find the letter K across the top or side and the number 21 on the side or top and follow the two lines until they meet). In that grid area, you will find the place you want.

Some of the most common general atlases are listed here:

Atlas of the World
New York: Oxford University Press, 1992. 2d ed. Incl. index.

Goode's World Atlas
Espenshade, Edward B., Jr., ed. Chicago: Rand McNally, 1993. 18th ed. Incl. index.

Hammond Atlas of the World
Maplewood, NJ: Hammond, 1992. Incl. index.

National Geographic Atlas of the World
New York: National Geographic Society, 1993. 6th ed. Incl. index.

The Times Atlas of the World
New York: Time Books, 1994. 9th comprehensive ed., rev. Incl. index.

Somewhat specialized atlases are found in nearly every library:

Historical Maps on File
New York: Facts on File, 1984. Looseleaf. Incl. index.
Intended to be photocopied and similar to *Maps on File* (below), these maps focus on world geography during the time of ancient civilizations, Europe to 1500, Europe 1500–1815, Europe 1815–present,the United States, the Western Hemisphere, Africa and the Middle East, Asia, and Australia.

Maps on File
New York: Facts on File, 1981– . 2 vols. Looseleaf. Incl. index.
Like most Facts on File looseleaf publications, these black and white outline maps are intended for photocopying. Students can fill in cities or other information on their copy. Both geographical and theme maps (population, natural resources, etc.) are included. Updated maps are issued annually.

Rand McNally Commercial Atlas and Marketing Guide
Chicago: Rand McNally. Annual. Incl. index.

This is a good source for locating small towns and local areas in the United States that are not listed in other atlases. It provides clear county outlines in each state, capitals, county seats, and similar vital information to users who may have a commercial point of view. Several statistical tables of business interest are also provided.

Rand McNally Road Atlas: United States/Canada/Mexico
Chicago: Rand McNally. Annual. Incl. index.

Familiar to most cross-country automobile and truck travelers, this atlas show all major routes through states and cities. Local roads are not shown. Mileage charts are provided and distances shown on maps.

As mentioned above, there are many types of specialized atlases. They can be useful when researching specific topics. A short list of examples follows:

Atlas of American Women
Shortridge, Barbara Gimla. New York: Macmillan, 1986. Incl. bibliography and index.

Atlas of North American Exploration
Goetzmann, William. Englewood Cliffs, NJ: Prentice-Hall, 1992. Incl. index.

The Atlas of the Ancient World: Charting the Great Civilizations of the Past
Oliphant, Margaret. New York: Simon & Schuster, 1992. Incl. bibliography and index.

The Atlas of the Crusades
Riley-Smith, Jonathan, ed. New York: Facts on File, 1991. Incl. index.

Atlas of Westward Expansion
Wexler, Alan. New York: Facts on File, 1995. Incl. bibliography and index.

First World War Atlas
Gilbert, Martin. New York: Macmillan, 1970. Incl. index.

Rand McNally Atlas of World History
Chicago: Rand McNally, 1992. Incl. index.

The Times Atlas of the Second World War
Keegan, John, ed. New York: Harper & Row, 1989. Incl. index.

A World Atlas of Military History
Banks, Arthur. New York: Hippocrene, 1973–1984. 4 vol. Incl. index.

Gazetteers (912)

Some common gazetteers are:

Chambers World Gazetteer
Munro, David, ed. New York: Cambridge University Press, 1988. 5th ed.

Columbia Lippincott Gazetteer of the World
Seltzer, Leon E., ed. New York: Columbia University Press, 1952.
A new edition of this outstanding place name dictionary will be published in three volumes in 1998: *The Columbia Gazetteer of the World*, edited by Saul Cohen.

Geo-Data: The World Almanac Gazetteer
Kurian, George Thomas. Detroit: Gale, 1989. Incl. bibliography and index.

The Statesman's Year-Book World Gazetteer
New York: St. Martin's, 1991. 4th ed.

Webster's New Geographical Dictionary
Springfield, MA: Merriam-Webster, 1988.
While the other gazetteers listed above concentrate on current place names, *Webster's* includes ancient, biblical, medieval, and pre–World War II place names.

Statistical Sources (317)

Demographic Yearbook
New York: United Nations. Annual. Incl. index.
This source concentrates on current population, birth, death, marriage, and divorce statistics, country by country, worldwide. Some charts compare statistics over ten or so years.

Europa World Year Book
Detroit: Gale. 2 vols. Annual. Incl. index.

This alphabetical listing of countries provides demographic and economic statistics and listings of government officers, media, business and industry, descriptions of government, constitutions, and other facts. Addresses are included in case you want to write to someone for information. There's a large section on international organizations with addresses.

The Statesman's Year-Book: A Statistical and Historical Annual for the States of the World
Hunter, Brian, ed. New York: St. Martin's. Annual. Incl. bibliographies and index.

This is a quick summary reference source for information on every country, major region in the world, and states or regions within individual countries. Information provided includes brief text and statistics in each of several categories: capital, seat of government, population, gross national product per capita; history; land area, boundaries, and population; climate; constitution and government, including a list of major officials; defense; international relations; economy and foreign economic relations; communication; justice; religion; education and welfare; diplomatic representatives and embassy and consulate addresses; and a bibliography. Energy, natural resources, agriculture, labor, and production are also covered. Every student sooner or later has to put together country reports or answer brief questions on basic facts about a specific country, and this is one of the best places to get the information needed.

Statistical Abstract of the United States
Washington, DC: U.S. Bureau of the Census. Annual. Incl. index.

This annual compilation of statistics from every aspect of American life is the first stop for numerical analysis. Every statistical table is numbered, so it's important to remember that the index refers to table numbers, not page numbers. Statistics are grouped by broad category: population, vital statistics, health and nutrition, education, law enforcement, geography and environment, parks, recreation and travel, elections, state and local government finances and employment, prices, banking and finance, business, energy, natural resources, and more. For each table, the source is cited, which helps if you need more detailed information on the topic. Most statistics come from the Census or other government data collection services. This is an extraordinary source that astounds with the information it provides. As with the *World Almanac,* many libraries keep this title indefinitely as a historical record, making it possible to compare statistics across the decades.

Statistical Abstract of the World
Reddy, Marlita A., ed. Detroit: Gale, 1994. Incl. index.
Statistical compilations and comparisons by country are presented in this volume on topics such as population, health, crime, government, economics, manufacturing, natural resources, military expenditures, and more.

Statistical Yearbook
New York: United Nations. Annual. Incl. bibliography and index.
This source compares statistics country by country for several years on many topics. Divided into broad categories (population and social statistics, economic activity, and economic relations), statistical tables review the numbers on education and literacy, childbearing and nutrition, labor force, wage and prices, manufacturing, agriculture, energy, trade, and tourism as well as other topics.

Examples of specific statistical sources:

Statistical Handbook on U.S. Hispanics
Schick, Frank L., and Schick, Renee, comps. and eds. New York: Oryx, 1991.

Statistical Record of Black America
Horton, Carrell Peterson, and Smith, Jessie Carney, comps. and eds. Detroit: Gale, 1991. Incl. bibliography and index.

Statistical Record of Women Worldwide
Schmittroth, Linda, comp. and ed. Detroit: Gale, 1991. Incl. bibliography and index.

Other General Reference Sources

Famous First Facts
Kane, Joseph Nathan. Bronx, NY: H. W. Wilson, 1981. 4th ed. Incl. index.
This volume lists the first known of everything and provides dates, names, and a brief description. Especially useful for inventions and discoveries. Indexed by days, years, personal names, and geographic location.

The Guinness Book of Records
New York: Facts on File. Annual. Incl. index.
Just what it's title says it is, this compendium lists all kinds of records in all kinds of areas, including science, space, entertainment,

sports, business, technology, animals, and nature. Some records are silly, of course, but others may be useful to spice up a report. For a report on tigers, for example, is there a listing for the oldest known or largest tiger?

Chronologies

These basic reference sources identify the sequence in which events occurred. As with most other reference sources, both general and specific chronologies have been published. Chronologies may be organized by date or by subject. They may provide a sentence or several paragraphs of information about each event. Some use symbols to identify topics. Chronologies will help you determine the sequence of significant events, and correlate events in different countries or different fields of endeavor that occurred at about the same time. They help you make sense of history. For example, did Shakespeare write plays before, during, or after the French Revolution? Were the Crusades fought while the Black Plague devastated Europe? Did Julius Caesar, Aristotle, and Attila the Hun live at the same time?

General historical chronologies are listed at the beginning of Chapter 10. Specific subject chronologies are listed in other chapters, such as *The Timetables of Science* on p. 204, Chapter 16.

Pro and Con

There are many series that present the pros and cons of debatable issues, such as abortion, flag burning, ozone, space exploration, and so on. *Opposing Viewpoints* is one such series. *Taking Sides* is another.

Opposing Viewpoint Series
San Diego, CA: Greenhaven Press.
This series is appropriate for middle school and high school students. Each book in the series is separately titled, focuses on one topic, and contains essays that explore both sides of different facets of the topic. For example, the title, *The 1960s: Opposing Viewpoints*, discusses "Vietnam and the Antiwar Movement" in Chapter 2, and "Social Unrest and Movements for Equality" in Chapter 4. In Chapter 2, an excerpt from President Lyndon Johnson's speech at Johns Hopkins University, April 7, 1965, is titled, "Americans Should Support the Vietnam War." Martin Luther King takes the opposite view in an essay titled, "Americans Should Oppose the Vietnam War," also excerpted from a speech. President Richard Nixon published an article in 1966, reprinted in Chapter 4 under the heading, "Rioters Should be Condemned for Re-

jecting Law and Order." In an essay reprinted from his book, *Rebellion in Newark,* Tom Hayden put forth the idea that "Riots Should be Understood as Social Revolutions." Most libraries these books and shelve them individually by subject.

Taking Sides: Library Index and Guide
Guilford, CT: Dushkin, 1994. 20 vols.
This set, which can sit together on a shelf in numbered volumes, like an encyclopedia, with an index volume as the last volume, differs from *Opposing Viewpoints* and other similar series. With *Opposing Viewpoints* each book stands on its own. Together they do not make an encyclopedia. Each book presents several pro and con arguments on several related issues, within a general topic, such as abortion or capital punishment. *Taking Sides,* by contrast, offers 734 pro and con essays discussing 367 controversial issues. For each question, a positive and negative argument are given, with the author and source listed. A subject index to the issues makes the articles accessible, no matter what volume they appear in. For example, under "Euthanasia," the question, "Is Physician-Assisted Suicide Ethical?" is published in the Bio-Ethics volume. "Should Doctors Ever Help Terminally Ill Patients Commit Suicide?" appears in the Health Issues volume. Both *Opposing Viewpoints* and *Taking Sides* provide valuable information on debatable subjects for students. Both, as well as similar series, will be widely used. *Taking Sides,* however, is more likely to be found in the reference section of the library.

CHAPTER 4

More Sources of Information: Magazines and Newspapers, Indexes and Interlibrary Loan

MAGAZINES AND NEWSPAPERS

Newspapers provide current, up-to-the-minute reporting on current events. So do magazines. Today's politics, wars, and weather become tomorrow's history. Newspapers published at the time of significant events, say the Civil War, are often considered primary source, material as the journalists usually witnessed the events, and their writing reflected the attitudes and biases of the time.

In science, the *New York Times* reports recent discoveries (on Tuesdays). Magazines like *Newsweek* and *Time* do the same. They occasionally make a big discovery the cover story. However, the specialty journals break the discoveries first. In science, journals such as *Science, Nature,* and others publish the original research as written by the discovering scientists themselves. In medicine, *JAMA (Journal of the American Medical Association)* and the *New England Journal of Medicine* publish scholarly research. Each field of study publishes very specific journals, which contain highly technical articles.

In physics, *Journal of Modern Physics, Physics Today, Progress in Particle and Nuclear Physics,* and *Physics of Particles and Nuclei* may carry articles pertinent to your research on the atom. However, only the largest public libraries, academic libraries with strong physics departments, and corporate libraries where physics research is important to product development carry these.

You can discover through such publications what the latest research has shown about the nucleus of an atom, for example. Not only do these magazines and newspapers serve to record the latest research, they also preserve it for future researchers to study and build upon. A backfile of *Science,* for example, might serve to enlighten you as to the development of research into the nucleus of an atom over the past five or ten years. The question then becomes, How do I find all the articles written in various magazines or newspapers on the particles of an atom over the last five or ten years? The answer: By using **indexes.**

INDEXES (016)

Just as a card catalog is a multifaceted index to a library's book collection, helping you find the specific books you need, and just as any book other than fiction is nearly useless without an index in the back that helps you quickly find information you need in the text without reading the entire book, magazine and newspaper indexes help you find the specific articles you need quickly, without thumbing through issue after issue.

Indexes can lead you to a wealth of information. As you get older and your research and writing skills improve, you will find your need to familiarize yourself with all the work done on a particular subject becoming greater. Indexes make this work easier.

General periodical indexes index the major news magazines: *Time, Newsweek,* and *U.S. News and World Report.* These report the big discoveries or events in any field, plus world news of the week. General indexes also index a broad selection of popular magazines, from a variety of fields of interest—business, sports, science, health, consumer information, hobbies, and others.

Computerized Indexes

Most indexes are now computerized, either online or CD-ROM. CD-ROM indexes are read-only databases, as described in the previous chapter. Many indexes can also be found online. **DIALOG**, a fee service, offers many newspapers, full text, online. They offer a search mechanism, OneSearch, that allows you to search the text of many newspapers and their backfiles simultaneously. It's a real timesaver. Some libraries have taken advantage of another option by loading index tapes onto their mainframe computers, allowing library users to access the indexes via the library's public access catalog terminals.

Some computerized indexes offer **subject searching,** some offer **keyword searching,** and some offer both. Keyword searching can be useful for hard-to-find information. You can search by one term or several. If you are interested in atoms in space, for example, you put in the terms "atoms space," and any article with those terms in the **bibliographic record** will be retrieved. You may or may not easily find articles on that topic under the subject term "atoms" or "space."

In addition to the benefits of keyword searching, computerized indexes search many years of magazines at once. Print indexes are usually published in annual volumes, so you have to search in each volume.

Not only do the databases index articles; frequently they provide at least **abstracts** and, increasingly, **full text** as well. **Abstracts** summarize the full article in a few lines and help you decide whether you really need to see the full article. **Full text** saves even more time because you don't have to hop from the index to the magazine or newspaper (which, when the librarian searches for it, may be missing or turn up perhaps with the article you need torn out). It's all right there in one-stop shopping, so to speak. Just print it out or download it, and take it home on a floppy disk to your computer.

As with computerized library catalogs, you may find any one of a variety of computerized indexes available in the library you use. They all operate a little differently, but basically if you can operate one system, you should be able to figure out any others. If you have difficulty, don't hesitate to ask the information librarian for assistance.

General Magazine Indexes

Magazine Index/InfoTrac
Menlo Park, CA: Information Access Corporation, 1976– .

Information Access Corporation (IAC) produces *Magazine Index*, also known as *InfoTrac*. It indexes 400 or so magazine titles of a general nature, plus many business and health titles and other titles from specific fields—for example, include *Business Horizons, Chicago, Country Living, Industry Week, Phi Delta Kappan,* and *Sporting News,* plus many of the same titles indexed by *Reader's Guide to Periodical Literature* (see below). *InfoTrac* is not available in print. In the late 1970s, it was a microfilm product. Since 1980, it has been available on CD-ROM and online. It offers both subject and keyword search options. It is currently divided into three parts—1982–1989, 1990–1993, and 1994–present—and it's updated monthly. Three searches, and you've found every article on your topic published in the magazines indexed in the past 15 or so years.

A search of the subject term "atoms" yielded many cross-references and subdivisions under the main topic. The subdivision "research" produced 45 **citations** from such publications as *Discover, Science World, Science News, Scientific American,* and *Science.* A cross-reference to "neutrons" produced 16 citations from titles like *Physics Today* and *Aviation Week and Space Technology,* as well as more subdivisions and cross-references. "Electrons" yielded 30 citations, "protons," 21. For example, *Physics Today* published "Where Does the Proton Really Get Its Spin?" (September 1995).

The term **citation** describes the article information found in the index: article title, publication title, date of issue, and pages. Here's a complete reproduction of the citation from InfoTrac:

Heading: PROTONS
    1. Where does the proton really get its spin? by Robert L. Jaffe il v48 Physics Today Sept '95 p24 (7)
        ABSTRACT/HEADINGS
      ABSTRACT (5 lines)
          The discovery that quarks account for only 20-30% of the spin of a proton and neutron spawned a spin crisis that led to a striking confirmation of quantum chromodynamics. In addition, it spurred experiments which produced rich data on the spin phenomena.
    -END-

It's important to understand the details of this citation. Citations from most indexes have the same or similar component parts. When in doubt, consult the introductory matter in the front of the print volume or use the Help function on the computer. Magazine title abbreviations are also listed in the introductory pages. To locate the magazine, you must know the full title. Many times a student has asked for a magazine by abbreviation and suddenly realized he or she had no idea what the abbreviation meant. This causes at least a temporary delay while the student retraces his steps to decipher the abbreviation.

Heading: PROTONS—The subject term used to find the citation.
1.—InfoTrac numbers each citation found under a subject. This is the first citation found.
Where does the proton really get its spin?—This is the title of the article, not the title of the magazine or other publication that published the article.
by Robert L. Jaffe—The author of the article.
il—An abbreviation for "illustration," meaning the article is accompanied by an illustration.
v48—Magazines and newspapers are usually given volume numbers, sometimes corresponding to the calendar year where each year is represented by a successive volume number. In this case, the September 1995 issue falls within volume 48. Issue numbers are sometimes given, too, such as v48, no 5.
Physics Today—The title of the magazine.
Sept '95—The month and year of the magazine issue. Keep in mind that some periodical publications are issued daily, some weekly, some two or three times per week, some biweekly, some monthly, some bimonthly. You must be date specific when searching for the magazine or

newspaper listed in your citation. *Newsweek,* for example, is a weekly. You will not meet with quick success if you ask for *Newsweek* September 1995.

p24—"p" means page number. This article begins on page 24.

(7)—InfoTrac uses this number in parentheses after the page number to indicate that the article is seven pages long. In the actual magazine, those seven pages may or not be printed consecutively.

ABSTRACT—A brief article summary is available. If you want to see it, select it and press Enter.

HEADINGS—Subject headings used for this citation are also available to see. Select Headings and press Enter. PROTONS was one heading. Other headings may lead you to other articles on the same topic.

TEXT—Not shown here. If offered, select Text and press Enter to view and/or print or download the full text of the article. Most computer indexes that provide text do not provide charts or illustrations.

InfoAccess provides a companion product to its index called *Magazine Collection.* Libraries that subscribe to the index may or may not subscribe to *Magazine Collection.* The collection consists of microfilm cartridges that contain the full text (photographed magazine pages, reduced in size) of entire magazines. Many (maybe 250) of the magazines indexed on InfoTrac are contained full text on the cartridges. Each citation on the index for a magazine on the collection includes a seven-digit code that sends you to the exact cartridge and frame on which the article begins.

Reader's Guide to Periodical Literature
New York: H. W. Wilson, 1901–   . Update monthly with annual cumulation.

Wilson is the venerable name in indexing. It produces many titles in print, CD-ROM, and online formats. The *Reader's Guide,* available in print, online, on tape, and on CD-ROM, indexes about 240 popular, well-known magazine titles and many specific titles as well from a variety of fields. Some of the magazines are *Atlantic Monthly, Aviation Week and Space Technology, Business Week, Christianity Today, Home Mechanix, International Wildlife, Ladies' Home Journal, Physics Today, Science, Time,* and *Women's Sports and Fitness.* An abstract edition is also available.

Other General Indexes

Access: The Supplementary Index to Periodicals
Evanston, IL: John Gordon Burke, 1975–   .
Indexes 108 that magazines *Reader's Guide to Periodical Litera-*
ture doesn't. Some titles, like *Boy's Life* and *Writer's Digest*, are indexed elsewhere, but many are not. The emphasis is on city, state, and
regional magazines, such as *Aspen, Atlanta, Cleveland, Connecticut,*
Seattle, and *Vermont Life.* Also featured are special interest magazines, such as *American Lawyer, American Photo, Elle, Family Circle,*
Outside, Smart Money, Spin, Spy, Village Voice, and *Wired.* If you
looking for information on specific places or from magazines not commonly cited, this is a good place. Available in print, online and on CD-
ROM.

Alternative Press Index
Baltimore: Alternative Press Center, 1970–   . Quarterly.
Subject access to 240 underground, alternative lifestyle, offbeat
magazines not indexed elsewhere. These publications lean left, as
would seem likely for a publication that began in the late 1960's. Subjects indexed include the environment, women's issues, sexual issues,
atheism, and animal rights. Definitely a place to check for the non-
mainstream subject, if you can find a library that subscribes to it.

Index to Black Periodicals
Boston: G. K. Hall, 1988–   . Annual
Indexes about 35 Afro-American periodicals of general and
scholarly interest, with a subject and author index arranged alphabetically. Indexing runs about two years behind the publications indexed.
Entries used can be inconsistent, so you may need to check under several
subject terms to find most articles you're interested in.

Magazine Article Summaries Full-Text Elite
Ebsco, one of the major names in supplying magazines to libraries,
produces a CD-ROM index to nearly 400 general magazines, from 1984 to
the present. It indexes the *New York Times* from 1989 and includes
full-text articles for 90 magazines. Updated monthly, it allows both
subject and keyword searching.

Magazines ASAP Plus
IAC's InfoTrac full-text upgrade of *Magazine Index.* Provides the
full text of articles or brief abstracts from 100 magazines while indexing
300 more from 1989 to present. Recent issues of the *New York Times* and
Wall Street Journal are also indexed on this CD-ROM.

Nineteenth Century Reader's Guide to Periodical Literature, 1890–1899
New York: H. W. Wilson, 1944. 2 vols.
Bridges the gap from Poole's (see the next entry) to the twentieth century.

Poole's Index to Periodical Literature, 1802–1881
Boston: Houghton, 1891, 2 vols.
The only place to look for the time period covered. Great for source material on the Civil War.

U.S. Government Periodicals Index
Bethesda, MD: Congressional Information Service, 1994–   . Quarterly.
Subject and author access to 180 federal publications of general interest, major research, or reference value. Proper name and subject access. **Superintendent of Documents (SuDoc) numbers** given for each periodical title indexed. (SuDoc numbers serve as organization and location codes for government documents, much as Dewey Decimal numbers do for books.) It should be found in academic libraries and in libraries serving as depositories for government publications. Available in print and on CD-ROM.

Newspaper Indexes

New York Times
The *New York Times* also covers significant events and scientific discoveries. It considers itself the historical record for the nation. Because of this, most college and public libraries carry it and subscribe to it in print and microfilm.

Most libraries that subscribe to the microfilm also subscribe to the *New York Times Index*. The print index is thorough but tricky to use. It gives only one main entry for an article. This entry includes description of the content, date, section, page, and column. Other entries for that article refer to the main entry by listing the subject and the date. It can also be tricky to find the corresponding article on the film. The print index is issued in monthly paperbound installments, periodically accumulated, then finally published in a hardbound annual edition. This means you have to know when an event that you are researching occurred. That way you look in the volume for the year it occurred. Other sources, chronologies, for example, may help you determine when the event occurred. (Refer to Chapter 3, p. 34, for more about chronologies.)

Let's look at an example. From the *Times* annual index for 1994, there were no entries listed under the subject word "atoms." Under the subject word "physics," however, were several entries including this:

International team of scientists working at Fermi National Accelerator Laboratory is expected to announce discovering convincing evidence for existence of top quark, last of 12 subatomic building blocks of all matter; discovery would mark major milestone for modern physics—validating theoretical Standard Model, which defines modern understanding of atom and its structure and is central to concepts of time, matter and the universe; diagram (M), Ap 26, A, 1:1.

A **main entry** such as this provides a lot of description about article content. It's the equivalent of an abstract. (M) means it's a medium-length story. The *Times* index uses (L) for a long story (more than three columns), (M) for a story between one and three columns, long and (S) for a short story, less than one column long. The month and day are then indicated. A means section A or the first section. Monday through Friday papers are normally published in four (recently, six) sections, lettered A, B, C, and D. Sections for Saturday and Sunday editions are normally numbered (more on sections below); 1:1 indicates page 1, column 1. Most indexes citing the *New York Times*, including its own, always cite the column it appeared in. The *Times* currently runs six columns.

If there had been a **"see also" cross-reference** (not a main entry but a cross-reference to a main entry) to this article under "atom," it would have read:

ATOM. See also Physics. Ap 26.

Following this lead, you turn to "physics" and hunt down the column of articles until you find the article cited April 26.

The *Times* is also available on its own CD-ROM disks. The disks are full text and are published by UMI, the same company that publishes the microfilm and the index. The CD-ROM disks do not reproduce photos or illustrations. They do allow topic and keyword searching. The articles found can be printed or downloaded to floppy disks. Libraries that subscribe to the full-text disks often drop their subscriptions to the print index but continue their subscriptions to the microfilm, if they can afford it, because of the photos, illustrations, advertising, and other matter not included on the disks. In any case, whether you use the *Times* disk as an index, use the print index, or find your citation to the *Times* in Ebsco, InfoTrac, or other index, you need to be aware of two details to make locating the article easier.

First, the *Times* publishes two editions; a local edition widely distributed throughout the Northeast and a national edition distributed everywhere else. Both editions may be indexed in the sources you use. If so, the citations will be designated by (L) for local and (N) for national. You then need to match the correct citation to the edition on the microfilm. The two editions are not identical. An article on page 1, section 1 in the local edition may be published on page 8, section 2 in the national edition. Articles from one edition may not appear at all in the other edition. Libraries subscribing to the microfilm and its print index should receive the corresponding matching edition for each.

The other trick pertains to sections of the newspaper. Either letters or roman numerals may be used in the index, but on the film or the newspaper itself, you may find the other used so that they don't seem to match. Just keep in mind that section A = section I, section B = section II, and so on.

A search for the word "atoms" in the *New York Times* CD-ROM for January–November 1995 produced 60 articles. They ranged from "Chih-Kung Jeh Is Dead at 89; Leader in Microwave Physics," by William Dicke, November 24, 1995, to "Deep Solar Rumblings May Offer Key to Sun's Inner Structure," by Malcolm W. Browne, October 24, 1995.

This last citation looks like this:

Access No. 9300050307 ProQuest—The New York Times (R) Ondisc
Title: DEEP SOLAR RUMBLINGS MAY OFFER KEY TO SUN'S
     INNER STRUCTURE
Authors: Malcolm W. Browne
Source: The New York Times, Late Edition—Final
Date: Tuesday Oct 24, 1995   Sec: C   Science Desk p: 1
     Length: Long (2061 words) Illus: Diagram, Photo
Subjects: SPACE; TELESCOPES 7 OBSERVATORIES; SUN;
     GLOBAL OSCILLATION NETWORK GROUP (GONG);
     SOUND
An abstract and full text follow.

Many other newspapers are indexed; some are available full text online through fee subscription services such as Dialog, America Online, and CompuServe. Many libraries index their local newspapers because the content is so valuable for local news yet it is not profitable for a commercial firm to do the indexing. Indexes are available for *Barron's* and the *Wall Street Journal*. UMI produces the *Wall Street Journal* and the *Washington Post* on CD-ROM as it does the *New York Times*.

NewsBank

NewsBank provides *NewsBank* and *Business NewsBank*. These products index newspaper articles from around the country by topics thought most appealing to most general researchers. The company photographed the articles and reproduced them on microfiche cards. Recently NewsBank started putting the newspaper full text directly on the CD-ROM disk. It now includes wire service articles, like those from the Associated Press, that are distributed to many subscribing newspapers.

A sample full-text article from NewsBank Newsfile/CD News-Bank looks like this:

Source: Washington Post
Headline: INSIDE THE INDIVISIBLE: QUARKS COLLIDE WITH
              THEORIES
              SCIENCE: PHYSICS
Date: February 19, 1996   Length: 1351 words
Page: A3   Edition: FINAL
                                  Section A SECTION
Author: Curt Suplee Washington Post Staff Writer
Index Terms: atoms
              physicists
              research
              quarks
         The full text follows.

A NewsBank citation that refers to microfiche looks like this:

MICROFICHE LOCATOR CODE: NewsBank 1992 SCI 41:E10
SOURCE: San Jose (California) Mercury News
DATE: December 8, 1992
ABSTRACT: Scientists from many disciplines are investigating the practical applications of nanotechnology, research into objects as as small as atoms.
INDEX TERMS:
NewsBank SCIENTIFIC RESEARCH
         nanotechnology
         charts

This citation does not offer full text. It was produced before News-Bank offered full-text CD-ROM products. Instead, the locator code refers to a microfiche card on which the newspaper text has been photographically reproduced. Microfiche cards are grouped by year, then color coded by subject. Business news articles, for example, are on one set of cards color coded yellow; science articles are on another set of cards color coded gray. All cards for the same year are filed together. On this card, SCI stands for "science." The card number is 41. The grid number is E10, meaning that the particular frame on the card that contains the *San Jose Mercury News* article described in the abstract can be found in row E, column 10. When you look at the microfiche card, it is clearly identified with the year and full locator code. First you find the year, then the subject, then the card number. Take the card, put it on the microfiche machine, and search for frame E10. When you look at the frames on the microfiche machine, you will find that each frame is clearly marked with the frame locator number and identified with the source name (*San Jose Mercury News*, in this case) and publication date.

Specialized Indexes

Depending on your topic, you may wish to consult a specialized index. H. W. Wilson produces many specialized indexes, including *Business Periodicals Index, Humanities Index, General Science Index, Social Sciences Index,* and *Art Index.* InfoAccess produces *Business Magazine Index, Health Reference Center,* and others. UMI produces *ABI/INFORM,* a business periodicals database. Each of these products indexes a hundred or more specialized publications within the topic indicated by the index's title. We'll discuss subject-specific indexes in more detail in the following subject chapters. Since we've been talking about atoms and physics, however, examples are given below to complete this chapter's theme.

Biology Digest

NewsBank's *Biology Digest* product is not limited to newspapers. Articles are full text on disk and come from both general and specific scientific publications, about 170 in all. *Biology Digest* covers scientific issues of all types (not just related to biology), including the environment; plant, animal, and insect life; and health and disease. Publications included can be popular like *Organic Gardening, Psychology Today,* and *Discover,* or highly technical, like *Journal of Immunopharmacology* or *Recombinant DNA Technical Bulletin.* A search on the keyword "atoms," for example, produced 39 articles. Of those, "The Classical Limit of an Atom" came from *Scientific American,* (June 1994), while "'Molecule of Life' Is Found in Space" came from *New Scientist* (June 11, 1994). One point of information about *Biology Digest:* Although some of the articles are full text, most are edited down. *Biology Digest* most commonly provides a lengthy summary, or "digest," rather than an abstract or full text. The digest may suffice even for serious students. If not, it serves as an index to the full article.

General Science Index

Biology Digest can lead to highly specific publications. So can specific indexes such as *General Science Index.* It indexes about 150 journals, such as *American Journal of Physics, Botanical Review, Contemporary Physics, Impact of Science on Society,* and *Quarterly Review of Biology.* More specific indexes are available, such as *Current Physics Index* and *Physics Abstracts,* but they're more for upper-level college physics majors, graduate students, or researchers.

To continue following the "atom" example, *General Science Index* for 1991–1992 produced citations for 11 articles on atoms, plus eight cross-references. *Physics Teacher* published "Seeing Atoms" in January 1992, for example. Under "electrons," the *Journal of Chemical Education* published "Describing Electron Distribution in the Hydrogen Molecule, a New Approach" by C. J. Willis (September 1991).

INTERLIBRARY LOAN

Suppose you want these articles. Suppose, judging by the title or the abstract, one of them seemed to be exactly what you needed for your research paper. Also suppose the library you're using is a medium-sized public library that doesn't subscribe to such technical journals. How can you get the article? The answer is interlibrary loan. Nearly all libraries participate in interlibrary loan, a program of exchange that allows libraries to access from each other materials they don't own for their customers. No library can own everything, so interlibrary loan is the next best thing. It can be slow, but it does work.

For articles, if they're not too long, fax machines have speeded things up considerably.

Interlibrary loan works for books too. The librarian can search the collections of other libraries through shared bibliographic systems that list the holdings of all participating libraries; through OCLC, a national bibliographic database listing the holdings of hundreds of libraries; or through the Internet, which allows access to the computerized catalog of one library at a time.

Sometimes there's a fee attached to interlibrary loan, especially for copies of articles and for materials from college libraries. Often there's no fee. If it's important enough to you, it may cost you. Just ask your information librarian about the procedure. The other option, if the library is near enough, is for you or the librarian to identify the library owning the material you need and for you to go there directly and use it, copy it, or borrow it if possible.

WHAT YOU SHOULD KNOW ABOUT MICROFILM

Not every computerized index offers full text on disk. Print indexes certainly don't. When you find an article listing, or **citation**, you will need to determine in what format the library holds that magazine or newspaper. Most libraries provide listings of their periodical subscriptions, the publication dates covered, the format in which they hold the publication, and perhaps, if it's a fairly large library, where they store the publication. The may have it in print, for example. You may be able to retrieve the print issue yourself on the public floor. If so, magazines and newspapers are often stored alphabetically by title, with each title stored by year and specific date of issue. If not available on the public floor, you will need to request the specific issue at the information desk because many libraries keep back files of periodicals stored in nonpublic areas.

Print, sometimes called **hard copy**, offers you text and the publication's original illustrations and advertising. Storing hard-copy back files of magazines and newspapers causes the library storage, retrieval, filing, and safety hazard problems, however. Specific issues can get lost, misfiled, torn, worn out, or cut out. Hard copy takes a lot of storage space, and most libraries don't have the room. Newspapers in particular become brittle with age and present a fire hazard. Many libraries choose to dispose of the original hard copy after a couple of years and replace it with a **microform** reproduction.

The microform, also called **microfilm**, allows a library to keep lengthy runs of the newspaper in a small space without the fire hazard of newsprint. University Microfilms (UMI) is one of the major companies that photographs newspapers, magazines, and journals from around the nation and world, page by page; reduces those photographs; and reproduces them on film in *micro* format. To use the film, you put it on a machine equipped with a magnifying lens. This enlarges the picture, allowing you to read the microprint easily. Most of these machines are also equipped with photocopiers so you can make a paper print of the article to take home.

Microfilm products come in three basic varieties in libraries. Microfilm generally means **roll film**, either **16 mm (wide)** or **8 mm (narrow)**; 16 mm is usually on **reels,** 8 mm packaged in **cartridges.** The term **microfiche** describes flat 4" x 6" film cards. Microfilm reproduces the entire publication, including all illustrations and advertising, but in black and white. Photocopies made from microfilm reproduce black and white. Text is fine, but illustrations, when viewed on a microfilm machine, appear in quality only slightly better than silhouette. The photocopied reproductions unfortunately lack clear detail. Color film and copiers are not currently available.

CHAPTER 5

Using the Internet to Conduct Library Research

Amy Terlaga

The Internet has a wealth of information. But because nearly anyone can create Web pages and post information on anything they choose, the quality and availability of research materials vary widely. You might get great support for one project but nothing (or very questionable) materials for another.

The Internet in general tends to have more complete and accurate information on cutting-edge technical-scientific issues. For information on telecommunication technology, The Net may be the best place to go for advanced information. For information on historical or literary topics, the more traditional print and electronic library resources are a better place to start. Sources like these will help you put your topic within the broader picture. In fact, there are few topics that shouldn't begin with an electronic overview.

That said, you will be amazed with just how much information you can find on practically anything under the sun when it comes to the Internet. You just need to know where and how to look.

GETTING STARTED

First, determine whether your library has an Internet connection and whether searching is permitted by its users. (Some libraries have Internet terminals only for staff to use.) Ask a librarian to show you where the Internet terminals are and how to access the Internet if it is not on the screen when you sit down to use it. Some libraries have some rules concerning Internet use; for instance, there may be a time limit for Internet searching, you may have a limit to the number of pages you can print, or you may have to download all information found onto your own floppy disk if you want to save anything.

Ask the librarian about these rule; it may save you the headache of interrupted research. Keep in mind, though, that you can always copy down the Web site addresses you find to check out later if you do run out of time in this first session.

Most people searching the Internet, are really searching one part of it, the World Wide Web, which has been and continues to be the fastest-growing part of the Internet. The Web is a collection of Web sites (or pages): text, pictures, and other information located on computers all around the world. To demonstrate what I mean by this, think of the page you are reading right now. Now imagine this page on a computer screen. Now imagine that some of the words on this page are a different color. When you put your mouse arrow over them, the little arrow turns into a hand. Those words are called hypertext links. When you click the mouse on any of these words, the computer will whisk you off to another page of text, maybe even a page at another Web site! The idea is to give you, the user, the power to investigate further based on the word(s) you clicked on. That's hypertext.

WHAT IS A URL?

Think of a URL (universal, or uniform, resource locator) as a Web site's address. You can track down any page on the Web if you have its Web address, its URL. A URL looks something like this:

http://www.sitename.com

The first part (http: //) is always at the beginning of any Web site address. (However, most browsers now accept the URL without the http: //.)

The "www" part is also very common for Web site addresses, although it doesn't have to be part of the formula. The rest, "sitename.com," usually is the company's name (e.g., Microsoft), with ".com" indicating what kind of a Web site it is. "Com" stands for commercial company, "org" is nonprofit, and "edu" is educational (usually a college or university).

Sometimes URLs can be much longer than these basic few parts. That's because many Web sites have additional directories, subdirectories, and files attached to them. As soon as you click on a word or image on that site's main (often called home) page, it will usually bring you to another directory at that site. The URL will now look something like this:

http://www.sitename.com/directoryname/ filename.html

The nice thing about URLs is you can use their directory or file addresses to get to the exact page you want to read without going through the home page address. Just type in this new and longer URL, and instantly you're there.

ON TO SEARCHING

Searching on the Web is getting easier and easier now that we have some good Internet searching tools at our fingertips. These tools come in the form of subject directories and word search engines.

A **subject directory** uses very broad subject terms to organize all of its Web site information. Subject directories are great places to start a search since someone has selected a few hundred (or thousand perhaps) sites from the millions out there and organized them into easily usable groups. Subject directories are useful for term papers and other school projects. For instance, consider the home page of the most popular subject directory site on the Web, Yahoo! (http://www.yahoo.com). After you type in the URL, you will see a screen like the graphics on pages 54 to 56.

Each of these main subject categories and their corresponding subcategories is clickable. Once you click on a subject, say Humanities, you are then brought to Yahoo's subdirectory, Humanities. All of the categories on Humanities are also clickable. Each one has its own Web page with its own links. Keep in mind that you are still in Yahoo! The numbers in parentheses after the subjects let you know just how many links will be on that subject page. Eventually a link will lead you out of Yahoo! and into the big, wide world of the Web. That is, in fact, your main objective: finding information on the Web. Yahoo! has just organized the Web site addresses so you can find your information in a logical manner.

The next few paragraphs will demonstrate how to search for information on Charlotte Brontë, a subject also explored in the next chapter. For instance, if we follow the link "Literature" on the Humanities page, we find another category, "Genre." If we follow that link, we come to another subcategory Yahoo! listing. One of the genres listed is Literary Fiction, the kind of genre Charlotte Brontë's work would fall under. Luckily, Authors is one of the subcategories on the Literary Fiction page. Following this Authors link, we see that Brontë, Charlotte (1816–1855), is indeed listed on this page. Following this link, we come to a screen as on the bottom of p. 56.

Happy New Year
College Bowls

Win Your Holiday Wish List! **VISA**
Click Here!

Holiday
Movie Guide

Search | options

Yellow Pages - People Search - Maps - Classifieds - Personals - Chat - **Email**
Holiday Shopping - My Yahoo! - News - Sports - Weather - Stock Quotes

- **Arts and Humanities**
  Architecture, Photography, Literature...

- **Business and Economy [Xtra!]**
  Companies, Finance, Employment...

- **Computers and Internet [Xtra!]**
  Internet, WWW, Software, Multimedia...

- **Education**
  Universities, K-12, College Entrance...

- **Entertainment [Xtra!]**
  Cool Links, Movies, Music, Humor...

- **Government**
  Military, Politics [**Xtra!**], Law, Taxes...

- **Health [Xtra!]**
  Medicine, Drugs, Diseases, Fitness...

- **News and Media [Xtra!]**
  Current Events, Magazines, TV, Newspapers...

- **Recreation and Sports [Xtra!]**
  Sports, Games, Travel, Autos, Outdoors...

- **Reference**
  Libraries, Dictionaries, Phone Numbers...

- **Regional**
  Countries, Regions, U.S. States...

- **Science**
  CS, Biology, Astronomy, Engineering...

- **Social Science**
  Anthropology, Sociology, Economics...

- **Society and Culture**
  People, Environment, Religion...

Yahooligans! for Kids - Beatrice's Guide - MTV/Yahoo! unfURLed - 3D Stock Viewer
What's New - Weekly Picks - Today's Web Events - Yahoo! Internet Life
Visa Shopping Guide - Yahoo! Store

World Yahoos Australia & NZ - Canada - Denmark - France - Germany - Japan - Korea
Norway - SE Asia - Sweden - UK & Ireland
Yahoo! Metros Atlanta - Austin - Boston - Chicago - Dallas / Fort Worth - Los Angeles
Get Local Miami - Minneapolis / St. Paul - New York - S.F. Bay - Seattle - Wash D.C.

Smart Shopping with **VISA**

How to Suggest a Site - Company Info - Openings at Yahoo! - Contributors - Yahoo! to Go

Top:Arts:Humanities:Literature

| | Search | Options |

◉ Search all of Yahoo ○ Search only in **Literature**

- **Yahoo! Net Events: Books and Literature** - today's author chats and programs.
- **Indices** *(42)*

- **Authors** *(39)*
- **Awards** *(29)*
- **Banned Books** *(18)*
- **Bestseller Lists** *(9)*
- **Book Arts** *(53)*
- **Classics@**
- **Companies@**
- **Countries, Cultures, and Groups** *(110)*
- **Criticism and Theory** *(91)*
- **Education** *(59)*
- **Electronic Literature** *(76)*
- **Events** *(57)*
- **Exhibits** *(54)*
- **Genres** *(4926)* NEW!
- **History of Books and Printing** *(55)*
- **Institutes** *(137)*

- **Journals** *(40)* NEW!
- **Libraries@**
- **Magazines** *(464)* NEW!
- **Mailing Lists** *(14)*
- **Museums** *(14)*
- **Online Forums** *(31)*
- **Organizations** *(86)*
- **Periods and Movements** *(217)*
- **Poetry** *(1875)* NEW!
- **Publishing@**
- **Reference** *(74)*
- **Reviews** *(132)*
- **Scripts** *(8)*
- **Storytelling@**
- **Television Shows@**
- **Writing@**
- **Usenet** *(20)*

- New York Times Books ☞ - includes the complete Sunday Book Review, daily book related news and reviews, a searchable archive of over 50,000 New York Times Book Reviews, bestseller lists, and more.

- Book Game - try to identify books by their first and last lines.
- BookBrowser - collection of fiction reading lists. Find the next book in a series, new works by your favorite author or new titles in your favorite genre.
- Booknotes - America's finest authors on reading, writing, and the power of ideas. Includes transcripts and and RealVideo clips from the C-SPAN show.
- Bookplex - excerpts of best-sellers and interviews with popular authors, such as Anne Rice, Clive Barker and Dominick Dunne.
- Booktalk - all the buzz about books.
- BookWeb ▶REVIEW◀ - author tours, bookstore directories, discussion groups, etc.
- BookWire ▶REVIEW◀ - bestseller lists, reviews and more.
- Chapter One - featuring full first chapters of books with reviews and discussions, from the Washington Post.
- Digital BookWorld - index of new and old books, by author, title or publisher, as well as links to

further resources.
- First Lines - your challenge is to name the book given the first line.
- Incipit - contains the first lines of various works of literature; site is in Italian, but the works are not restricted to Italian authors.
- Just So Postcards - literary email postcards, with quotes from Kipling, Carroll, Baudelaire, Anna Akhmatova, Pushkin, Cervantes, Rimbaud and many others.
- Literary HyperCalendar - this day in literary history...
- Literary Locales - pictures links to some places that figure in the lives and writings of famous authors: Bede's World, Wordsworth's Lake District, Joyce's Dublin, etc.
- Reader's Corner, The - for readers of fantasy, romance and mystery stories. Our site and our free e-mail publication include lots of genre fiction and theme material.
- Real Fiction - a listing of novels published by small presses. We welcome readers and authors.
- UNCAT: Catalog of Uncataloged Titles - Publications, video and audio cassettes, from businesses, nonprofit groups, self-publishers, covering art, education, finance, health, history, products, self-development, services, travel, "other."
- Watch File (Writers and Their Copyright Holders) - database containing the names and addresses of copyright holders for English-language authors whose papers are in US and UK libraries and archives.
- FAQ - rec.arts.books ▸REVIEW◂

BEATRICE ASKS, "Looking for this?"

| Relationships ▼ | Click here |

Top:Arts:Humanities:Literature:Genres:Literary Fiction:Authors: Bronte, Charlotte (1816-1855)

| | Search | Options |

⦿ Search all of Yahoo ○ Search only in **Bronte, Charlotte (1816-1855)**

- Brontë Sisters, The
- Charlotte Brontë: An Overview
- Jane Eyre
- Life of Charlotte Bronte, The - text of the biography by Elizabeth Gaskell.

All of the links on this page will bring you to Web sites not at Yahoo! For instance, the second one, Charlotte Brontë: An Overview, has the URL,

http://www.stg.brown.edu/projects/
hypertext/landow/victorian/cbronte/
bronteov3.html

And its home page looks like this:

Charlotte Bronte: An Overview

- Works
- Literary Relations
- Biographical Materials
- Artistic Relations
- The Cultural Context: Victorianism
- Religion and Philosophy
- Social and Political Contexts
- Science and Technology

THEME AND TECHNIQUE

- Themes
- Characterization
- Imagery, Symbolism, and Motifs
- Narration and Point of View Setting
- Genre and Mode

Search Engines

Internet search engines are provided for users to search one or many databases for specific information. There are many different kinds of search engine sites on the Web. Some search for personal e-mail addresses, others for e-mail discussion groups, and still others for very homogeneous, specialized databases, like dictionaries or almanacs. The kind of search engines you want to use for your library research are World Wide Web search engines. Web search engines usually require the user only to input a keyword or two, then click a search button;

search results are displayed in a matter of seconds. These search results usually consist of the URLs of Web pages that contain your keywords somewhere on the page. Sometimes the search engine site also gives a brief summary of the site. (See pages 59 to 61 for an example of a search engine site and search result.) This is a nice plus when searching: it saves a great deal of time if you can determine whether a site has relevant information. All you need to do is look at the summary instead of visiting the site itself.

There are over 40 Web search engine sites in existence in the Internet. Most offer their search services for free. Remember, though, that not everything that a search engine brings back as a result will be relevant to your research, and a lot of what is brought back will be junk. Keep in mind that you must critically evaluate all the information you find on the Internet. *Consider the source.* In other words, if PBS (Public Broadcasting Service) provides information on the Cuban missile crisis, confidence will most likely be high that this information is true. But if you get your information from a site called Kevin's Internet Encyclopedia, you may want to verify the information found there by checking into another source.

Search Techniques

You can use many of the same skills you've learned in searching the library electronic catalog when searching the Internet with the aid of a search engine. When choosing your keywords, try to use those that define your search uniquely. You won't want to waste your time sifting through a lot of irrelevant information just because a Web page had the word **Cuban** on its page 20 times. Also look for search engine sites that allow for phrase searching. Phrase searching allows you to input a number of keywords, then have them linked together as a phrase, so that only Web pages that have those words linked together on their pages will be brought back.

Let's use **Cuban missile crisis** as an example. Searched as a phrase, you are guaranteed to get only Web pages that have "Cuban missile crisis" somewhere on the page. For a search engine site that does not allow phrase searching, you may end up with pages that have *Cuban* in the first paragraph, *missile* in the third paragraph, and *crisis* in the title. Granted, chances are that this site will probably pertain to your topic, but there are many instances in which the words will not be so uniquely linked as a concept or specific person. Of course, you could always put in more keywords to clarify what you are looking for. The problem with this approach is that you may end up with nothing. Too many words may equal too specific.

There will be times when your search at a site will not provide much. If you don't succeed, try again with another search engine. There are plenty of them, and no two work exactly the same way. Take the time to read the search Help link provided at each search engine site the first time you visit it. It only takes a few minutes and may save you time in the long run. If you use the proper syntax, your search results will be more on target. It won't take long for you to find a favorite site, and you'll also find that some sites are better than others, for different reasons. One may be easy to use and give you quick results, while another may give you the best results time and time again.

CITING WEB RESOURCE INFORMATION

When it comes time to write your paper, you'll need to footnote any information you retrieved from the Web. The following Web sites can be referred to for some professionally recognized formats:

"Bibliographic Formats for Citing Electronic Information" includes examples of new guidelines that are included in Xia Li's and Nancy B. Crane's book, *The Official Internet World Guide to Electronic Styles* (http://www.uvm.edu/~xli/reference/estyles.html). Also see "MLA-Style Citations of Electronic Resources," by Janice R. Walker (http://www.cas.usf.edu/english/walker/mla.html).

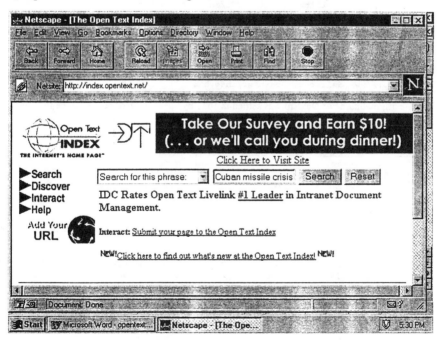

Open Text search from http://index.opentext.net. Reprinted by permission of Open Text Corporation, 1996.

The Open Text Index found **236** pages containing: cuban missile crisis

You can improve your result or start a new search.

pages 1-10 (of 236)

1. **Cuban Missile Crisis** (score: 1206, size: 2.4k)
   From: http://choo.fis.utoronto.ca/FIS/Courses/LIS2149/Case97/Cuban.html
   LIS 2149: Case Analysis and Presentation of The Cuban Missile Crisis. The United States and
   Soviet Union: "Eyeball to Eyeball" by Sandra Shoufani and Judith Zoltai. Abstract: On October
   16, 1962, American aerial photographs revealed that the Sovie
   [Visit the page]

2. **31st Fighter Wing History** (score: 104, size: 10.5k)
   From: http://www.avi.af.mil/hh/31fw.html
   The Life and Times of the 31st Fighter Wing. The wing has a long and proud heritage that spans
   several decades at multiple locations. World War II Post World War II Cuban Missile Crisis Viet
   Nam Recent History A New Home... A New Mission. World War II. The
   [Visit the page]

3. **La morte di Mattei - Pag9** (score: 104, size: 4.2k)
   From: http://www.bookline.gvo.it/10001/mattei/pag9.htm
   Proprio dell'Italia si parlò, in termini molto drammatici, in quella riunione dello ExComm, come
   probabile obiettivo, insieme alla Turchia, di una ritorsione sovietica. "un'azione di forza a Cuba
   potrebbe comportare un attacco ai missili in Tur
   [Visit the page]

4. **Del Rio Chamber of Commerce Information** (score: 103, size: 5.3k)
   From: http://www.delrio.com/chamber/info.html
   The Devil's River just north of Lake Amistad. © 1996 by Blake Trester History San Felipe del
   Rio, the original name of Del Rio was settled in 1635 by Spanish missionaries. Since then, this
   area has seen indian attacks, the coming of the railroads, Judge
   [Visit the page]

5. **Del Rio Chamber of Commerce Information** (score: 103, size: 5.3k)
   From: http://server.delrio.com/~delriotx/info.html
   The Devil's River just north of Lake Amistad. © 1996 by Blake Trester History San Felipe del
   Rio, the original name of Del Rio was settled in 1635 by Spanish missionaries. Since then, this
   area has seen indian attacks, the coming of the railroads, Judge
   [Visit the page]

6. **Graduate Course: POLS630 International Politics (Requirements & Policy)** (score: 102, size:
   10.8k)
   From: http://www-polisci.tamu.edu/dept/classes/danilovic/policy630.htm
   POLS 630 International Politics Spring 1997 Professor: Vesna Danilovic Course Requirements
   and Policy Required Materials The following required texts are available for purchase at the
   University Bookstore (only the course packet should be purchased at Notes
   [Visit the page]

7. **College of Humanistic Studies** (score: 102, size: 2.5k)

From: `http://www.mursuky.edu/college5.htm`
Murray State University College of Humanistic Studies Research the Cuban Missile Crisis or
delve into Chaucer's Canterbury Tales. Study the development of human societies or embark on a
summer study in Florence, Italy. Examine the ethical responsibiliti
[Visit the page]

8. **DCC: Connection: Item of the Week** (score: 102, size: 2.1k)
From: `http://www.discovery.ca/connection/itemweek/0615_url.htm`
The Item of the Week for June 15 - June 22. This is the American U2 Spy Plane The U2, under
the auspices of the CIA, played a pivotal role twice during the 1960s. First, when Francis Gary
Powers was shot down in a U2 (near Sverdlovsk, USSR, on May 1, 1960)
[Visit the page]

9. **Cold War Letters: Preface** (score: 102, size: 3.2k)
From: `http://www.sjcme.edu/wellehan/cldwrpr.htm`
The following is excerpted from the preface of The Cold War Letters. These copies of letters
written over a period of little more than one year preceding the Cuban Missile Crisis of 1962, have
been made for friends who might be expected to understand someth
[Visit the page]

10. **Crimson Tide** (score: 102, size: 5.0k)
From: `http://www.xtravision.ie/crimson.html`
When a volatile Russian nationalist and a rebel faction of the former Soviet Army seize control of
a nuclear missile base, it triggers the greatest global emergency since the Cuban Missile Crisis in
the dramatic action adventure film, Crimson Tide. With the
[Visit the page]

More...

Open Text search from http://index.opentext.net. Reprinted by permission of Open Text
Corporation, 1996.

CHAPTER 6

Sample Library Searches

LITERATURE: RESEARCHING CHARLOTTE BRONTË AND *JANE EYRE*

This is an example of how to use a library for a specific term paper topic in English. Let us suppose you have selected Charlotte Brontë's novel *Jane Eyre* as your literature topic. In a library with an automated card catalog, start by going to an OPAC terminal. After selecting the "author" choice on the menu screen, type in "Brontë, Charlotte." You will see on the screen a variety of books by her. Go to the individual screen on each book to see if it is in or out of the building. Often these screens show the date the book is due to be returned. (Sometimes the books are not returned on time, however.) Print out the full information about the books or, if there is no printer, copy down the Dewey Decimal call number for the books, which will usually be found at the beginning of the citation. Brontë's fiction books will not usually have a Dewey number but are arranged alphabetically by author on the shelves in the fiction section of the library.

Before you leave the terminal, you will need to do some more searches. Select the search option "subject." Type in *Jane Eyre* this time to see if there is a whole book about this novel. Since this is the title of a novel, type in *Jane Eyre,* and do not reverse the name by typing in "Eyre, Jane" as you would if this was an author. Print out the full information about the books (if there is no printer, copy down the Dewey Decimal call number).

Select the search option "subject." Type in "Brontë, Charlotte" again. Now the screen will show books about the author, such as biographies or literary criticism. Many of these will be in the 823.8 section of the library, which contains books about English authors of fiction who lived in the Victorian period—roughly 1800–1900. Go to the individual screen on each book to see if it is in or out of the building. This so-called full record screen may also tell you some useful things about the book that may influence your selection. For instance, books with bibliographies will help to identify other books to look for; the number of pages may be helpful to weed out brief books.

There are often more complex search strategies that the librarian can help you with, so don't think that you have finished with catalog searching. For example, when you search by subject and get several hits, these are often in chronological sequence so that the most recent ones can be quickly seen, and you can highlight several topics or books at one time to get group printouts. You can sometimes combine terms for searching in categories in which there are many titles.

If you can't find anything in the OPAC under "Brontë" or *Jane Eyre,* the library may still have useful material in other books on English literature. These may be found both in the reference and circulating sections of the library.

Shelf Searching

Go to the shelves and look at the books. Here you may select the books by the reputation of the author, the most recent publication date, the length, or the particular relevance to your critical approach to the topic.

When you are deciding which books to look at in detail, check these parts of the book:

The **Introduction** or **Preface** may give you an idea of what the author is writing about.

The **Table of Contents** in the front of the book lists major topics in order. Look to see if the book has a chapter on *Jane Eyre.*

In the **Index** in the back of the book, look under "J" (not "E") for "*Jane Eyre.*" Don't reverse the name because in this case it is a title, not the name of a person If there is no listing under "Jane Eyre," check the "Brontë, Charlotte" heading and look for a subheading under *Jane Eyre.*

The **Bibliography** in the back of the book lists other books you may find useful.

A **Chronology** may place your book in historical context.

Footnotes are sometimes found at the bottom of each page in the body of the book, in a separate section at the end of each chapter, or at the back of the book. They tell you about books the author researched to find material to write the book. They can be very helpful in telling you what other books to look for. Footnotes are sometimes called *citations* because they cite other materials.

Books about English Fiction (823)

If one of the call numbers is 823, when you get to the shelves, also look at nearby books. Some of these may be books about English fiction writers and may have articles or sections in the books about Brontë. See especially the subdivision 823.8. Here you may find:

The Brontë Novels
Craik, W. A. New York: Methuen, 1968.
A source focusing on Brontë's novels exclusively. This criticism compares *Jane Eyre* to *Wuthering Heights*.

The Brontës: A Collection of Critical Essays
Gregor, Ian. Englewood Cliffs, NJ: Prentice Hall, 1970.
In the table of contents you can find: page 76, "The Place of Love in Jane Eyre and Wuthering Heights" by Mark Kinkead Weekes; and page 110, "Fire and Eyre: Charlotte Brontë's War of Earthly Elements," by David Lodge.

Charlotte Brontë
New York: Twayne's Masterwork Studies, 1987.
This short book comments on the historical context, importance, and critical reception and includes a chapter entitled "A Conscientious Study of Art," which theorizes that the places where Jane lived— Lowood, Thornfield, and Marsh End—corresponded to stages in Jane's mental development and artistic vision. This book also has a bibliography or list of other works about *Jane Eyre*.

The Scribner Companion to the Brontës
Evans, Barbara, and Lloyd, Gareth. New York: Scribner's, 1982.
In the index under "Jane Eyre" you will find a commentary on the natural and unnatural themes in *Jane Eyre,* as well as a synopsis, a list of characters, and a list of places.

B—Biography Books

If some of the books have the letter "B" as part of the call number, they are biographies of Brontë in a special biography section of the library, where books are arranged alphabetically by the person who is the subject of the biography. All books about Brontë will be in the "B" section of biography.

Fact Outline Inventory

By now you will have accumulated some notes about Brontë that may be helpful in further research. From the terminal, you have a list of books by and about Brontë that this library owns. You know her birth and death dates from the terminal, and you may have found out that she lived in a particular part of England. Her biography may include an outline of her life with other dates, places, and people. Now use your fact outline to meet with the librarian. Tell her or him what you've found out and ask for any suggestions on where else to look. The librarian should be able to identify additional sources in the library and other sources in other libraries and perhaps even on the Internet.

Reference Books

If some of the books have "R" or "Ref" before the Dewey Decimal call number, that means they are in the reference section of the library. This is usually designated by signs on the shelves, and it is often located close to the reference desk. Look at the other books in the 823 section of reference and see if they have articles in them about Brontë. You will have to look in the front of each book to see if the Table of Contents includes Brontë and in the back of the book to see if Brontë is listed in the index. In the reference section in the 803, area you may find the following books.

Benet's Reader's Encyclopedia
Murphy, Bruce. 4th ed. New York: HarperCollins, 1996.
Under "Brontë, Charlotte," we find out that she lived from 1816 to 1855 and was one of three sisters who also collaborated together on other books written under the name of "Bell." We learn that *Jane Eyre*, her best-known and most successful novel, was published in 1847. At the end of the "Charlotte Brontë" entry, we are referred to an entry about her brother Patrick who was Charlotte's tutor and who was an opium addict. Also in the *Reader's Encyclopedia* under "Jane Eyre" we find that in *Jane Eyre* Brontë introduced in both hero and heroine two new types to English fiction. Jane is a shy, intense little orphan, not the superficial beauty and charmer that marked the conventional heroine of English fiction; her lover, Edward Rochester, is strange and violent without the conventional courtesy of most heroes of English fiction.

The Cambridge Guide to Literature in English
Ousby, Ian. Cambridge: Cambridge University Press, 1988.
Includes 3,100 entries on authors, titles, characters, and literary

terms, with critical comments. This book is similar to *Benet's Reader's Encyclopedia* (the previous entry.)

A Handbook to Literature
Holman, C. Hugh, and Harmon, William. New York: Macmillan, 1986. 5th ed.
On page 535 is an outline of literary history showing that the 1847 publication of *Jane Eyre* coincided with writings by Tennyson, Thackeray, and Dickens in England and Emerson and Longfellow in America. In the index to this book under "Brontë, Charlotte," we find that she wrote in the early Victorian age and that during that period there was a lessening of the romantic and an increase in realism.

Bibliographies

Brontë Bibliography
Yablon, G. Anthony, and Turner, John. New York: Bowker, 1987.
An effort to list all of the Brontës' works, as well as critical and biographical material.

Reference Works in British and American Literature
Bracken, James K. Englewood, CO: Libraries Unlimited, 1990–1991. 2 vols.
Volume 1 annotates over 500 magazine indexes, bibliographies, biographical sources, and research libraries in these fields. Volume 2 includes reference works on 637 authors arranged alphabetically.

As you are browsing in these bibliographies and in books on criticism, you may find that reference is made to particular books more frequently than to others. This is an important clue to their value. For example, a very early biography was written by Mrs. Gaskell and is still frequently referred to:

The Life of Charlotte Brontë
Gaskell, Mrs. New York: Harper, 1900.

Now move to the R820 section of the Reference area of the library. You will recall that 820 is the English literature section. A book very similar to *The Readers' Encyclopedia* but limited to English literature is:

The Oxford Companion to English Literature
Drabble, Margaret, ed. New York: Oxford University Press, 1995.
The editor, Margaret Drabble, is a prominent English novelist of

the 1980s. This book has articles on Charlotte Brontë that reveal the circumstances surrounding the writing and publishing of *Jane Eyre* and mentions that it was originally published under the pseudonym Currer Bell. *The Oxford Companion* also has an article under *Jane Eyre* that summarizes the plot and gives a brief critical history.

English Literary Criticism

In the 820.9 part of the reference section are several multivolume literary criticism series.

The Chelsea House Library of Literary Criticism
Bloom, Harold, ed. New York: Chelsea House, 1988.
This set is arranged chronologically so it is important to have the author's dates. In the case of Charlotte Brontë, we know from our earlier research that she lived from 1816 to 1855, so we can find her in Volume 7, dealing with the earlier Victorian period. (In English history, the nineteenth century is often called the Victorian period, after Queen Victoria, who reigned for most of the nineteenth century.) In this volume, pages 4194–4229 contain a variety of critical essays on Charlotte Brontë, including several on *Jane Eyre*. In 1974 Thomas Langford wrote "Prophetic Imagination and the Unity of *Jane Eyre*," and in 1977 Nancy Pell wrote "Resistance, Rebellion, and Marriage: The Economics of *Jane Eyre*." These are useful essays that reveal how critics dealt with the novel and show you what a critical essay looks like. It is very important not to plagiarize, or copy the exact words of other critics, for your paper, but it is acceptable to quote from these other works, attributing the work to the author by using footnotes telling where you found the quote. These other critical essays can suggest a possible approach for your paper. You can agree with other critics or disagree by criticizing the critic.

An earlier and still useful compendium of critical essays also found in the R820.9 section of the reference library is:

Moulton's Library of Literary Criticism Through the Beginning of the Twentieth Century
New York: Frederick Ungar, 1966. Reprint.
This multivolume series contains excerpts from critical writings, most published before 1900. Although this is not criticism at the time the novel was first published, it does represent older critical views of the novel and, taken together with the Chelsea House series, it provides a historical perspective on how the criticism of *Jane Eyre* has changed over the years. Again, you will have to know the author's

dates in order to pick out the correct volume, which is Volume 3, *Nineteenth Century Victorianism.*

Another huge compendium of criticism is:

Nineteenth Century Literature Criticism: Criticism of the Works of Novelists, Poets, Playwrights, Short Story Writers, Philosophers and Other Creative Writers Who Died between 1800 and 1899 from the First Critical Appraisals to Current Evaluations
Lazzari, Margaret, ed. Detroit, MI: Gale, 1981–   .
In Volume 8, page 51, under *"Jane Eyre,"* there is an introduction and several excerpts from criticisms arranged chronologically from 1847 to 1979, and a bibliography on page 93.

You will recall that the third number in the literature section of the Dewey Decimal system signifies the type of literature, and "3" means fiction, so books in 823 are about English fiction. In the reference section under R823.9 we find:

British Writers
Scott-Kilvert, Ian, ed. New York: Scribners, 1982.
Volume 5 contains a long essay about the Brontës by Winifred Gerin, in which the author discusses shaping influences, education, and many other topics. Starting on page 137 there are four pages on *Jane Eyre.*

The English Novel: 20th Century Criticism
Dunn, Richard J., ed. New York: Swallow Press, 1976.
Volume 1 is subtitled *Defoe through Hardy,* with a chronological arrangement, so in order to find the section on Charlotte Brontë, you have to know that Defoe wrote in the eighteenth century and Hardy in the twentieth century, with Charlotte Brontë in between. This book does not contain the actual articles; instead, it is a bibliography, or listing of articles, which you will then have to look up in the card catalog (if they are books) or in a periodical index (if they are magazine articles). There are 20 items listed under *Jane Eyre,* thus yielding a rich source of future references.

Electronic Resources

Arts and Humanities Citation Index
Philadelphia: Institute for Scientific Information, 1990–Compact disc edition updated three times a year.

More than 1,100 periodicals are indexed by author and keyword. Citations show what books have been cited in other books.

Books in Print Plus
New Providence, NJ: Bowker, 1979– .
A CD-ROM database found in larger libraries that lists books recently published together with reviews of the books. Using this database, we find 56 items listed under "Charlotte Brontë."

DiscLit: American Authors
New York: G. K. Hall, 1991– .

DiscLit: British Authors
New York: G. K. Hall, 1992– .
These useful CD-ROM sources contain the full text of the Twayne series of critical introductions to the lives and works of major authors —over 140 in each set. They also include citations to books by and about the authors and may be searched by every word in the texts and bibliographies.

DISCovering Authors: Biographies and Criticism on 300 Most Studied Authors
Detroit, MI: Gale, 1994.
This CD-ROM includes criticism and bibliographical and biographical information on specific authors from all time periods and many different countries. It may be searched by theme, time period, characters, and genre. A more extensive set is also offered by Gale, with over 1,200 authors.

Library of the Future
Three discs for Sony's Data Discman contain the full texts of hundreds of classic books. On CD-ROM as the *Electronic Home Library*.

Scribners Writers Series on CD-ROM
New York: Scribner's, 1993.
Full texts of essays on over 500 writers from many time periods and nationalities. Includes bibliographies and can be searched by genre, language, nationality, time period, race, and combinations of these.

WILSONLINE
New York: Ongoing.
In this CD-ROM database, you may find the most recent magazine articles on this topic. This includes the *Humanities Index*, which is specifically devoted to indexing magazine articles on humanities top-

ics. You may want to look in the "J" section, for material on *Jane Eyre*, and in the "B" section, for material on Charlotte Brontë.

Further Research

In selecting other resources to search, useful criteria might be:

• Intended audience—some of the books may be written for younger children.
• Subtitle—this may give a clue to the contents. Is it a critical study or a biography?
• Date of publication—Is it up-to-date in its research?
• Publisher—If it is a university press, it may be intellectual in its approach.

If you have the time and are beginning to think that literary research may be your field, you may want to look at:

Handbook of Literary Research
Miller, R. H. London: Scarecrow Press, 1995.
This slender volume includes a Quick Reference Bookshelf listing ten basic reference books and a series of articles on various methods for locating literary books. In the section on manuscripts, a book in progress is listed: Croft, P. J., et al., eds. *Index of English Literary Manuscripts.* This title would be useful for locating Brontë manuscripts.

Literary Research Guide: A Guide to Reference Sources for the Study of Literatures in English and Related Topics
Harner, James L. New York: Modern Language Association of America, 1989.
This is the definitive guide for researchers in this field. It annotates dozens of books, journals, library collections and catalogs, and computer programs and databases and includes name, title, and subject indexes.

Modern Philology
This periodical has a section "Victorian Bibliography." It is periodically cumulated into volumes covering several years.

A Reference Guide for English Studies
Marcuse, Michael J. Berkeley: University of California Press, 1990.
This book covers a huge list of specific topics in English and American literature, focusing on frequently recommended works in each topic.

Victorian Studies

This magazine publishes a bibliography each summer with the most up-to-date research on literary topics of the Victorian period.

The Internet

See also Chapter 5.

Using the Yahoo! search engine reveals several Brontë sites, including Arts: Humanities: Literature: Genres: Literary Fiction: Authors: Brontë, Charlotte.

Writing Your Paper

When you begin to write your paper, you may want to consult a style book to have an authoritative guide to how your paper should be written.

The Elements of Style

Strunk, William Jr., with White, E. B. New York: Macmillan, 1979.

This delightfully written volume guides you on how to write clearly, briefly, and boldly.

A Manual for Writers of Term Papers, Theses and Dissertations

Turabian, Kate L. Chicago: University of Chicago Press, 1987.

This useful manual includes sections on parts of the paper, footnotes, bibliography, and punctuation. It is an abridgment of *The Chicago Manual of Style,* Chicago: University of Chicago Press, 1993. 14th ed.

HISTORY: RESEARCHING

Preparing a Paper for a Class in Modern History

This is an example of how to use a library for a term paper in history. Suppose the assignment is to write a paper on a topic of your choice in the field of modern European history. The paper must be ten, typewritten double-spaced pages and must incorporate documentary primary source materials on the topic. You have just completed a class assignment on the French Revolution and were intrigued by how the revolution ended. What happened to the revolutionary spirit of the people? Stirred at first by the excesses of a wealthy aristocracy and monarchy who cared little about the suffering and poverty of the average French citizen, they rebelled and adopted a democratic constitution, but the chaotic murdering frenzy of the various factions disillusioned the people and made them prey to a reactionary force of new leaders. In your readings, the text mentions a revolutionary movement led by Babeuf, known as the Conspiracy of Equals, that attempted to restore the revolutionary constitution. The powerful Directory planted spies and suppressed them. You are interested in finding out more about this conspiracy as a possible term paper topic. Use this sequence to find some general facts about your topic, dates, people, and a brief history, and then begin to develop the detail by looking at more specialized sources:

General articles and terminology
General bibliography
Special subject bibliography
Shelf search
Catalog search
Type of literature search
Internet search
CD-ROM multimedia search

General Articles and Terminology

You need a precise time line for the events, and you need to know more about the people involved, as well as topics for further research. A general orientation to the period in greater depth than your modern European history text-book may be found in a general encyclopedia. These are in the reference section of the library in the 030 area (if the library uses the Dewey Decimal classification).

General Bibliography

As you use each of these books, search in the bibliographies at the end of each article or at the end of the book and copy down the titles of books to search later.

Special Subject Bibliography

Since you are already in the reference area of the library, try a few other sources. A more specific European history encyclopedia or a French history reference book would be useful. *The Encyclopedia of World History* has useful information on the French Revolution in general and will refine your time line. *The New Cambridge Modern History* is more scholarly and also useful. Both will yield further detail and a more specific time line.

Shelf Search

If you know the letter or number code, you can go directly to the shelves and quickly browse through materials rather than going back and forth from the terminals or card catalog.

Dewey Decimal system numbers for history research are:

030—General works such as encyclopedias
900—Books on history in general
940—Books on Western European history
944—Books on French history
944.04—Books on the French Revolution

Remember that reference books have their own separate sequence, so you have to look for 944.04 in reference as well as the circulating books. If you are in an academic library or a very large public library that uses the Library of Congress (LC) system, the letter code for non-U.S. history is D and for French history is DC.

Now try the circulating collection. This may be frustrating and disappointing if the topic was assigned to a large class because many of the materials may be checked out. Use the Dewey numbers you used in the reference collection. Start with 944.04, the number for the French Revolution. Go to the shelves in this area and browse for books on the French Revolution. Look inside the books:

Table of Contents—Located in the front of the book just after the title page, this shows the sequential contents of the book. See if you can find material on your period.

Index—Located in the back of the book, this lists specific topics and people and tells the pages in the book where more information can be located.

Bibliography—Located in the back of the book, this is a list of books the author used in writing the book. The bibliography may be arranged according to the chapters in the book or alphabetically. Use this to find other books on your topic.

Footnotes—These are found in the book itself or in the back of the book. These are useful clues on where to go for further information on a topic.

Catalog Search

In addition to a simple shelf search under Dewey numbers, it is useful to use the terminals for the library catalog under subject and under keyword. Your research in the references already mentioned and in the books you found on the shelves will give you a variety of subjects to look up in the card catalog—for example:

The French Revolution—for books on the revolution in other parts of the collection, such as political science.

The Directory—for information on this form of government.

Babeuf—for biographical information.

If you search under keyword, you will find additional information not found under subject because keyword searches include all words, not just subject headings.

Type of Literature Search

After you have browsed the 944 .04 shelves, also look under:

Biography

If your earlier research gave you names of important people, try biography. Many libraries arrange their biographies alphabetically by the name of the subject, but some libraries shelve historical biographies with history books of the same period. Look up "Babeuf," "Napoleon," "Danton." Use the indexes to these biographies to find specific topics. Most biographies are chronological, so you can read the chapters just for the period you identified from your earlier time line research.

Essays

These useful and often very specific short written pieces are a wonderful way to research topics, but more difficult to use than other methods because they are not always grouped together by consistent similar subjects. To get at them, browse the shelves using your French history number/letter code, or you can use an index.

Indexes

These are much more specific but similar to subject classification systems. The big difference is they are inside the books in most cases. There may be recent articles on French history listed in the *The Read-*

er's Guide to Periodical Literature or *Magazine Index,* but you may have better luck in a more specific index such as:

Essay and General Literature Index

This is a cumulating index that goes into essay books and lists each article. It can be tedious to wade through the many volumes. Perhaps the best general article on Babeuf and the Conspiracy of Equals is in a book of essays by Edmund Wilson, *To the Finland Station,* which deals with the history of socialist theory.

Creative Topic Brainstorming

Looking directly under the specific topics and names is the easiest research method, but related topics are often helpful, and the period of the French Revolution was a rich one for experiments in government. An entirely different research topic would be political science and government. Here the Dewey classification number is 320 (in LC, the letter is J.) Histories of political systems might yield a new perspective and give you some useful documentary primary source information. Documentary histories are also be a useful source. Since Babeuf was a forerunner of socialist thought, histories of socialism or communism might also mention his contribution.

Internet Search

The Internet provides access to hundreds of libraries, which may give you immediate access. Direct digital access to print articles is possible with recently published materials. See the chapter in this book on Internet searching.

CD-ROM Multimedia Search

Multimedia resources are in their infancy, but videotapes and audiotapes may be possible sources for some topics. Indexing may be a problem here, but film indexes do exist that list films on the French Revolution, and audio books on the subject are available.

History Research Paper: Recent History Example

The same search sequence will be useful in researching a modern history topic. The example here will be for the Cuban Missile Crisis.

General Articles and Terminology

A general resource such as an encyclopedia will yield some basic information on this incident and the people involved.

America in the 20th Century
Humphrey, Paul. Tarrytown, NY: Marshall Cavendish, 1995. 11 vols.
Each volume covers a decade and looks at medicine, media, literature, art, sports, and the environment. Included are photographs, cartoons, advertisements, biographies, bibliography, and an index.

Dictionary of Recent American History
New York: McGraw-Hill, 1979.
An overview of modern American History.

The Encyclopedia of American Facts and Dates
Carruth, Gordon. New York: Harper, 1987.
Tables of events and dates on government, politics, history, literature, art economics, sports, science, and entertainment.

Encyclopedia of American History
Morris, Richard B., ed. New York: Harper, 1982.
Within the chronological presentation are articles on special topics, such as science, inventions, and Supreme Court cases.

Twentieth-Century America: A Primary Source Collection from the Associated Press
Danbury, CT: Grolier, 1995. 10 vols. Illustrated, index.
Associated Press correspondents' reports during the past 95 years arranged chronologically. Includes politics, sports, and crime. Each volume has a time line, photographs, and an index. In addition there is an index to the entire work.

General Bibliography

Look in a general American history bibliography for a list of related books and magazines.

America: History and Life
Santa Barbara: CA: ABC-CLIO, 1964–   . Seven issues per year. Cumulative indexes. Available online.
An index to 2,000 magazines includes abstracts or citations on the history of Canada and the United States. Part A is abstracts and cita-

tions. Part B is an index to book reviews. Part C is a bibliography, including dissertations. Part D is an annual index.

Writings on American History
1902–   . American Historical Association. Annual bibliography and index.
Classified by topic with author, title, and subject index. Varying coverage.

Special Subject Bibliography

Look in the general bibliographies to see if there is a special subject bibliography on the missile crisis.

Shelf Search

Libraries arrange their history books by nation, then chronologically by date. In order to find the shelf number for American history, look in the catalog terminal under United States History ("American History" is not the term used by catalogers). The Dewey Decimal number for this period is 973.922 (the Library of Congress letter and number for modern United States history is E740).
Go to the shelves where books on the same period of history are arranged chronologically. Look at some of these books. One of the 973.922 books is *The Missiles of October*—just what you are looking for.

Table of Contents

Look in the front of the books under the Table of Contents. See if the sections cover your time period: October 1962. Several of these nearby books may supply additional useful information on the crisis.

Bibliographies

Look in the back of this book for a bibliography. Luckily, there is a list, and it also includes a wonderful list of articles from magazines and newspapers, so even if the books are not available, the newspapers and magazines might be.

Indexes

Pick some of the nearby books off the shelves and look in the rear of the books for the index and see if they refer to the Cuban missile crisis.

Catalog Search

The computer lists two books under this subject:

In the Eye of the Storm
Lechuga, Carlos. Melbourne, Australia: Ocean Press, 1995.

On the Brink
Blight, James G. New York: Hill and Wang, 1989.

Select a time when you think the librarian will be least busy, wait for a quiet moment, and then tell the librarian about your topic: "I'm writing a paper on the Cuban missile crisis, and I have looked it up on the library computer under that term. The computer lists two books: 973.922, James G. Blight, *On the Brink,* and 973.922, Carlos Lechuga, *In the Eye of the Storm.* The computer says this book is checked out. How can I find the book that is in the library?" The librarian will direct you to the largest book stack section of the library where the numbered sequence 973.922 books are located.

Creative Brainstorming —Other Related Topics

You have focused your search so far on books in American history, but there were several other nations involved in the missile crisis. It might be useful to try the history of the Soviet Union. By searching in the library computer terminal, you find that Soviet Union history has the Dewey Decimal number 947, so you return to the shelves, looking this time in the 947 section. There you find the books arranged chronologically, with modern Soviet Union history for the Khrushchev era under 947.085.

Khrushchev
Medvedev, Roy. New York: Doubleday, Anchor Press, 1983.
This book on Krushchev's participation in the Cuban missile crisis is written from the point of view of a dissident Russian author.

Khrushchev and the First Russian Spring
Burlatsky, Fedor. New York: Scribners, 1988.
This book devotes a chapter to the Cuban missile crisis.

Also in 947.085 we find:

Khrushchev on Khrushchev
Khrushchev, Sergei. Boston: Little, Brown, 1990.
This useful book reveals the missile crisis from the Russian prime minister's point of view.

Reference Books

Having accomplished the request process, tell the librarian what you have found and ask if there are any other places you should look. The librarian will tell you that in addition to the 973.922 section of **circulating books,** there is another 973.922 section of **reference books** that cannot be checked out but may contain a lot of useful information on your topic. You go to the reference section and find:

Dictionary of Recent American History
New York: McGraw-Hill, 1979.
On page 80 of this book is a two-page summary, a useful place to start your research because it will give you some useful facts to begin to make connections for further research. These facts shape your research and give useful clues to guide you to further information. What are the exact dates? October 16–October 28, 1962. Knowing these dates makes it possible to search newspaper and magazine articles more easily. The article mentions John and Robert Kennedy, Adlai Stevenson, U Thant, Khrushchev, and Fidel Castro. Now you can look for brief biographies of the players in the great drama.

Nearby on the reference shelves you see a large set of reference books:

Twentieth-Century America: A Primary Source Collection from the Associated Press
Danbury, CT: Grolier, 1995. 10 vols. Incl. index.
That's your period, so you browse through this set and find a volume entitled *Civil Rights and the Great Society 1961–1967*. You check the index, and on page 46 there begins a multipage article on the Cuban missile crisis. Better still, you find a number of documents in the book that are primary sources written at the time of the crisis.

In this same reference section of the library you will be able to find some of the materials revealed in the bibliographies you found earlier. In addition you will find such biographic reference tools as:

Current Biography
New York: Wilson, 1940–   .
A multivolume set listing some of the people you identified earlier.

Finally, you can use the list of articles to find magazines and newspapers on the topic. These are often in computer databases or in micrographic form requiring machines in the reference area, which the librarian will help you use.

A really comprehensive source is:

John F. Kennedy: A Bibliography
Giglio, James N., comp. Westport, CT: Greenwood Press, 1995. Incl. indexes.
There are 4,349 entries arranged chronologically, with an index to authors and subjects.

Remember to search general indexes to periodicals such as *The Magazine Index* and *The Reader's Guide to Periodical Literature.*

The Internet

Having completed your research in the reference section, you may now want to go beyond the confines of this particular library. You can identify and borrow books from other libraries if they are available to be checked out. In addition you can find up-to-date information by asking the librarian to conduct a remote search on the library connection to the Internet. This may yield up-to-date research on your topic. Be careful, as it can also yield rumors and semifactual information from questionable sources that needs to be authenticated before use. In all cases, you will need to list your sources by using specific footnotes for each of your facts or by listing all sources in your bibliography.

CD-ROM Multimedia Search

Electronic reference materials on CD-ROM computers may give you up-to-date and authentic material. Many of these encyclopedias are now updated online by library computers connected to the Internet. These sources are increasingly multimedia, containing sound, pictures, and even video clips that you can download onto your own floppy disc.

Sound and pictures consume very large quantities of your disc space, so be selective about including those media.

PART II

Reference Sources by Topic

Now that you have a good idea how to use the library and conduct research, you need to know what reference sources will help you fulfill the requirements of your homework and term paper assignments. Part Two lists and annotates core library reference resources by subject. It is organized alphabetically by subject. Within each chapter, sources are grouped in subcategories. Dewey Decimal numbers are provided within chapters, by subject, as another means of helping you find additional resources on the subject you are researching.

CHAPTER 7

The Arts (700–793)

Sources for Information on
Architecture (720), Sculpture (730),
Drawing/Handicrafts/Furniture (740),
Painting (750), Graphic Arts (760),
Photography (770), Music (780),
Movies (791.43), Theater (792),
Dance (792.8, 793.3)

Art assignments may involve comparing and contrasting: compare and contrast the painting styles of Gauguin and Van Gogh, of surrealism and impressionism, of nineteenth-century France with sixteenth-century Italy. The role of art and crafts in specific cultures begs for exploration: Native Americans, prehistoric Europeans, African tribes. In the study of film and theater, various acting styles might be discussed. The role of photography in other fields, such as astronomy, is worthy of review, as is the role of photography during a specific period, such as the Civil War. The art and life of a specific photographer, like Brassai, may be explored. There are thousands of topics possible within the arts, and many of them can be related to time periods, countries, cultures, world events, or other areas of study, as well as to each other. Art and crafts tell us something about ourselves: beauty and learning, combined and inseparable. The following resources will help you with your research.

ART ENCYCLOPEDIAS AND DICTIONARIES (703)

The Dictionary of Art
Turner, Jane, ed. New York: Grove's Dictionaries, 1996. 34 vols. Incl. bibliographies and index.

The 6,700 contributors and 15,000 illustrations provide "comprehensive coverage of the visual arts of every culture and civilization from prehistory to the present." This book examines "works of art within the social, cultural, historical, religious, and economic contexts in which they were created," according to *Booklist* (December 15, 1996). There are nearly 21,000 biographies, exceeding any other English-language art publication. Length of entry varies according to the significance of the artist. The illustrations include artwork and objects, architectural designs and archaeological sites, as well as maps and charts. The text represents the most recent scholarship available. A truly magnificent source.

Encyclopedia of World Art
New York: McGraw-Hill, 1959–87. 17 vols. Incl. bibliographies and index.

Big, handsome volumes with full-page plates of illustrations, covering all art objects from every country and throughout history. Thorough discussion of artists—their work and specific works and their lives. The master work, though superseded in 1996 by Grove's *The Dictionary of Art,* (see previous entry), which does the same thing, only better.

Oxford Companion to Art
Osborne, Harold, ed. New York: Oxford University Press, 1970. Incl. bibliography.

The 3,000 entries on the fine arts cover styles, movements, biographies, and techniques. Articles range from brief descriptions to longer overviews. No handicrafts or other practical arts are included.

Oxford Illustrated Encyclopedia of the Arts
Norwich, John Julius, ed. New York: Oxford University Press, 1990.

Short entries on artists from all fields: music, literature, drama, painting, sculpture, architecture, cinema, and decorative arts. Major works, style and technique, country, and period are provided. Many cross-references and black and white and color photographs. One-stop shopping for brief amounts of information.

SYMBOLS (704)

The Book of Signs
Koch, Rudolf. New York: Dover, 1955.
According to the cover, the book contains "493 symbols used from earliest times to the Middle Ages by primitive peoples and early Christians," Grouped by type or style, each symbol is explained by a sentence or paragraph.

A Dictionary of Symbols
Cirlot, Juan Eduardo. New York: Philosophical Library, 1971, 1962. 2d ed. Incl. bibliography and index.
This respected dictionary explains the meanings of symbols and includes some illustrations. The listing is thorough, covering symbols taken from art and religion and from cultures around the world and throughout history. Articles vary in length from a long paragraph to several pages.

Dictionary of Symbols
Liungman, Carl G. Santa Barbara, CA: ABC-CLIO, 1991. Incl. bibliography and index.
This source arranges 1,500 symbols into 54 shape groups to aid readers in discovering a specific symbol. Line drawings illustrate each symbol, and a paragraph or more of explanation is provided for each. A word index and a picture index are valuable tools for locating a specific symbol.

ART HISTORY (709)

Gardner's History of Art
Tansey, Richard, and Kleiner, Fred. New York: Harcourt, 1996. 10th ed.
A standard history focusing on exemplary work over the ages and now including African and Etruscan art and more illustrations.

History of African-American Artists: From 1792 to the Present
Bearden, Romare, and Henderson, Harry. New York: Pantheon Books, 1993.
"A major contribution to the literature on African-American history and to the annals of American art," according to *Booklist*, this source discusses the lives and works of Henry O. Tanner, Aaron Douglas,

Edmonia Lewis, Jacob Lawrence, and many others. It provides 250 black and white and 61 color reproductions of their work. Hard-to-come-by information, obtained "through great perseverance and determination," combined with "vivid biographical portraits," and "forgotten artwork."

History of Art
Janson, H. W., and Janson, Anthony F. New York: Abrams, 1995. 5th ed. Rev. and expanded.

Completely revised and expanded by the author's son, Anthony, this college text is one of the standards on the subject. Anthony Janson has improved the readability, added more color reproductions, and included chapters on postmodernism and contemporary art and artists. Just about anything worth knowing about Western painting, sculpture, architecture, and photography is in this book. A great reference for high school students too. For grades 5–9, try the Jansons' *History of Art for Young People*, New York: Abrams, 1992. 4th ed.

The Oxford History of Classical Art
Boardman, John, ed. New York: Oxford University Press, 1993. Incl. bibliographical references.

An excellent overview of Greek and Roman art up to the end of the Roman Empire. Lots of plates and explanations of changing styles, plus discussion or historical and social context.

Art History by Country and Time Period (709.3–709.9)

Art and Architecture in France, 1500–1700
Blunt, Anthony. New Haven, CT: Penguin; Yale University Press, 1981. 4th ed. Incl. bibliography.

Art, architecture, and painting, plus individual artists of the period are studied in this source.

Art and Architecture in Italy, 1600–1750
Wittkower, Rudulf. New Haven, CT: Penguin; Yale University Press, 1980. 3d rev. ed. Incl. bibliography.

Individual artists and architects during the baroque period are studied.

The Art and Architecture of Ancient Egypt
Smith, William S. Rev. by Simpson, William K. New Haven, CT: Penguin; Yale University Press, 1981. Incl. bibliography.

This text shows the development of art and architecture in ancient Egypt.

The Art and Architecture of China
Sickman, Laurence, and Soper, Alexander. New Haven, CT: Penguin; Yale University Press, 1968. 3d ed. Incl. bibliography.
This source follows the development of art and architecture from the Shang dynasty to the modern era.

The Art and Architecture of Islam: 650–1250
Ettinghausen, Robert, and Graber, Oleg. New Haven, CT: Penguin; Yale University Press, 1987. Incl. bibliography.

The Art and Architecture of Islam: 1250–1800
Blair, Sheila, and Bloom, Jonathan. New Haven, CT: Yale University Press, 1994. Incl. bibliographic references.
These two books trace the development of art and architecture as Islam spread through the Middle East.

The Art and Architecture of Japan
Paine, Robert Treat, and Soper, Alexander. New Haven, CT: Penguin; Yale University Press, 1975. Rev. ed. Incl. bibliography.
How cultural forces influenced simplicity in Japanese art and encouraged a sensitivity to form are shown in this text, covering the pre-Buddhist period to the modern day.

Art and Architecture of Russia
Hamilton, George Heard. New Haven, CT: Penguin; Yale University Press, 1983. Incl. bibliography.
From the Byzantine empire to the modern day, the development of Russian art is examined.

Greek Art
Boardman, John. New York: Praeger; Thames and Hudson, 1973. Rev. ed. Incl. bibliography.
Classical and Hellenistic Greek art, its origins and influence, are reviewed.

A History of Far Eastern Art
Lee, Sherman. New York: Abrams, 1982. 4th ed. Incl. bibliography.
Art traditions of China, Japan, and India from 5000 B.C. to 1850 are studied in chronological order.

Mexico: Splendors of Thirty Centuries
New York: Metropolitan Museum of Art, 1990. Incl. bibliographic references.

Painting, sculpture, textiles, and ceramics throughout Mexican history are studied.

A Short History of African Art
Gillon, Werner. New York: Facts on File, 1984. Incl. bibliography.
Art from the earliest times is examined by region and culture. Sculpture, pottery, jewelry, and textiles are included, along with painting and architecture.

Art Biography (709.2)

A Biographical Dictionary of Artists
Gowing, Lawrence, ed. New York: Facts on File, 1995. Rev. ed. Incl. bibliographies and index.
The 1,340 alphabetical entries cover ancient Japanese to Western pop artists and discuss each artist's life and work. Clear and vivid descriptions also include analysis of style, stages of development, and intent of the work. Generally, the more important the artist, the longer the entry. Excellent color reproductions; a glossary and chronology are included.

A Biographical Dictionary of Women Artists in Europe and America since 1850
Dunford, Penny. Philadelphia: University of Pennsylvania Press, 1989. Incl. bibliography.
This source provides brief biographical information reviewing the accomplishments of 1,700 artists. Of particular interest are comments on how an artist chose to balance major life decisions, such as marriage and childbearing, against the demands of her art.

Dictionary of Women Artists: An International Dictionary of Women Artists Born before 1900
Petteys, Chris. Boston: G. K. Hall, 1985. Incl. bibliographic references and bibliography.
This source provides biographical sketches of 21,000 women painters, sculptors, printmakers, and illustrators.

Who's Who in Art: Biographies of Leading Men and Women in the World of Art Today
London: Art Trade Press. Biennial.
This source provides brief biographical data on mostly British artists, designers, craftsmen, and others in or connected to the world of art.

World Artists, 1950–1980
Marks, Claude, ed. New York: H. W. Wilson, 1984.
World Artists, 1980–1990
Marks, Claude, ed. New York: H. W. Wilson, 1991.

In the first volume, 312 world-renowned artists are profiled. The second profiles 120 artists. Artists represent a variety of styles and movements, their work is discussed and commented on, and formative influences are mentioned. A list of each artist's works and major exhibits is provided. Art critics and artists alike are quoted. *American Reference Books Annual* calls these volumes "authoritative and readable" and recommended for high school students.

ARCHITECTURE (720)

See also Art History by Country and Time Period, p. 88

American Architecture since 1780: A Guide to the Styles
Whiffen, Marcus. Cambridge, MA: MIT Press, 1992. Rev. ed. Incl. index.

This book describes and illustrates 40 architectural styles. Arranged by time period, it provides a brief history for each style.

A Field Guide to American Architecture
Rifkind, Carole. New York: New American Library, 1980. Incl. bibliography.

This survey of American architectural styles over three centuries is arranged chronologically and covers buildings of all types, including houses, churches, governmental, business, and utilitarian examples.

Identifying American Architecture
Blemenson, John. New York: Norton, 1981, 1990. Rev. ed.

Arranged by time period, the details and characteristics of 39 architectural styles are identified by illustration and description in this source. Students will find it useful because of the many photographs and illustrations.

Macmillan Encyclopedia of Architects
Placzek, Adolf, ed. New York: Free Press, 1982. 4 vols. Incl. bibliographies and indexes.

This exceptional work provides biographical information on 2,400 architects from ancient times to the present. Significant contributions are provided, as is a list of buildings for each architect. Indexes provide access by name and to the architectural structures. Appendixes list architects by date and geographical area. A glossary of 600 terms and more than 1,400 illustrations are included.

Master Builders: A Guide to Famous American Architects
Maddex, Diane, ed. Washington, DC: Preservation Press, 1985. Incl. bibliography and index.

This volume provides four-to six-page biographies of 40 American architects. Beginning with William Thornton, designer of the U.S. Capitol, the book is arranged chronologically. Selected architects represent a cross-section of American architectural history. Major characteristics of each architect's work are presented. Portraits and illustrations of each architect's designs are included.

Native American Architecture
Nabokov, Peter, and Easton, Robert. New York: Oxford University Press, 1989. Incl. bibliography and index.

In pictures and words, this source describes North American Indian structures of all types. It notes materials used and construction techniques. An important book for students.

The Penguin Dictionary of Architecture
Fleming, John, et al. New York: Penguin Books, 1991. 4th ed.

This essential dictionary defines terms and provides information on building styles, movements, ornamentation, materials, and types of building and supplies biographical information on significant architects.

Sir Bannister Fletcher's History of Architecture
Fletcher, Bannister, and Musgrove, John, eds. Boston: Butterworths, 1987. 19th ed. Incl. bibliographies and index.

This valuable source, first published in 1896, provides a worldwide review of architectural history and includes lots of illustrations.

The World Atlas of Architecture
Norwick, John, ed. Boston: G. K. Hall, 1984. Repr. New York: Portland House, 1988. Incl. bibliography and index.

Extensively illustrated with plans, diagrams, photographs, and drawings, this source is arranged by time period. It covers mostly the Western world from early civilization to the present.

Church Architecture (726)

The Gothic Cathedral: The Architecture of the Great Church, 1130–1530
Wilson, Christopher. London: Thames and Hudson, 1990. Incl. bibliography and index.
Style and development are discussed in this book, which includes 220 photographs and drawings. An excellent source.

The House of God: Church Architecture, Style and History
Norman, Edward R. London: Thames and Hudson, 1990. Incl. index.
This book covers the entire history of church architecture from the earliest days of Christianity to the present. Lavishly illustrated. Significant chapters cover Gothic, Renaissance, baroque, and Enlightenment styles.

SCULPTURE (730)

History of World Sculpture
Bazin, Germain. Greenwich, CT: New York Graphic Society, 1968. Repr. Secaucus, NJ: Chartwell Books, 1976. Incl. index.
This source is arranged by time period and includes an overview essay plus color illustrations of more than 1,000 works, each with descriptive text.

Sculpture
Opie, Mary-Jane. New York: Dorling Kindersley, 1994. Eyewitness Art Series. Incl. index.
In only 64 pages, this book provides an excellent overview of the subject, with a mix of superb photographs, numerous captions, and text. Examples are taken worldwide from prehistory to the present. Also included are tools, models, sketches, and techniques. A great introduction made interesting, informative, and understandable.

DRAWING /COMICS AND CARTOONS (741)

The World Encyclopedia of Cartoons
Horn, Maurice, ed. Detroit: Gale, 1980. 2 vols. Incl. bibliography and indexes.
Alphabetically arranged entries include artists' biographies, characters, cartoon plots, and content.

The World Encyclopedia of Comics
Horn, Maurice, ed. New York: Chelsea House, 1976. Incl. indexes.
The 1,200 entries, alphabetically arranged, provide a "vital source of information on comics and their creators."

PAINTING (750–759)

Encyclopedia of Painting: Painters and Painting of the World from Prehistoric Times to the Present Day
Myers, Bernard S., ed. New York: Crown, 1979. 4th rev. ed.
A thorough one-volume encyclopedia, alphabetically arranged, providing definitions of painters' terms, tools, techniques, schools, styles, time periods, brief biographies of significant painters worldwide, outlines of their work, and often a line or two of critical assessment. Examples are given in 1,000 illustrations.

The Story of Painting
Beckett, Wendy. New York: Dorling Kindersley, 1994. Incl. index.
Contains 400 full-color reproductions of paintings, some with detail close-ups, plus an informative review of the history of painting, through time periods, movements, and styles, from before the Renaissance to the twentieth century. Specific works and details are discussed, and time lines and chronologies are provided. A lively, straightforward writing style includes details of painters' lives, the times they lived in, and personal aspects of each painting. The author, a nun with her own TV show in England, has a knack for making everything interesting. Students will find the theme index most useful, as well as the index by painting title.

The World's Master Paintings
Wright, Christopher. New York: Routledge, 1992. 2 vols. Incl. bibliographies and indexes.
The lengthy subtitle describes the contents and coverage: *From the Early Renaissance to the Present Day: A Comprehensive Listing of Works by 1,300 Painters and a Complete Guide to Their Locations Worldwide.* The coverage is limited to Western painting, and although it does provide biographical information and specific information about each artist's works, it is primarily a listing and a guide to the museums and other places that own the paintings.

PHOTOGRAPHY (770)

The Focal Encyclopedia of Photography
Stroebel, Leslie, and Zakia, Richard, eds. Boston: Focal Press, 1993. 3d ed.
A standard in the field, in A–Z format, this excellent resource defines terms and techniques and provides historical articles as well as articles on the art and use of photography.

The ICP Encyclopedia of Photography
New York: Crown, 1984. Incl. bibliography.
Though now 14 years old and needing to catch up with recent technologic developments, this source nevertheless discusses history and the development of photography, techniques, processes, and applications, all valid information. It also provides biographies of inventors and photographers. Ansel Adams, Daguerre, Cartier-Bresson, Matthew Brady, Steichen, and Stieglitz are among the 230 photographers from the nineteenth and twentieth centuries whose lives and careers are profiled.

World History of Photography
Rosenblum, Naomi. New York: Abbeville Press, 1984. Incl. bibliography and index.
Lavishly illustrated, this history discusses photography from its beginning. Chapters cover time periods and movements within time periods. Techniques and technical developments are also included.

MUSIC (780)

Music Encyclopedias and Dictionaries (780.3)

The New Grove Dictionary of Music and Musicians
Sadie, Stanley. New York: Stockton Press/Grove's Dictionaries, 1980. 6th ed. 20 vols. Incl. bibliographies and index.
Extensive articles on composers, performers, time periods and styles, types of music, and biographies. An excellent source for background and depth on any musical topic. It covers the history of music and instruments, as well as popular, folk, and classical music throughout history. It emphasizes biographies of individual composers, performers, conductors, writers, and instrument makers. The best and most comprehensive source available.

New Harvard Dictionary of Music
Randel, Don M., ed. Cambridge, MA: Belknap/Harvard University Press, 1986. 3d ed. Incl. bibliography.

This standard source explains music history worldwide, including popular music. It describes instruments and defines musical terms and concepts. No biographies.

The Oxford Dictionary of Music
Bourne, Joyce, ed. New York: Oxford University Press, 1994. 2d ed.

Nearly 12,000 alphabetical entries explain and define all types of musical terms, styles of music, individual composers, performers, and orchestras.

Music History (780.9)

The New Oxford History of Music
New York: Oxford University Press, 1954–1900. 10 vols.

Spanning musical history from ancient times to 1960, these 10 volumes are the authoritative, comprehensive source on the topic. Readable and interesting.

American Music History (780.973)

The New Grove Dictionary of American Music
Hitchcock, H. Wiley, and Sadie, Stanley, eds. New York: Stockton Press/Grove's Dictionaries, 1986. 4 vols.

The 5,000 articles cover all American music—popular and classical, native and African-American, jazz, rock, and country, folk, political and patriotic music—in depth. The definitive work on the subject, this source provides thorough biographical and career information on composers, performers, conductors, and many others in and associated with music. It includes photographs and illustrations.

Music Biography (780.92)

American Songwriters: One Hundred Forty-Six Biographies of America's Greatest Popular Composers and Lyricists
Ewen, David. New York: H. W. Wilson, 1986. incl. index.

The 146 biographies, alphabetically arranged, cover all the greats from Stephen Foster and George Gershwin to Bob Dylan, Chuck Berry, and Carole King.

Baker's Biographical Dictionary of Musicians
Slonimsky, Nicolas. New York: Schirmer, 1992. 8th ed.

High school students will benefit from this source, which profiles 13,000 musicians including classical and popular figures throughout the world and throughout history. Coverage includes composers, performers, conductors, instrument makers, and others significant in music. Biographies range from a few lines to several pages. Bach is included, and so is Elvis.

Biographical Dictionary of Afro-American and African Musicians
Southern, Eileen. Westport, CT: Greenwood, 1982. Incl. index.

This source provides biographical information on 1,500 musicians, composers, and performers during the period 1640–1945.

Blues Who's Who: A Biographical Dictionary of Blues Singers
Harris, Sheldon. New York: Da Capo Press, 1981. Incl. bibliography and indexes.

This source profiles 571 blues singers from 1900 to 1980.

The Great Composers I and II
North Bellemore, NY: Marshall Cavendish, 1987. 11 vols.; 1990, 5 vols. Incl index.

Greater depth, color portraits and other pictures, readable text, and attractive layout distinguish these sets from other biographies and makes them useful to middle and high school students. The lives, works, and times of 40 composers from the seventeenth to twentieth centuries are discussed.

The Norton/Grove Dictionary of Women Composers
Sadie, Julie Anne, and Samuel, Rhian. New York: Norton, 1995.

This title discusses the lives and works of 1,000 women composers of Western classical music.

Ethnic Music (781.7)

World Music: The Rough Guide
Broughton, Simon, et al., eds. London: Rough Guides, 1994. Incl. index.

This 720-page book provides excellent background on specific types of music within countries and regions worldwide. Coverage includes history, current status, and major performers both old and new. Each chapter covers a geographic area: Celtic music (Ireland and England), West Africa, the Far East, Native American, the Caribbean, and Australia aborigines. Discographies list specific recordings of some of the best samples of each region's music. An excellent source for teachers who want musical background to support a country research project.

Musical Instruments (781.9)

The Illustrated Encyclopedia of Musical Instruments
Dearling, Robert, ed. New York: Schirmer, 1996. Incl. bibliography and index.

A good source for students, in part because of its profusion of illustrations and boxed facts set off from the main text. Coverage from early instruments to modern electronic instruments, as well as non-Western instruments. Arranged by family of instruments, the text is well written and informative. Drawings and photographs of construction of instruments and instruments in use during performance increase the informative value of the text.

The Scribner Guide to Orchestral Instruments
Diagram Group. New York: Scribner's, 1983. Incl. index.

Lots of illustrations and graphics help explain orchestral instruments old and new, their similarities and differences, their evolution, anatomy, range, how they're made and played, and how they fit together to form an orchestra. Originally published as part of *Musical Instruments of the World*.

Opera (782)

New Grove Dictionary of Opera
Sadie, Stanley, ed. New York: Grove's Dictionaries, 1992. 4 vols. Incl. bibliographies and indexes.

Grove's subject dictionaries usually serve as the authoritative reference source on the topic, and this one is no exception. Plot summaries, personalities, historical information, and worldwide coverage are all here.

Song Indexes (782.42)

Song Index: An Index to More Than 12,000 Songs
Sears, Minnie, ed. New York: Wilson, 1926. Reprint Services Corp., 1990.
Song Index Supplement: An Index to More Than 7,000 Songs
Sears, Minnie, ed. New York: Wilson, 1934. Shoe String Press, 1966 (reprint).

These two volumes were reprinted in one volume in 1966 by Shoe String Press. This work broke ground as no indexes of this type, except what libraries did for themselves, existed before. Indexes 177 song collections by title, composer, and author with first line cross- references.

Index to Top Hit Tunes (1900–1950)
Chipman, John, comp. Boston: Humphries, 1962. Incl. bibliography.
This source is really a title list of 3,000 songs popularized during the first half of the twentieth century. Each song sold over 100,000 copies of sheet music or records. Composer, author, publisher, and publication date of each song are identified, along with key of the music and the name of the film or musical that may have featured the song. An appendix lists the songs by year.

Popular Music (784.5)

Encyclopedia of Rock Stars
Rees, Dafydd, and Crampton, Luke. New York: DK Publishing, 1996. 1st American ed.
This source is arranged alphabetically by group or performer. Within each listing is a year-by-year overview of activities and recordings from the beginning to the end of performance career. It's thorough, detailed, and excellent. A general chronology is published in the front of the book. No index.

The New Grove Dictionary of Jazz
Kernfeld, Barry, ed. New York: Stockton/Grove's Dictionaries, 1988. 2 vols.
The standard source on the topic, it covers everything about jazz in a style suitable for high school students.

The New Rolling Stone Encyclopedia of Rock and Roll
Romanowski, Patricia, and George-Warren, Holly, ed. New York: Fireside, 1993. Rev. and upd.
Contains 1,800 alphabetically arranged entries on rock groups and individual performers. Coverage includes awards, MTV, videos, musical terms, and the Rock and Roll Hall of Fame.

Oxford Companion to Popular Music
Gammond, Peter. New York: Oxford University Press, 1991. Incl. indexes.
A dictionary-style source that provides brief paragraphs on musicians, composers, and others in the field, describes their careers, and covers songs, types of music, famous places, and terms. Three indexes access "people and groups," "shows and films," and "songs and albums."

The Harmony Illustrated Series:

The Harmony Illustrated Encyclopedia of Classical Music
Gammond, Peter, ed. New York: Harmony/Crown, 1989. 2d ed.
Incl. index.
This title is divided into sections on the orchestra, the opera, the composer, chamber music, musical instruments, and medieval and Renaissance music and recorded music.

The Harmony Illustrated Encyclopedia of Country Music
Dellar, Fred. New York: Harmony/Crown, 1994. 3d rev. ed.
The 700 alphabetical entries of single and group performers are accompanied by 500 color photographs. Biographical information, career highlights and low lights, and recording history are provided.

The Harmony Illustrated Encyclopedia of Jazz
Case, Brian, and Britt, Stan. New York: Harmony/Crown, 1986. 3d ed. Incl. index.
Lush with color photographs reproducing album covers, this source profiles 500 jazz performers and includes biographical information, as well as career history and discographies.

The Harmony Illustrated Encyclopedia of Rock
Clifford, Mike, ed. New York: Harmony/Crown, 1992. 7th ed.
This source provides an alphabetical arrangement of 900 single and group performers with substantial biographical information, evaluation, and discography. Numerous color photographs add to the book's interest.

National Anthems (784.71)

National Anthems of the World
Reed, W. L., and Bristow, M. J., eds. London: Blandford, 1993. 8th ed.
Updated regularly, this source provides the anthems of 178 nations with musical score, lyrics in native language and English and a brief history of the song.

Top Hits (789.9)

The Billboard Book of Number One Hits
Bronson, Fred. New York: Billboard, 1992. Rev. and enl. 3rd ed.
Incl. indexes.
Hits from 1955–1992, plus song history and performer background.

Hit Parade, 1920–1955
Tyler, Don. New York: William Morrow, 1985. Incl. index.
The subtitle describes the book: "An Encyclopedia of the Top Songs of the Jazz, Depression, Swing and Sing Eras." Of historical value, this source also provides biographies of performers and writers.

PERFORMING ARTISTS BIOGRAPHY (790.2092)

Performing Artists
Severson, Molly. Detroit, MI: UXL, 1995. 3 vols. Incl. bibliography and index.
Written for students, this set profiles "120 popular singers, actors, dancers, comedians, musicians, and television personalities who have made an impact on the performing arts," according to the Preface. A photograph of each artist is included, and students will find interesting the mention of each artist's early life and motivation.

MOVIES (791.43)

Leonard Maltin's Movie and Video Guide
New York: New American Library. Annual.
This paperback provides release date, plot summaries, characters, actors, directors, and so on for most movies.

Magill's Cinema Annual
Englewood Cliffs, NJ: Salem Press 1982–1994; Detroit: Gale, 1995– Annual. Incl. bibliographic references and index.
This source reviews about 500 films per year. Gale has enlarged and illustrated the format. Each review is originally written from other review sources, which are listed at the end of the article. Some reviews are quite lengthy; others are just a few lines. Awards are listed along with production credits.

New York Times Directory of the Film
New York: Arno Press/Random House, 1971. Incl. index.
Arranged by year from 1924–1970, a full reprint of the original *Times* review for each of the ten best films of the year is provided. A section of film star photographic portraits is included.

TELEVISION (791.45)

Les Brown's Encyclopedia of Television
Brown, Les. Detroit: Visible Ink, 1992. 3d ed. Incl. bibliography and index.

In dictionary format, this book covers television programs, networks, rules and regulations, technology, people, and terms.

THEATER (792)

The Cambridge Guide to World Theatre
Banham, Martin, ed. New York: Cambridge University Press, 1988. Incl. bibliographies.
This title surveys national theater developments emphasizing non-United States, non-European countries.

The Oxford Companion to the Theatre
Hartnoll, Phyllis, ed. New York: Oxford University Press, 1983. 4th ed.
Covering the world, this source offers historical background of theater by country, defines theater terms, provides biographies of theater personalities, and gives background on famous theaters and theater companies.

Shakespeare: An Illustrated Stage History
Bate, Jonathan, and Jackson, Russell. New York: Oxford University Press, 1996.
Essential for students researching Shakespeare for reports, this book covers 400 years of stage presentation of Shakespeare's plays. It covers the theaters, actors, props, and acting, and, most important, it provides photographs, reproductions, and drawings, which will serve to increase the understanding of Shakespeare through the ages.

MUSICAL THEATER (792.6)

Ganzl's Book of the Broadway Musical
Ganzl, Kurt. New York: Schirmer, 1995. Incl. index.
Subtitled *75 Favorite Shows from H.M.S. Pinafore* to *Sunset Boulevard*, this source provides details and story lines from mostly modern Broadway shows.

Ganzl's Book of the Musical Theatre
Ganzl, Kurt, and Lamb, Andrew. New York: Schirmer, 1989. Incl. indexes.
This source provides plot summaries and production details for 300 musical plays, produced anywhere in the world between 1728 and 1987.

DANCE (792.8, 793.3)

Biographical Dictionary of Dance
Cohen-Stratyner, Barbara. New York: Schirmer, 1982.
This book profiles 2,900 figures from 400 years of European and American dance, including many types of dance, dancers, choreographers, and other personalities associated with dance.

The Dance Encyclopedia
Chujoy, Anatole, and Manchester, P. W., comps. and eds. New York: Simon & Schuster, 1967. Rev. and enl. ed.
In dictionary format, this source provides historical and international coverage from ancient to modern times, includes biographical information, discusses types of dance, looks at dance in many countries, provides plot summaries of classic and modern dance works, defines dance terms, and reviews technique.

Dictionary of the Dance
Raffe, W. G., and Purdon, M. E. New York: Barnes, 1964. Incl. bibliography and index.
Covering all dance throughout the world and throughout history, this text defines terms, dances, forms, and techniques.

CHAPTER 8

Computers (004)

Librarians often prefer to use Yahoo! when searching the World Wide Web. This site organizes material by subject, much the same way that libraries do. This usually yields more relevant items but often fewer hits than other search engines. Alta Vista generally provides more hits and ranks them by relevancy. The HotBot and Excite engines also analyze hits for their relevancy. Some newer search engines provide thesauruses, which automatically include similar terms in the search.

This subject changes so rapidly that the best source of information is the Internet itself. Most libraries catalog material on computers in the 004 area of the library. Remember to look in both the circulating and reference sections. (For more information on the Internet, see Chapter 5.) The following sources will get you started.

ENCYCLOPEDIAS AND DICTIONARIES (004.03)

Computer Dictionary
Spencer, Donald. Ormond Beach, FL: Camelot, 1993.
The 5,800 terms include biographies.

Dictionary of Computer and Internet Terms
Downing, Douglas, ed. Hauppauge, NY: Barrons, 1996.
Over 1,800 terms are defined. Includes cross-references and a table of characters and symbols.

Encyclopedia of Computer Science
New York: Van Nostrand, 1993. Incl. bibliography and index.
   Contains 605 definitions. Subject categories include acronyms, computer science and engineering, glossary, time line, name, and general indexes.

INDEXES (004.16)

Computer Select
New York: Information Access, 1991–   .
   This CD-ROM source indexes and provides abstracts of articles for about 100 computer industry publications. It provides full text of articles for about 50 more computer industry periodicals. Disks are issued monthly. Each disk adds the most current month of a publication and drops the earliest month, so there are always 12 months of publications on disk. Coverage includes products, evaluations, companies, and more. It allows keyword searching or searching by publication, by date, by author or title of article. A great all-in-one source for computer industry information.

Microcomputer Index
Learned Information, 1980–   . Available online.
   Quarterly index to 75 popular computing magazines sections on software and hardware reviews, buyer and vendor guides, columns, and feature articles. Author, company, product, and subject indexes. Annual cumulative index.

Full Text Sources Online: For Periodicals, Newspapers, Newsletters and Newswires. 1988–   .
   Bibliodata annual alphabetical listing of title, service and date coverage.

COMPUTER REFERENCES (004.165, 621.3916)

Troubleshooting Your PC
Aspinall, Jim and Todd, Mike. New York: MIS Press, 1997.
   This book is a complete PC reference guide. Highly readable, it promotes self-maintenance with guides and technical support and helps users improve system performance, set-up, and repairs.

INTERNET AND WORLD WIDE WEB (004.67)

Cyber Dictionary: Your Guide to the Wired World
Morse, David. Santa Monica, CA: Knowledge Exchange, 1996.

A useful guide written in clear language. Contains over 900 key cyberspace words, phrases, and names. Includes how the Internet works, how and where to use it, and definitions. With illustrations.

The History Highway: A Guide to Internet Resources
Trinkle, Dennis A. Armonk, NY: M. E. Sharpe, 1997.
Includes general history, ancient, medieval, world, scientific and technical, military, and religious, history; electronic journals; and maps. Uniform resource locators (URLs) are given for each site.

Home Sweet Home Page: An Easy Guide to Creating Your Own Family Web Site
Williams, Robin. Berkeley, CA: Peach Pit Press, 1996.
This book shows how to create a personal Web site. This easy-to-use guide cuts through the usual jargon of getting on the Web and gives creative ideas for Web pages in a friendly, nontechnical way.

Internet International Directory
Emeryville, CA: Ziff-Davis, 1995.
This book comes with accompanying CD-ROM. It includes hardware and software, Internet accounts, addresses, netiquette, security, searching, World Wide Web, personal connections, and research. Part II, on international Internet sites, deals with multiuser dungeons, defined as simple, interactive online games. An appendix lists service providers, print resources, and children's resources.

McKinley Internet Yellow Pages
Maxwell, Christine. Indianapolis, IN: New Riders,1995.
This major Internet guide is divided into 15 major subject categories, including Mailing Lists, News Groups, Commercial On-Line, and Whimsical Tour. Starred ratings show items rated "good" by McKinley. Appendixes include providers, glossary, keyword, and audience.

The Whole Internet User's Guide and Catalog
Kroll, Ed. Sebastopol, CA: O'Reilly & Associates Inc. Corrected through 1995.
A very popular introductory guide. Includes remote Login, Moving Files, Electronic Mail, Network News, Finding Files, Finding Someone, Gophers, Databases, World Wide Web, and appendixes on Getting Connected, Acceptable Use, Unix Primer, and List of Internet Access Providers.

DIRECTORIES AND GUIDES (005.3–005.7)

The Online 100
O'Leary, Mick. Wilton, CT: Pemberton Press, 1995.

A guide to *Online* magazine's 100 most important databases. Topics include general and business news, business, U.S. and international companies, current events, law and government, general and physical sciences, life sciences and medicine, technology and computing, intellectual property, patents, social sciences and humanities, and general reference. For each database, it includes time span, producer, availability on the Internet, CD-ROMs, and search costs.

CHAPTER 9

Economics (330–339) and Business (650–659)

High school and middle school student assignments on business and economic topics may not center entirely on one or the other but may be included as part of a broader assignment. For example, a teacher may want to see that a student doing a country study understands that country's monetary and economic systems. A history assignment might include information on the way of life in the time and place studied, such as how much was a farm worker in colonial America was paid in today's dollars. At some point before graduating from high school, most students study the stock market—its role in national and world economies, the importance of investment to economies and to individuals—and learn how to read and interpret stock reports. Many sources offer this information, not all of them in the business or economics sections of the library. A brief description of a country's economic and financial system can be found in *Statesman's Yearbook,* for example. Longer discussions can be found in a source such as *Political Handbook of the World* or *Worldmark Encyclopedia of Nations.* Economic statistics, inflation rates, and other data may be found in the *Statistical Abstract of the United States,* among other sources. The following resources can be used to answer business and economics questions.

ECONOMICS ENCYCLOPEDIAS AND DICTIONARIES (330.03)

Atlas of the World Economy
Freeman, Michael J. New York: Simon & Schuster, 1991. Incl. bibliography.

The 250 maps, charts, graphs, and tables in this book are divided among eight broad categories: population, agriculture, energy, industry, national income, transport and trade, labor, and multinationals. Useful for visual representations, though maps are in black and white.

A Field Guide to the U.S. Economy
Folbre, Nancy. New York: Pantheon/Random House, 1987.

This book, valuable for students, uses charts, graphs, and tables to explain key economic issues and demonstrate how the United States economy works. It makes a complex topic fun and easy to understand.

Harper Dictionary of Economics
Pass, Christopher, et al. New York: HarperPerennial, 1991.

This source provides 1,700 clearly written definitions, describes organizations, and provides biographies of important economists. Contains 200 illustrations.

The McGraw-Hill Encyclopedia of Economics
Greenwald, Douglas, ed. New York: McGraw-Hill, 1993. 2d ed. Incl. bibliographies and indexes.

Alphabetically arranged articles discuss and explain basic concepts and theories in economics, such as supply-side economics; institutions, such as Medicare and the International Monetary Fund; and history, such as the Great Depression. This updated edition covers new developments in the world, including "Decline of the Soviet Economy," "German Unification," and "Going Private and Leveraged Buyouts." No biographies.

The New Palgrave: A Dictionary of Economics
Eatwell, John, et al., eds. New York: Stockton Press, 1987. 4 vols. Incl. bibliographies and index.

Comprehensive, even scholarly coverage of theoretical and applied aspects of economics is provided in this multivolume source intended for serious and knowledgeable students. There are 700 biographies. Although high school students may do better consulting *The McGraw-Hill Encyclopedia of Economics* (see the previous entry), since it is easier to read and covers popular economic topics, this remains the authoritative source.

BIOGRAPHIES OF ECONOMISTS (330. 09)

Great Economists before Keynes: An Introduction to the Lives and Works of 100 Great Economists of the Past
Blaug, Mark. Atlantic Highlands, NJ: Humanist Press International, 1986. Incl. index.
Great Economists since Keynes: An Introduction to the Lives and Works of 100 Modern Economists
Blaug, Mark. Totowa, NJ: Barnes and Noble, 1985. Incl. index.
Both books describe in an interesting, light, fair manner the lives and contributions of the world's most important economists. Arranged alphabetically, the books include photographs or illustrations of the subjects.

STATISTICS (330.9)

ACCRA Cost of Living Index
Alexandria, VA: ACCRA. Quarterly.
This source, arranged by place and item, gives comparative prices around the country for grocery items, utilities, transportation, health care, and housing. It's very specific, giving prices, for example, for movies, shirts, and haircuts.

American Cost of Living Survey
Darnay, Arsen J., and Fisher, Helen S. Detroit: Gale, 1994. Incl. bibliography.
While *The Value of a Dollar* (the last entry in this section) compares costs of goods and services and wages across the years, *American Cost of Living Survey* compares costs and wages in towns and cities across the United States currently. This source, intended for people and businesses considering locating in other parts of the country, will help students with economics and home economics assignments. For example, where in America can you find the best housing buys? Where in America is it best to live if you are a biologist? Does inflation affect all parts of the country equally? Why or why not?

Commodity Prices
Friedman, Catherine, ed. Detroit: Gale, 1991. 2d ed. Incl. index.
Commodities—for example, steel, copper, wheat, and coffee—are the raw materials that businesses and manufacturers use to produce their products. Investors buy commodities, often before they're harvested or produced, and sell them later—at a profit, they hope. This book lists the prices of commodities at different periods of time. It will help

students with their understanding of markets, investments, and even the importance of and dependencies of people and nations on commodities.

CPI Detailed Report
Washington, DC: Bureau of Labor Statistics. Monthly.

The government collects price and wage information from around the country and uses them to produce the Consumer Price Index (CPI). This is the number used to determine whether the cost of living is going up or down or staying the same. The *Detailed Report* compares numbers for specific items, services, and labor in different parts of the country, as well as averaged nationwide.

The Economist Book of Vital World Statistics
New York: Times Books, 1990. Incl. bibliography.

This source will help students compare statistics country by country and category by category. Within chapters of broad categories, such as agriculture and food, employment, education, and health, countries are statistically compared. The book will support papers and answer questions pertaining to such things as coffee or wheat production or consumption, vehicle ownership, working hours, cost of living, standard of living, school enrollment, foreign debt, and so on.

The Value of a Dollar: Prices and Incomes in the United States, 1860–1989
Derks, Scott, ed. Detroit: Gale, 1994. Incl. bibliography.

Invaluable for students who are often asked to support their studies of periods in United States history with facts and statistics that connect to their own experience. What was the price of beef or a haircut during the Civil War, the Great Depression, or the 1950s, for those who lived during those times, as compared with what we pay now? What wages were paid to a carpenter or a cab driver? These statistics make it personal. This source has them in well-organized, easy-to-read charts. Every student will use this book sometime during his or her schooling.

LABOR (331)

The ABC-CLIO Companion to the American Labor Movement
Taylor, Paul F. Santa Barbara, CA: ABC-CLIO, 1993. Incl. bibliography and index.

This source covers, according to the Preface, "labor leaders, major unions, landmark court decisions and legislation, key events, and the opposition of American business." A chronology is included.

The ABC-CLIO Companion to Women in the Workplace
Schneider, Dorothy, and Schneider, Carl J. Santa Barbara, CA: ABC-CLIO, 1993. Incl. bibliography and index.

Alphabetically arranged, this history of paid employment of women covers America from colonial times. Entries include information on people, events, organizations, court cases, and movements.

Biographical Dictionary of American Labor
Fink, Gary M., et al., eds. Westport, CT: Greenwood, 1984. 2d ed. Incl. bibliography and index.

This source provides 725 biographies of union leaders, radicals, intellectuals, lawyers, politicians, and others who a had major impact on the American labor movement. Women and African Americans are well represented.

Labor Conflict in the United States: An Encyclopedia
Filipelli, Ronald, ed. New York: Garland, 1990. Incl. bibliographies.

This source discusses 250 major labor conflicts between 1661 and 1988. Entries are alphabetically arranged, and a chronology and glossary of terms are included.

CAREERS (331.702)

Encyclopedia of Careers and Vocational Guidance
Chicago: J. G. Ferguson Publishing. 1997. 10th ed. 4 vols. Incl. index.

Similar to *Occupational Outlook Handbook* (the following entry), this set provides pretty much the same information. It covers more specific jobs and provides industry profiles. Jobs and careers are arranged alphabetically. Students should examine this and *Occupational Outlook,* if possible. Both are accurate in their job descriptions and assessments.

Occupational Outlook Handbook
Washington, DC: U.S. Department of Labor, Bureau of Labor Statistics. Annual. Incl. index.

This source is the standard for providing summary information on hundreds of careers. Articles describe the nature of the work, working conditions, current employment figures and projections for the future, training and qualifications required, likely and potential earnings, paths and opportunities for advancement, related jobs, and sources of information. Introductory chapters examine the world of work today based on statistics and offer a projected overview for the near future.

Guidance on how to look for a job, the resumé, cover letter, and interview process is also provided.

FINANCE AND INVESTMENT (332)

Barron's Finance and Investment Handbook
Hauppauge, NY: Barron's Educational Series, 1990. 3d ed. Incl. index.

This one volume explains everything you need to know: investment opportunities, how to read annual reports and financial pages, terms, additional sources of information, and financial statistical data charted over time. An excellent resource for students needing explanations of the arcane world of finance.

Common Stock Newspaper Abbreviations and Trading Symbols
Jarrell, Howard R. Metuchen, NJ: Scarecrow Press, 1989. Supp. One, 1991.

This book is very useful for identifying stock symbols. There are three sections, each arranged alphabetically and serving as an index to the other two listings. You can look up the company name and find its trading or ticker symbol used on Wall Street, its newspaper abbreviation, and the stock exchange on which the company is traded. If you know the trading symbol, you can look it up that way and find the company name, newspaper abbreviation, and stock exchange. If you know the newspaper abbreviation, you can access the company, trading symbol, and stock exchange that way. Abbreviations and symbols don't always easily designate the company name. This book removes the mystery.

The Dow-Jones Irwin Guide to Using the Wall Street Journal
Lehmann, Michael B. New York: Dow Jones–Irwin, 1990. 3d ed. Incl. bibliographic references.

Students will find this book useful for interpreting the *Wall Street Journal* as a guide to the U.S. and world economies. Emphasis is on key economic indicators: what they are, how they are computed, what they mean, and when they're published.

Encyclopedia of Banking and Finance
Munn, Glenn G., et al. Detroit, MI: St. James Press, 1991. 9th ed. Incl. bibliographies.

A standard source providing 4,200 entries that define and explain all aspects of the world of money. Statistics, laws, charts, and illustrations are included. Problems such as bank failures and the collapse of the savings and loan industry are discussed.

Moody's Handbook of Common Stocks
New York: Moody's Investors Service. Quarterly.

This quarterly paperback provides information similar to *Standard and Poor's Stock Reports* (see below in this section). One-page summaries chart stock performance and provide financial data, company history, recent developments, and future prospects.

Moody's Manuals
New York: Moody's Investors Service. Annual with looseleaf updates.

These cover all publicly traded companies, divided into volumes on industrial, bank and finance, transportation, public utilities, over-the-counter, and international companies. History, officers, address and telephone numbers, business description, product listings, plant locations, subsidiaries, financial statistics, and more are provided. Looseleaf volumes, updated biweekly, accompany each title. Also available on CD-ROM. This source will inform students fully about public corporations, providing invaluable information for those developing a business and investment awareness. A soft-cover master index to all volumes is published separately, similar in appearance to a slim magazine.

Morningstar Mutual Fund Sourcebook
Chicago: Morningstar. Weekly. Looseleaf.

This source tracks mutual funds the way *Value Line Investment Survey* (see below, this section) tracks stocks. Performance summaries, histories, and predictions are of most interest, supported by statistics, charts, graphs, portfolio analysis, and written analysis.

Standard and Poor's Stock Reports
New York: Standard and Poor's. Weekly.

These reports come in looseleaf binders that are updated weekly. They provide stock price reports and brief assessments of the specific corporation—its history, business, performance in the recent past, and present and expected near future performance. The New York and American Stock Exchanges, and over-the-counter exchanges are covered. This source will give students the ability to track stock and company performances over time with an eye to the future.

Value Line Investment Survey
New York: Value Line. Weekly. Looseleaf.

This source tracks close to 2,000 companies on the major stock exchanges, providing regularly updated statistical and financial data, ratings and reports, industry overviews, stock prices, and projects.

Wall Street Words
Scott, David Logan. Boston: Houghton Mifflin, 1988.
This source defines 3,600 terms and provides examples of application through case studies.

COMMERCE AND TRADE (380)

World Chamber of Commerce Directory
Loveland, CO: World Chamber of Commerce Directory. Annual.
Every student at one time or another has to write for information to chambers of commerce, tourist bureaus, or embassies. All the addresses and telephone numbers are in this book for the United States and most other countries. It even includes addresses and telephone numbers of members of the United States Senate and House of Representatives. An invaluable resource.

BUSINESS (650)

Brands and Their Companies
Edgar, Susan, ed. Detroit: Gale, 1996. 15th ed. 2 vols. Annual.
Who makes Rice Krispies? Is Mr. Coffee a product or a company or both? How do I contact the manufacturer? This source is comprehensive, and makes the answers easy. Although many business reference sources include brand name indexes, this is the one book that exceeds the others. It includes about 326,000 consumer brands and 68,000 manufacturers and distributors. There are no brand histories, just alphabetical access by product name and identification of the company that makes it. The last third or so of Volume 2 is an alphabetical list of company names with addresses and telephone numbers. Simple, useful, and thorough.

Directory of Corporate Affiliations
New Providence, NJ: National Register. Annual. 5 vols. Incl. indexes.
The best source for for tracking who owns what—that is, what company owns what other company or companies. Most large corporations have such a multitude of subsidiaries and other business relationships that it's difficult to keep track of the parent companies. This source makes it easy. Addresses, officers, sales volume, employees, and product listings are included for each entry. A master index provides easy access to the separate volumes on public, private, U.S., and international companies. Also included is a brand name index identifying the maker of a brand product and a nearly 20-year listing of mergers, acquisitions, and business name changes. Does Ford Motor Co. own Hertz Rent-a-Car, or not? Look it up! Also available on CD-ROM.

Dun's Business Rankings
Parsippany, NJ: Dun's Marketing Services. Annual.
Great for determining which companies are largest (ranked from largest to smallest) by sales volume or number of employees within a specific industry or by state.

Encyclopedia of Consumer Brands
Jorgensen, Janice, ed. Detroit, MI: St. James Press, 1994. 3 vols. Incl. bibliographies and index.
A similar service to *Brands and Their Companies* (above), this set provides more information per brand but covers fewer (600) brand name products. Articles on each brand give company history, market performance, and advertising information.

Hoover's Handbook: Profiles of over 500 Major Corporations
Hoover, Gary, et al., eds. Emeryville, CA: Publishers Group West, 1991.
An excellent, easy-to-read and-understand, graphically inviting resource for students and others needing brief, accurate, summary information on major corporations. Alphabetically arranged by company name, each one-page summary provides historical background on the company, products made, significant people involved in the company, financial statistics over the past several years, rankings (such as on the Fortune 500), and names of competitor companies. Several helpful lists are included, such as "The 100 Largest Companies," "The 100 Most Profitable Companies," and "The 100 Largest Employers." Hoover has put his name on several other useful business resources such as *Hoover's Handbook of American Business 1996: Profiles of 750 Major U.S. Companies; Hoover's Guide to the Top New York Companies; Hoover's Global 250; Profiles of Major European, Asian, Latin American and Canadian Companies; Hoover's 500: Profiles of America's Largest Business Enterprises; Hoover's Handbook of Emerging Companies: Profiles of 250 of America's Most Exciting Growth Companies; Hoover's Handbook of World Business;* and *Hoover's Guide to Computer Companies.* All of these, and there are others, follow the same format and are useful to job seekers, investors, and students researching companies for career projects or financial and economic studies.

Market Share Reporter
Detroit: Gale. Annual.
Does what it says: provides market share statistics on products on companies. Useful for figuring out who, for example, has more market share: Kellogg's or Post.

U.S. Industry Profiles: The Leading 100
Sawinski, Diane, ed. Detroit: Gale, 1995. Incl. bibliographies and index.

This source provides overview and outlook information by broad industrial and service industry categories, arranged alphabetically. Coverage includes discussion of the industry's workforce, functional aspects of the industry, impact of research and technology on the industry, global influences, reference to other sources of information, and statistical and market share information.

BUSINESS INDEXES (650.016, 016.65)

ABI/INFORM Ondisc
Louisville, KY: UMI/Data Courier. Monthly on CD-ROM. Updated weekly online.

This product indexes 800 business and management journals and includes lengthy abstracts. Very useful to students because the abstracts may satisfy their need. Found mostly in large public libraries with good business divisions and in academic libraries. Online access offers full text rather than abstracts.

Business Magazine Index
Menlo Park, CA: Information Access Corp., 1980– . Monthly on CD-ROM and online.

Various versions of the product are offered to libraries. Students may find the index that coordinates with microfilm copies of the magazines or versions of full text on CD-ROM covering the current three-year period or other versions, which offer more or less periodical coverage over longer or shorter periods of time or offer variations of full text and abstracts. Any version is useful to the student because coverage includes hundreds of trade and business-specific periodicals.

Business NewsBank
New Canaan, CT: NewsBank, 1985– . Monthly on CD-ROM.

Disks now provide full text of business articles from wire services and newspapers from around the country. Earlier disks provided indexing and reference microfiche reproductions of newspaper articles. Disks can be searched by subject or keyword. Students will find this an excellent source, complementing those listed above, since local newspapers are used as sources rather than the *New York Times* and *Wall Street Journal.*

Business Periodical Index
New York: Wilson, 1958–   . Monthly with annual cumulation.

Also available on CD-ROM, this service indexes business and business-related periodicals, covering such subjects as accounting, marketing, advertising, banking, insurance, retailing, public relations, industries and trades, real estate, finance, communications, chemical industries, and petroleum and gas industries.

Wall Street Journal/Barron's
Ann Arbor, MI: University Microfilms, 1957–   . Monthly with quarterly and annual cumulations.

Available full text on CD-ROM and online, this service indexes both the *Wall Street Journal* and *Barron's*. Green pages belong to *Barron's*. Corporate news and general news are indexed separately. Both newspapers are superb for keeping up with business developments. The indexes are of great help to student researchers.

CHAPTER 10

History (900) and Biography (920, B)

Popular research assignments in history include ancient life in Rome, Greece, and Egypt; the Renaissance; the Middle Ages; the world wars; the American Civil War; the French Revolution; country studies; life in colonial America; and the Irish potato famine. Often teachers want students to fold in daily life details. How were children in ancient Greece or colonial America taught? What did they eat? How much did bread cost? How much did a cobbler earn? And so on. The answers to these and many more questions can be found in sources listed below.

What about America's westward expansion, the Mormon trail, the Trail of Tears, the Underground Railroad? Some of these you can research using the term, such as "Underground Railroad." But often you have to use the name of the country, subdivided by "history," and then subdivided by the time period, as in "United States—History—1861–1864," the years during which the Civil War occurred. The sections in this chapter will lead you to the sources for your questions about history.

BIBLIOGRAPHY (901.6)

Reference Sources in History
Fritze, Ronald H., ed. Santa Barbara, CA: ABC-CLIO, 1990. Incl. indexes.

This guide to the major reference works is arranged by format, subdivided geographically and by period. It is indexed by broad field, author, and title.

CHRONOLOGIES (902)

Almanac of Dates: Events of the Past for Every Day of the Year
Millgate, Linda. New York: Harcourt Brace Jovanovich, 1977.

This source follows every day of the year with a list of years and a sentence describing a significant event that occurred on that day in that year. All of known history is included.

Chronicle of the Twentieth Century
Daniel, Clifton, ed. Liberty, MO: JL International, n.d. Incl. index.

Organized by year and month, pages are set up to look like newspaper pages. News photos are included. A vertical column lists significant events by day for the month. Three to six brief, newspaper-style articles elaborate on selected significant events of the month.

Frew's Daily Archive: A Calendar of Commemorations
Frew, Andrew, comp. Jefferson, NC: McFarland, 1984. Incl. indexes.

Similar to the *Almanac of Dates* (see above, this section), this source provides a line of text on significant events by day and year. It also includes commemorative days. For example, April 22 is Arbor Day and Oklahoma Day. It's also Lenin's birthday. The construction of the Bastille began in Paris in 1370. George Washington went to the circus on this day in 1793. An index of birthdays is useful for determining who was born on a day, and there's an index of commemorative days.

New York Public Library Book of Chronologies
Wetterau, Bruce. Englewood Cliffs, NJ: Prentice-Hall, 1990. Incl. bibliography and index.

This book is organized by subject and by year within the subject chapters. Subjects include nations and empires, technology, arts, science, sports, and accidents and disasters.

The People's Chronology: A Year-by-Year Record of Human Events from Prehistory to Present
Trager, James. New York: Holt, 1992. Rev. and upd. ed. Incl. index.

This source provides paragraphs of text on significant events by year. Symbols next to the paragraph indicate in what field of endeavor the event occurred and help you spot specific types of information (e.g., food and drink are symbolized by a crossed fork and spoon and daily life by the face of an old-fashioned alarm clock). This source is useful for determining common events as well as major historical events. An example of daily life in 1798 stated that John Hetherington made the first silk top hat in London, thus reducing the demand for beaver pelts.

ENCYCLOPEDIAS AND DICTIONARIES (903)

Dictionary of Twentieth Century History: 1914–1990
Teed, Peter, ed. New York: Oxford University Press, 1992.
Nearly 2,000 brief entries on major countries, terms, people, movements, events, culture, technology, and social and economic affairs. No index.

Encyclopedia of World Cultures
Levinson, David, ed. Boston: G. K. Hall, 1991–1996. 10 vols. Incl. bibliographic references and indexes.
This is the best source for information on indigenous peoples, tribes, and cultural groups worldwide. The volumes are organized by geographic region. Within each volume, the cultural groups are listed by name. Entries range from a few lines to several pages. The way of life of each group is emphasized, and change over time is recorded. According to the Preface, "a mix of demographic, historical, social, economic, political, and religious information" is provided. From the Hmong to the Sioux, this is the source to use.

Encyclopedia of World Facts and Dates
Carruth, Gordon, ed. New York: HarperCollins, 1993.
Arranged in categories (e.g., war, politics). Tables list events and dates on government, politics, history, literature, art, economics, sports, science, and entertainment. Chronologically arranged by year in four columns, each column covers several subjects, such as exploration, wars, disasters, drama, publishing arts, entertainment, business, and sports.

Encyclopedia of World History: Ancient, Medieval, and Modern Chronologically Arranged
Langer, William Leonard. Boston: Houghton Mifflin, 1972. Maps and genealogical tables.
Geographical arrangement, with a political, military, and diplomatic emphasis.

New Cambridge Modern History
Cambridge: Cambridge University Press 1979. 14 vols. Incl. bibliographies and index.

Covers 1493–1945, with chapters written by scholars. Each volume is indexed. Bibliographies are in a separate volume, and Volume 14 is an atlas.

ANCIENT HISTORY (930–939)

Atlas of Classical History
Talbert, Richard J. A., ed. New York: Macmillan, 1985.

An excellent source for geographical material. It includes 100 maps, a list of Roman emperors, a gazetteer of places, and a basic chronology.

Cambridge Ancient History
Cambridge: Cambridge University Press, 1923– . 12 vols. in progress. 5 vols. of illus. Incl. bibliographies and index.

The Cambridge University histories are considered the basic reference volumes in their subject fields. Each volume is written by a specialist in the era.

Greek and Roman Life
Jenkins, Ian. Cambridge, MA: Harvard University Press, 1987.

An excellent source for material on the everyday life of ancient Greeks and Romans. This book includes material on dress, education, home life, and history.

Larousse Encyclopedia of Ancient and Medieval History
Dunan, Marcel, ed. Feltham, England: Hamlyn, 1964. Incl. index.

Color and black and white photographs and illustrations are found on every page in this source. Chapters cover prehistory to the fifteenth century. Ancient Greece and Rome, the barbarian invasions, and the rise of Europe from the thirteenth through the fifteen centuries are given strong emphasis. While not a daily life source, students will find the history of the Middle Ages well documented and useful.

Oxford History of the Classical World
Boardman, John, et al., ed. New York: Oxford University Press, 1986. Incl. index, maps, illus.

Illustrated history of Greece and Rome that covers politics, social history, literature, philosophy, and art. Divided into three sections: Greece, 900–336 B.C.; Greece and Rome, 336 B.C.–14 A.D.; and Rome, 14–476 A.D.

Perseus
An Internet World Wide Web site that includes Greek classics and thousands of pictures of art objects.

MIDDLE AGES (909.3, 940.1)

Cambridge Medieval History
Cambridge: Cambridge University Press, 1911–1936. 8 vols.
Narrative histories written by specialists in each topic. Bibliography and index in each volume. New edition of vol. 4 in two volumes, 1966–67.

Dictionary of the Middle Ages
Strayer, Joseph R. New York: Scribner's, 1982–1989. 13 vols. Incl. bibliographies.
This book covers European history from the sixth through sixteenth centuries with 5,000 entries on political, cultural, and religious history.

The Oxford Illustrated History of Medieval Europe
Holmes, George. New York: Oxford University Press, 1988.
A useful single-volume survey of history covering the period 500–1500.

MODERN ERA (940.2– 940.5)

Holocaust (940.5318, 940.5472)

Encyclopedia of the Holocaust
Gutman, Israel. New York: Macmillan, 1990. 4 vols. Illus., maps. Incl. bibliographies.
An alphabetical compendium of long articles on countries, people, sites of camps and massacres, documentation centers. The article on Auschwitz is 10 pages, with photos and maps.

Industrial Revolution (909.81, 940.28)

The ABC-CLIO World History Companion to the Industrial Revolution
Stearn, Peter N., and Hinshaw, John H. Santa Barbara, CA: ABC-CLIO, 1996. Incl. bibliography and index.
Arranged in alphabetical one-volume encyclopedia style, this source's entries range from a quarter-page to two pages in length. Most entries conclude with one to four bibliographic references. Coverage is

worldwide, from 1760 to the present, and includes the details of mechanized industrial development as well as social, political, and economic impact. The book is illustrated with black and white photographs and includes a chronology. A valuable source.

Technology (609)

History of Technology
Singer, C. J. Oxford: Clarendon Press, 1954–1978. 7 vols.
A magnificent scholarly work with many illustrations. The definitive history of technical changes through history. Includes people and inventions.

World War I (940.3)

An Illustrated Companion to the First World War
Bruce, Anthony. London: Michael Joseph, 1989. Incl. bibliography.
An A–Z popularly written encyclopedia, this source covers biographies, military equipment, battles, casualties, and political events relevant to the war. Photographs and maps illustrate the text for better comprehension, and a chronology concludes the book.

World War One Source Book
Haythornthwaite, Philip J. London: Arms and Armour, 1992. Incl. bibliography and index.
A solid one-volume source that covers the war chronologically and examines each front by year. Weaponry is studied in some detail and for all nations. Biographies of significant figures are provided. The book is illustrated, and maps are included. Entries average about a half-page, but many are longer. The government and administration of each warring state are examined, with emphasis on their military organizations. Definitely a useful source.

World War II (940.53, 940.54)

Encyclopedia of the Second World War
Hogg, Ian V., ed. Novato, CA: Presidio, 1989. Incl bibliography.
Dictionary of campaigns, battles, warships, aircraft, and so forth. Includes illustrations and maps. Cross-referenced, but no index.

Oxford Companion to World War II
Foot, M.R.D., ed. New York: Oxford University Press, 1995. Incl. bibliography.

Analytical articles on campaigns, armaments, social issues, tactics, and biography. Cross-referenced and illustrated.

COUNTRIES (910–919, 941–999)

Encyclopedias and General Sources

Country Studies (Area Handbook Series)
Federal Research Division, Library of Congress. Washington, DC: U.S. government Printing Office. Incl. bibliography and index.
Basic facts on social, economic, political, and military conditions in many different countries. These are detailed studies written by government experts to orient diplomatic and military officers to conditions in each of these countries.

Worldmark Encyclopedia of the Nations
Sachs, Moshe Y., ed. New York: Wiley, 1988. 5 vols.
Volume 1 covers the United Nations and other international organizations, as well as world statistics, United Nations online databases, and the polar regions. Volumes 2–5 are essays on countries arranged geographically by continent. Includes history, topography, climate, flora and fauna, finance, language, ethnic groups, and government.

Africa (916, 960)

Cambridge Encyclopedia of Africa
Oliver, Roland, and Crowder, Michael. Cambridge: Cambridge University Press, 1981. Incl. bibliography and index.
A section on the African continent as a whole and a section on the African past, which treats the history of each country. The final section on Africa and the world discusses the relationship of Africa with other countries and the colonial aspect. Part of a series on countries and continents done in narrative format with illustrations, maps, tables, and photos.

Arab Nations (915.3, 953)

A History of the Arab Peoples
Hourani, Albert. Cambridge, MA: Belknap Press of Harvard University Press, 1991. Incl. index.
A general survey of the history of Arab-speaking peoples from the seventh century to the present. Illustrated with maps.

Asia (915, 950)

Cambridge Encyclopedia of India, Pakistan, Bangladesh, Sri Lanka, Nepal, Bhutan, and the Maldives
Robinson, Francis, ed. Cambridge: Cambridge University Press, 1989. Incl. bibliography and index.
This work includes topical sections on land and peoples, economics, politics, religion, and cultural history. Illustrated and includes maps.

Encyclopedia of Asian History
Embree, Ainslie. New York: Scribners, 1988. 4 vols. Incl. photos, bibliographies, maps, index.
From Iran to Indonesia and from the earliest times in a thematic outline. Profiles of over 1,200 persons. Includes events and places. A two-part synoptic outline includes concepts and historic eras and an outline of countries by region.

Canada (917.1, 971)

The Canadian Encyclopedia
Marsh, James M., ed. Edmonton, CN: Hurtig, 1988. 2d ed. 4 vols. Incl. illus., index.
A comprehensive look at history, people, geography, economy, and government. The 9,700 entries, on people, places, politics, and the myths and legends of the Inuits (Eskimos), are arranged alphabetically.

China (915.1, 951)

Cambridge Encyclopedia of China
Hook, Brian, ed. Cambridge: Cambridge University Press, 1991. 2d ed. Incl. bibliographies. Illus. with maps.
Broad topics include land and resources; peoples; society; philosophy; religion; continuity (history), including a list of key emperors and their accomplishments; mind and senses; art and architecture; science and technology; a guide for visitors; government and military; and further readings. Includes tables.

Cambridge Illustrated History of China
Ebrey, Patricia B. Cambridge: Cambridge University Press, 1996. Incl. index.
This book is part of a new series. Each book in the series provides a general survey of a country in one volume, with many illustrations in a colorful, easy-to-read format.

France (914.4, 944)

Cambridge Illustrated History of France
Jones, Colin. Cambridge: Cambridge University Press, 1994. Incl. index.
Part of the same series as *Cambridge Illustrated History of China*, (see above), and others.

Historical Dictionary of the French Revolution
Scott, Samuel F., and Rothaus, Barry, eds. Westport, CT: Greenwood, 1985. 2 vols. Incl. bibliography and index, chronology.
A comprehensive dictionary of people and places. A bibliography at the end of each article includes many sources in the French language.

Germany (914.3, 943)

A History of Germany
Carr, William. 2d ed. New York: St. Martin's Press, 1979.
Modern Germany, 1870–1979.

Historical Dictionary of Germany
Metuchen, NJ: Scarecrow, 1994. Incl. bibliography.
Chronology, persons, political parties, events, terms. Includes cross-references.

Great Britain and Ireland (914.1, 914.2, 941, 942)

The Cambridge Historical Encyclopedia of Great Britain and Ireland
Haigh, Christopher, ed. Cambridge: Cambridge University Press, 1985.
Articles on the history and culture of England, Ireland, Scotland, and Wales.

The Course of Irish History
Moody, T. W., and Martin, F. W., eds. Niwot, CO: Roberts Rinehart, 1994. Rev. and enl. ed. Incl. bibliography and index.
This illustrated text covers Irish history from prehistory to 1994. Each chapter is written by a historian specializing in the specific century (e.g., "The Great Famine, 1845–1850"). So successful is this source that it serves as the core text on Irish history in Irish schools, according to the cover notes. A chronology is included.

India (915.4, 954)

See Asia, p. 128

Ireland

See Great Britain and Ireland, p. 129

Japan (915.2, 952)

Kodansha Encyclopedia of Japan.
Itosaka, gen. ed. Japan: Kodansha, 1983. 9 vols. Incl. index, illus., cross-references.
This is a master reference including materials on theater, art, religion, and history.

Latin America (917.2, 918, 972, 980–989)

Cambridge Encyclopedia of Latin America and the Caribbean
Collier, Simon, et al., eds. New York: Cambridge University Press, 1992. 2d ed. Incl. bibliographic references and index.
This series is in narrative format with illustrations.

Middle East (915.6, 956)

Cambridge Encyclopedia of the Middle East and North Africa
Mostyn, Trevor, ed. New York: Cambridge University Press, 1988. Incl. bibliographies and index.
This series is in narrative format with illustrations.

Muslim Nations (915.5, 916, 955, 960s)

Muslim Peoples: A World Ethnographic Survey
Westport, CT: Greenwood, 1984. 2 vols. Incl. bibliographies.
Articles on all groups of 100,000 or more. Maps.

Russia (914.7, 947)

Cambridge Encyclopedia of Russia and the Soviet Union
Brown, Archie, et al., eds. New York: Cambridge University Press, 1994. 2d ed. Incl. bibliographic references and index.
This series is in narrative format with illustrations.

A History of Russia
Riasanovsky, Nicholas V. New York: Oxford University Press, 1984.
A political, social, and cultural history into the Stalinist period.

Spain (914.6, 946)

Spain: The Root and the Flower
Crow, John A. Berkeley: University of California Press, 1985. 3d ed.
Political and cultural history to the early 1980s.

AMERICAN HISTORY (973)

African American History (305.8, 973)

American Historical Images on File: The Black Experience
Smith, Carter, exec. ed. New York: Facts on File, 1990. Incl. index.
This source reproduces images from black American history—photographs, drawings, woodcuts, and so forth—that illustrate the black experience. Arrangement is chronological, beginning with the kidnapping in Africa and transportation to America in chains, to the American Revolution, continuing through slavery, the Civil War, into the 1950s, the civil rights movement, to the present. The intent of the collection is for clear copyright-free reproduction. These images can enhance student reports.

Black Firsts: 2,000 Years of Extraordinary Achievement
Smith, Jessie Carney, ed. Detroit: Visible Ink, 1994. Incl. bibliographic references and index.
This source is a chronology of significant events in black history arranged by subject and then by date. Illustrated with photographs and charts, there is also a calendar of firsts by month and day and a foldout time line.

The Reference Library of Black America
Estell, Kenneth. Detroit: Gale, 1994. 5 vols.
This source, based on the sixth edition of the *African American Almanac*, includes chronology, documents, and landmarks in Volume 1. Volume 2 covers a history of Africa, people of Africa, country profiles, Africans in America 1600–1900, civil rights, and black nationalism. Volume 3 is about politics, demographics, family, education, and religion. Volume 4 deals with literature, media, and the performing arts.

Volume 5 covers popular music, fine and applied arts, science, medicine, sports, and the military.

African American Statistics (317)

Statistical Record of Black America
Horton, Carrell P., and Smith, Jessie Carney, comps. and eds. Detroit: Gale, 1995. 3d ed. Incl. bibliography and index.

This source provides statistical charts, graphs, and tables on a wide variety of topics, including population, family, health, religion, education, crime, values, and labor. A must for students who need statistics conveniently located in one source.

Atlases (910–912)

American Heritage Pictorial Atlas of United States History
New York: American Heritage, 1966. Incl. illus. and maps.

Chronological arrangement with a useful historical narrative accompanying maps. Sections on agriculture, resources, Revolutionary and Civil War battles, World War II operations, the Vietnam War, and national parks.

Bibliographies and Indexes (973.01)

America: History and Life
Santa Barbara, CA: ABC-CLIO, 1964– . 7 issues per year. Cumulative indexes. Available online.

An index to 2,000 magazines includes abstracts or citations on the history of Canada and the United States. Part A is abstracts and citations. Part B is an index to book reviews. Part C is a bibliography including dissertations. Part D is an annual index.

Guide to the Study of the United States of America
Washington, DC: Library of Congress, 1960; Supplement 1956–1965.

Annotated bibliography of books on American life and thought. Brief biographies of authors.

Chronologies (973.02)

American Chronicle, 1920–1990
Gordon, Lois G. New York: Atheneum, 1994.

This useful reference source has nine pages per year on prices, news, notable quotations, television programs, movies, fashion, and advertising.

American Decades
Detroit, MI: Gale, 1930– . Incl. illus., index to photos, general index.

Covers recent American history by decade. Includes world events, arts, business and economics, education, law, lifestyle, medicine, religion, science and technology, sports, biographies of headline makers, and publications.

America in the 20th Century
Humphrey, Paul. Tarrytown, NY: Marshall Cavendish, 1995. 11 vols. Incl. bibliography and index.

Each volume covers a decade and looks at medicine, media, literature, art, sports, environment, and biographies. Illustrations include photographs, cartoons, and advertisements.

Day by Day: The Forties
Leonard, Thomas M. New York: Facts on File, 1977. Incl. index.

Day by Day: The Fifties
Merritt, Jeffrey D. New York: Facts on File, 1979. Incl. index.

Day by Day: The Sixties
Parker, Thomas, and Nelson, Douglas. New York: Facts on File, 1983. 2 vols. Incl. index.

Day by Day: The Seventies
Leonard, Thomas, et al. New York: Facts on File, 1988. 2 vols. Incl. index.

Day by Day: The Eighties
Meltzer, Ellen, and Aronson, Marc. New York: Facts on File, 1995. 2 vols. Incl. index.

This very detailed series is organized by year and day. The text describes significant events in several categories: world affairs; U.S. politics and social issues; U.S. economy and environment; science, technology and nature; culture; and leisure and life style.

Civil War (973.7)

The Civil War CD-ROM
Indianapolis, Ind.: Guild Press.

This monumental reference source includes the 128-volume *Records of the Union and Confederate Armies* and Fred Dyer's *Compendium of the American Civil War* with histories of all Union regiments. It may be searched by name, document, date, and combinations.

The Civil War Day by Day: An Almanac,1861–1865
Long, E. B. Garden City, NY: Doubleday, 1971. Incl. bibliography and indexes.
An outline day by day of events of the war, including personal narratives from diaries and other sources. Each month opens with a summary to place the events in context, and headlines of significant events make scanning for information easy. Statistics on population and casualties are also provided, giving depth, detail, and significance.

The Civil War Source Book
Katcher, Philip. New York: Facts on File, 1992. Incl. index.
Another in the source book series (see *World War One Source Book,* p. 126), this is similarly organized with chapters covering each theater of the war by year, weaponry used in the war by both sides, military life, analysis of each component of the military forces of both sides, examination of militias from every state, biographies of significant participants, and a look at some details, such as military pay and uniforms. Articles are readable and understandable. A glossary is included, as are maps and other illustrations. A useful reference and overall review of the war of great value to students.

The Constitution (973.4)

See also Chapter 13, p. 181

Encyclopedia of the American Constitution
New York: Macmillan, 1986. 4 vols. Incl. bibliographies and index.
Contains 2,100 signed articles on law, including people, judicial decisions, public acts, and historical periods. Chronologies, plus index by case name and subject.

Diplomatic History (327.73)

Dictionary of American Diplomatic History
Findling, John E. Westport, CT: Greenwood, 1988. 2d ed. Incl. index.
Contains 1,200 entries with more than 500 biographies. Includes treaties, incidents, interventions, conferences, places, terminology, and events in foreign relations of the United States through mid-1988. Bib-

liographical references and useful appendixes. For each president, lists key diplomatic personnel.

Encyclopedias and Dictionaries (973.03)

Dictionary of American History
Ketz, Louise B. New York: Scribner's, 1976. 8 vols. Incl. bibliography and index.
Brief articles on topics and incidents. No biographies. The bibliography is extensive but dated.

Encyclopedia of American History
Morris, Richard B., ed. New York: Harper, 1982.
Within the chronological presentation are articles on special topics such as science, inventions, and Supreme Court cases.

Everyday Life

Almanacs of American Life: Modern America 1914 to 1945
Gregory, Ross. New York: Facts on File, 1995. Incl. bibliography and index.

Almanacs of American Life: Revolutionary America 1763 to 1800
Purvis, Thomas L. New York: Facts on File, 1995. Incl. bibliography and index.

Almanacs of American Life: Victorian America 1876 to 1913
Shifflett, Crandall. New York: Facts on File, 1996. Incl. bibliography and index.
Each title in this series reviews every aspect of American life during the period. Chapters cover climate, religion, health and food, education, economic details from prices and income to work and production, crime, holidays, recreation, population details, and government. Illustrations, statistical tables, and maps add to the value of the text. Biographies of important Americans are included, as is a chronology of significant events. There is a great emphasis in this series on statistics, prices, wages, and similar data that are difficult to pull from other sources. A broader range of topics is covered than in other sources.

General Sources

Harvard Guide to American History
Freidel, Frank, ed. Cambridge, MA: Harvard University Press, 1974. 2 vols. Incl. name, author, and subject index.

This basic reference covers the political, social, economic, and constitutional history of America. Volume 1 includes research methods, biographical materials, comprehensive and area histories, and special subjects (politics, demography, immigration, ethnicity, reform, education, religion). Volume 2 is a chronological guide, ending in 1953, and includes materials published through mid-1970.

Oxford Companion to American History
Johnson, Thomas Herbet, ed. New York: Oxford University Press, 1966.
Alphabetically arranged biographical and historical guide includes labor, art, science, commerce, literary movements, social protests, associations, education, law, sports, and entertainment, plus the entire text of the Constitution and its amendments. Contains 4,710 entries and 1,835 biographies. No index.

Native American History and Biography (970.00497)

Encyclopedia of North American Indians
Hoxie, Frederick E. Boston: Houghton Mifflin, 1996. Incl. bibliography and index.
This encyclopedia includes maps and illustrations. It covers 100 tribes and five languages and provides 100 biographies of prominent Indians.

Great North American Indians: Profiles in Life and Leadership
Dockstader, Frederick J. New York: Van Nostrand Reinhold, 1977. Incl. bibliography and index.
Contains biographies of 300 American Indian leaders, with tribal listing, chronology, illustrations, portraits, and index of names.

Reference Encyclopedia of the American Indian
Klein, Barry T. West Nyack, NY: Todd Publications, 1986. 5th ed. 2 vols.
Sections include a directory for the United States and Canada, an author and subject bibliography of 4,000 items, and biographies of 2,000 Indians. Museums, libraries, reservations, tribal councils, periodicals, schools, and government agencies are included.

Political History (320.973)

Encyclopedia of American Political History
Greene, Jack P. New York: Scribner's, 1988. 4 vols. Incl. bibliographies and index.

Ninety studies of the principal movements and ideas, with articles on the Constitution, issues, and institutions.

Primary Sources

Annals of America
Chicago: Encyclopaedia Britannica, 1968–1987. 21 vols. Incl. bibliography and index.
There are 2,200 selections from speeches, diaries, books, journals, and articles documenting American history.

Documents of American History
Commager, Henry Steele. Englewood Cliffs, NJ: Prentice-Hall, 1974. 2 vols. Incl. index.
Documents are arranged chronologically, 1492–1973. Index by topic and personal name.

Twentieth-Century America: A Primary Source Collection from the Associated Press
Danbury, CT: Grolier, 1995. 10 vols. Incl. indexes.
Each volume in this series covers a decade (approximately). The chapters proceed in general chronological order covering the major events of the time. Articles are actual reprints of Associated Press wire service news articles—hence the subtitle, *Primary Source Collection*. Primary sources are created at the time of the event, usually by witnesses or participants. Documentary photographs heighten the you-are-there feeling. This is an excellent source for students writing about significant events in our century.

The Revolution (973.3)

Encyclopedia of the American Revolution
Boatner, Mark Mayo. New York: David McKay, 1974. Rev. ed. Incl. bibliography and index.
Biographies, battles, and issues on the Revolution. Includes illustrations and maps.

The Encyclopedia of Colonial and Revolutionary America
Faragher, John Mack, gen. ed. New York: Facts on File, 1990. Incl. bibliographic references and index.
Intended as a quick reference, this alphabetically arranged source serves students quite well. Articles can be a half-page long, while major topics are considerably longer. Good cross-references and a topic guide,

and the longer articles include bibliographies. Biographies of significant persons, including women, are provided. A solid source.

Who Was Who in the American Revolution
Purcell, L. Edward. New York: Facts on File, 1993. Incl. bibliography and index.

There are 1,500 alphabetically arranged biographies of major figures from all sides of the war. Details on birth, death, and life before, during, and after the war are provided. Soldiers, generals, political leaders, traitors and diplomats, women, and French and British figures are all covered. Cross-references aid users in finding information.

Statistical Sources (310–319)

Historical Statistics of the United States, Colonial Times to 1970
Washington DC: U.S. Department of Commerce, Bureau of the Census, 1975. 2 vols.

This excellent reference provides definitions of terms, a descriptive text, and 12,500 statistical "time series" (comparisons of statistics on a specific subject over time). There are a subject arrangement and index. Some tables go down to the state or regional level. Detailed annotations are useful aids in understanding the numbers.

Historical Statistics of the United States: Two Centuries of the Census, 1790–1990
Dodd, Donald B., comp. Westport, CT: Greenwood, 1993.

This reference provides state statistics for 18 data items for each of the census years (every ten years). At the end of the volume are tables for agriculture, manufacturing, and other areas.

BIOGRAPHICAL REFERENCE SOURCES (920, B)

African American Biography (305.8, 920)

The Biographical Dictionary of Black Americans
Kranz, Rachel C. New York: Facts on File, 1992. Incl. bibliography and index.

This alphabetically arranged source provides biographical background on 200 black Americans from all walks of life, from colonial days to the present. Entries range from half a page to three pages in length and include basic information on birth, death, family, childhood, and achievements. Most entries include a list for further reading. Portraits are included for most entries. An occupation index is provided.

Black Women in America: An Historical Encyclopedia
Hine, Darlene Clark, ed. New York: Carlson, 1993. 2 vols. Incl. bibliography and index.

Presents 641 biographies and 163 articles on general topics and organizations in A–Z format with the intent of drawing a historical overview of black women in America. General topics include the anti-lynching movement, black nationalism, composers, education, and the Harlem Renaissance. Substantial articles will prove valuable to students.

Contemporary Black Biography: Profiles from the International Black Community
LaBlanc, Michael L., ed. Detroit: Gale, 1992–   . Annual. Incl. bibliographic references and index.

In-depth biographies average around four pages each. The articles are written from other sources, listed at the end of each article. A photographic portrait is included for each individual, and there are sometimes additional photographs. Coverage is what the title says it is, with subjects coming from all fields. Indexes are by nationality, occupation, subject, and cumulative by name. Valuable for contemporary world figures.

Dictionary of American Negro Biography
Logan, Rayford W., and Winston, Michael R., eds. New York: Norton, 1982.

An excellent resource despite the unfortunate title. Signed articles, some quite long, with additional references and primary source materials. Includes only persons who died prior to January 1, 1970.

Notable Black American Women
Smith, Jessie Carney, ed. Detroit: Gale, 1992. Incl. index.

Provides substantial biographies of 500 women of significance, though not necessarily the most well known or important. Portraits of close to 200 women are included. The women cover a wide range of backgrounds and fields of endeavor, with the oldest having been born around 1730 and the youngest in 1956. This is an important source, especially for uncovering lesser-known yet important black American women. The arrangement is alphabetical by name, with additional access by area of endeavor.

General Biographical Sources

Biography and Genealogy Master Index
Detroit: Gale, 1980. With supplements. 8 vols.

Part of the Gale biographical index series on many different areas. Index to over 5 million biographical sketches in 350 books and periodicals. Very brief entries for sources.

Biography Index
New York: H. W. Wilson, 1947– . Incl. indexes.
A current quarterly index arranged alphabetically by the person, with annual and three-year cumulative indexes. Includes biographies in 2,600 periodicals and books. Indexed by profession and occupation. Available online.

Current Biography
New York: H. W. Wilson Co., 1940– . Incl. portraits and indexes.
Sixteen to eighteen brief biographies of people in the news are published monthly. These are accumulated into an annual bound volume, organized alphabetically by last name. Each annual volume includes about 150 biographies—usually 2,500-word articles. Each volume is indexed by name and profession, and a 10-year index is also published.

Dictionary of American Biography
Garraty, John A. New York: Scribner's, 1957–1988. 20 vols. Incl. index.
Sponsored by the American Council of Learned Societies, this is the classic reference work on dead American men. Includes 18,000 biographies. Index by occupation, birthplace, school, and subject, with authors of articles in one alphabetic sequence.

Dictionary of National Biography
New York: Oxford University Press, 1982– . 22 vols. plus 8 supplements and additional complementary volumes. Each supplement includes a complete index.
Notable dead inhabitants of the British Isles and colonies, with bibliographies after each article.

The Discoverers: An Encyclopedia of Explorers and Exploration
Delpar, Helen, ed. New York: McGraw-Hill, 1980. Incl. index.
Twenty-eight contributors have written 250 signed articles on explorers, geographical concepts, and discussions of the impact of exploration. Illustrated with bibliographical references. Cross-references, maps, portraits, photos. Emphasis on Western Europeans.

Webster's New Biographical Dictionary
Springfield, MA: Merriam, 1983.

Contains 30,000 brief biographies from ancient times to 1983. Pronunciation, dates, and chief contribution.

Women in American History (920, 973.092)

Notable American Women, 1607–1950: A Biographical Dictionary
James, Edward T., ed. Cambridge, MA: Belknap Press, 1971, 1980. 3 vols.

Articles with bibliographies on 1,350 dead women. Similar to *Dictionary of American Biography* (see p. 140). A separate volume on the modern period, 1950–1975, adds 442 women who died from 1951 to 1975.

CHAPTER 11

Language (400) and Literature (800)

Research assignments having to do with language often center around the origins of language and languages, the origin of writing and specific forms of writing (cuneiform, Arabic); the development of alphabets; comparing and contrasting how language is used to achieve specific purposes, as with advertising language and political language; the tracing of historical and regional expressions, clichés, phrases, and idioms; and, of course, the origin of words. Dictionaries and other sources in this chapter will help answer these questions. Some questions may require general encyclopedias and beyond. When searching library catalogs, use terms such as "English Language—Encyclopedias and Dictionaries" or "English Language—History."

Literature assignments focus on specific authors—their biographies, writings, and criticism of their writings. American authors from Washington Irving to Maya Angelou, British authors from Chaucer and Shakespeare to the Brontës, Jane Austen, and Dickens, are commonly explored. Short stories can be compared and contrasted. Themes of novels can be revealed. What themes did Sophocles, Euripides, Henrik Ibsen, Anton Chekhov, Arthur Miller, and Eugene O'Neill explore in their plays? Sources listed in the literature section will get you started.

LANGUAGE (400)

Dictionaries (403, 423)

Abridged Dictionaries

The American Heritage Dictionary of the English Language.
Soukhanov, Anne H. Boston: Houghton Mifflin, 1992. 3d ed.
With 200,000, words this dictionary is larger than the other abridged versions. It places the most commonly sought meanings first and includes 4,000 illustrations. The type is a clear, bold sans serif typeface that is easy to read. Usage notes explain how the word should be used, word histories show how meanings evolved, and notes explain regional dialects. One of the most useful features is the synonym paragraph after many words, which calls attention to words with similar meanings. The synonyms are followed by antonyms, which mean the opposite. This dictionary includes obscene and slang words. Thumb indexes are indented into the pages for ease of use.

Random House Webster's College Dictionary
New York: Random House, 1991.
This briefer version of Random's unabridged has 180,000 entries, with tightly packed text pages and fewer illustrations than the *American Heritage Dictionary.* Definitions are given, with the most common meaning first.

Unabridged Dictionaries

The Oxford English Dictionary
New York: Oxford University Press, 1989. 2d ed. 20 vols.
Defines 500,000 words and includes 2.4 million quotations showing how the meanings of words have evolved. This book emphasizes English spelling and usage, which sometimes differs from American spelling and usage. Available on CD-ROM in a version that makes possible searches by date, author, title, or definition.

Random House Dictionary of the English Language
Flexner, Stuart Berg, editor in chief. Rev. 2d ed, New York: Random House, 1993.
This is more up-to-date than *Webster's* and emphasizes accuracy and clarity. It seeks to strike a balance between a descriptive dictionary, which attempts only to list definitions without recommending a particular definition, and a prescriptive dictionary such as Webster's *New Twentieth Century Dictionary of the English Language Un-*

abridged, 2d edition, which sought to arrive at the correct definition. The most common meaning is given first. The first date of use is given, as well as usage labels and notes. It includes slang, dialects, synonym and antonym lists, scientific terms, people, places, works of art, music, and literature. The appendix includes a basic manual of style, which has a section on writing a term paper. It also has a historical sketch of the English language, pictures, diagrams, maps, and brief dictionaries of French, Spanish, Italian, and German words. Available on CD-ROM.

Webster's Third New International Dictionary of the English Language Unabridged
Gove, Philip Babcock, editor in chief. Springfield, MA: G. and C. Merriam Co., 1968.

In the introduction, the editor says that the guiding principles for this dictionary are accuracy, clearness, and comprehensiveness. This edition includes over 450,000 words. Definitions are given in historical order, with the oldest first, followed by later meanings in chronological order. Over 6 million examples of usage were examined to derive the definitions. When this edition first appeared, it stirred up a hornet's nest of criticism because it sought to emphasize description of word meanings rather than prescribe the most correct meaning, as the second edition had done. Nevertheless, it is the still the world standard for American dictionaries. The second edition is sometimes retained by libraries since it is less permissive and directs users to the preferred meanings of each word. It includes illustrations, some in color, including a color frontispiece of Noah Webster, the originator of this dictionary. The Merriams bought the company from Webster in 1847. An addendum for 1962–1967 in the front of the dictionary brings the 1961 list up to 1967. There are no biographical or geographical names.

Language Tools (Including Thesauruses) (423.1)

A Dictionary of Slang and Unconventional English Colloquialisms and Catch Phrases
Partridge, Eric. New York: Macmillan, 1984.

Known to librarians as "Partridge" because it is used so frequently, this is an excellent source for finding 6,000 words or phrases that may not be in a conventional dictionary because they are used only in regional common speech and are not generally accepted as correct English.

The Oxford Companion to the English Language.
McArthur, Tom. New York: Oxford University Press, 1992.
This useful guide to English-language information is helpful for

usage, grammar, sexist language, history of language, and biographies of the great lexicographers. It contains 5,000 entries.

Roget A to Z
Chapman, Robert L., ed. New York: HarperCollins, 1994.
This version of the title that follows arranges the words alphabetically for easier finding.

Roget's International Thesaurus
Chapman, Robert L., ed. New York: HarperCollins, 1992. 5th ed. Incl. index.
This classic reference work helps authors to find the word by which an idea may be best described. It deals with the context of words. It also helps to vary vocabulary by finding words similar in meaning. It does this by dividing knowledge into 15 classes: the body and the senses; feelings; place and change of place; measure and shape; living things; natural phenomena; behavior and the will; language; human society and institutions; values and ideals; arts; occupations and crafts; sports and amusements; mind and ideas; and science and technology. Each heading organizes words into a context. There are word lists that group words (e.g., the bones in the human body, kinds of sweaters). Slang is labeled. There are numerous cross-references.

General Usage (428)

NTC's Dictionary of Easily Confused Words: With Complete Examples of Correct Usage
Williams, Deborah K. Lincolnwood, IL: National Textbook/NTC Publishing Group, 1995.
A handy guide to straighten out confusion resulting from several hundred words that are sometimes used incorrectly. The various words are carefully distinguished from one another. They may sound alike or may just be confused in usage.

Grammar (428)

Errors in English and Ways to Correct Them
Shaw, Harry. New York: HarperCollins, 1993. 4th ed.
Common mistakes in writing are explained and corrected in this useful guide. The book consists of guides to grammar, word usage, sentence structure, punctuation, mechanics, and spelling. Includes examples and practical exercises with wrong and right uses.

LITERATURE (800)

Electronic Resources

Art and Humanities Citation Index
Institute for Scientific Information, 1990– . Compact disc edition updated three times a year.
More than 1,100 periodicals are indexed by author and keyword. Citations show what books have been cited in other books.

Books in Print Plus
New York: Bowker. Updated monthly.
A CD-ROM database found in larger libraries that lists books recently published, together with reviews of the books.

DiscLit: American Authors
New York: G. K. Hall, 1991– .

DiscLit: British Authors
New York: G. K. Hall, 1992– .
These useful CD-ROM sources contain the full text of the Twayne series of critical introductions to the lives and works of major authors—over 140 in each set. They also include citations to books by and about the authors and may be searched by every word in the texts and bibliographies.

DISCovering Authors: Biographies and Criticism on 300 Most Studied Authors
Detroit: Gale, 1994.
This CD-ROM includes criticism and bibliographical and biographical information on specific authors from all time periods and many different countries. It may be searched by theme, time period, characters, and genre. A more extensive set is also offered by Gale including over 1,200 authors.

Scribners Writers Series on CD-ROM
New York: Scribner's, 1993.
Full texts of essays on over 500 writers from many time periods and nationalities. Includes bibliographies and can be searched by genre, language, nationality, time period, race, or combinations of these.

English Literary Criticism (820–829)

British Writers
Scott-Kilvert, Ian, ed. New York: Scribner's, 1982. 8 vols. Cumulative index for 8 vols. and supplements.
Lengthy essays on each of the writers, with bibliographies of works by and about the authors. The authors within each volume are listed on the spine of the book so you can easily select the appropriate volume. Two supplementary volumes bring the coverage up to 1992.

The Chelsea House Library of Literary Criticism
Bloom, Harold, ed. New York: Chelsea House, 1988.
A useful collection of critical essays on a variety of authors. The editor is a distinguished critic.

Moulton's Library of Literary Criticism Through the Beginning of the Twentieth Century
New York: Frederick Ungar, 1966. Reprint.
This multivolume series contains excerpts from critical writings, mostly before 1900. Although this is not criticism at the time the novel was first published, it does represent older critical views of the novel, and taken together with the Chelsea House series (see the previous entry), it provides a historical perspective on how the criticism has changed over the years. You will have to know the author's dates in order to pick out the correct volume. (While the Chelsea House series reprints long articles, Moulton's are shorter excerpts.)

Nineteenth Century Literature Criticism: Criticism of the Works of Novelists, Poets, Playwrights, Short Story Writers, Philosophers and Other Creative Writers Who Died between 1800 and 1899 from the First Critical Appraisals to Current Evaluations
Lazzari, Margaret, et al., eds. Detroit: Gale, 1981–   .
To date, this series, an American Library Association "Outstanding Reference Source," has covered "more than 300 authors representing 29 nationalities and over 17,000 titles," according to the Preface. A thorough survey of "critical reactions to nineteenth-century authors and literature," *NCLC*, as it is known, organizes and reprints commentary, and "helps students develop valuable insight into literary history, promotes a better understanding of the texts, and sparks ideas for papers and assignments."

Indexes (016.8)

Book Review Digest
New York: H. W. Wilson, 1905– . Annual. Incl. index.
This index locates reviews of significant books published in a given year. For many reviews, it provides a brief synopsis of the review, which may be enough for students. The full citation for the review is always given, so the *Digest* functions as an index too. Some libraries may own *Book Review Index,* published annually by Gale, which is purely an index without brief summaries.

Essay and General Literature Index
New York: H. W. Wilson, 1934– . Annual. Incl. index.
This source indexes essays in books and magazines. Arranged alphabetically by subject, it is an excellent tool for quickly finding opinion pieces and similar writings on a variety of topics.

Short Story Index
New York: H. W. Wilson, 1950– . Annual. Incl. index.
This important source indexes short stories in collections and periodicals. It not only locates stories by title and author, for those occasions when a teacher assigns a story that's difficult to find; it also indexes by subject. When a teacher says to write a paper about a story concerning a father-son relationship or to find a short story about fear, for example, this source will locate it.

Other Fields of Research in Literature

Drama (812, 822)

Critical Survey of Drama
Magill, Frank, ed. New York: Salem Press, 1985–1987. Incl. bibliography.
There are series on English-language authors and foreign-language authors and supplement. Contains commentary, biography, and criticism.

McGraw-Hill Encyclopedia of World Drama
Hochtman, Stanley, ed. New York: McGraw-Hill, 1984. 4 vols. Incl. index.
Contains 900 entries for authors, theater movements, genres, styles, and surveys of national dramas, with a glossary and illustrations.

The Shakespeare Handbook
Fox, Levi. Boston: G. K. Hall, 1987. Incl. index.

This useful handbook includes sections on the Elizabethan world, Shakespeare's life, the Elizabethan and Jacobean theater, the plays, and Shakespeare in performance, poetry, music, song, and film. There is a reading list and cross-references after most articles.

Poetry (811, 821)

Columbia Granger Index to Poetry
Hazen, Edith, and Fryer, Deborah. New York: Columbia University Press, 1990.

Contains 100,000 poems indexed from over 500 anthologies. The CD-ROM version has keyword searching and full texts of 8,500 poems.

Contemporary Poets
Riggs, Thomas, ed. Detroit: St. James Press, 1996. 6th ed.

This book includes 779 living poets with brief biographies, bibliographies, personal statements by the poets, and signed critical essays.

Critical Survey of Poetry
Magill, Frank, ed. Pasadena, CA: Salem Press, 1992. Rev. ed. 8 vols. Incl. bibliographic references and index.

Eight volumes arranged alphabetically by poet with topical essays in the final volume. There are also series on foreign-language authors and a supplement. It includes commentary, biography, criticism, and bibliography.

The English Poetry Full-Text Database
Chadwick-Healey, 1993–1994.

A CD-ROM product with the full texts of 1,350 poems, 600–1900 A.D.

Poem Finder 95: The Ultimate Poetry Reference on CD-ROM
Great Neck, NY: Roth Publishing: 1995.

Less comprehensive than *Columbia Granger Index to Poetry* (see above), this CD-ROM can be searched by first line, last line, author, title, keyword, subject and even poem date.

Research Guides

Benet's Reader's Encyclopedia
Murphy, Bruce. New York: HarperCollins, 1996. 4th ed.
First published by Thomas Y. Crowell in 1948 and edited for years

by William Rose Benet, this is a worthy inheritor of the tradition established by Ebenezer Cobham Brewer's *Reader's Handbook* and later continued by Crowell's *Handbook for Readers and Writers*. This volume contains short biographies of the most famous authors, together with information about literary terms, famous characters, places, and unusual terms encountered in reading literature (e.g., "dowsabell," a common name for a sweetheart in Elizabethan times).

Literary Research Guide: A Guide to Reference Sources for the Study of Literatures in English and Related Topics
Harner, James L. New York: Modern Language Association of America, 1989.

The definitive guide for researchers in this field of studies. It annotates dozens of books, journals, library collections and catalogs, and computer programs and databases and includes name, title, and subject indexes.

The Oxford Companion to English Literature
Drabble, Margaret, ed. New York: Oxford University Press, 1995.

This fifth edition of a standard work includes entries for authors, works, critics, terminology, nonliterary figures, and important magazines in the literary field. Includes authors born through 1939. Foreign authors important to English literature are also included. Appendixes are on censorship, copyright, and the calendar. There is also a concise edition. Margaret Drabble herself is a famous English author. The Oxford Companion series covers American, to French, German, and Canadian literature.

Special Topics in Literature

African American Literature

Oxford Companion to African-American Literature
New York: Oxford University Press, 1997. Incl. index.

Bibliographies after each entry. Contains 400 authors, 150 books summarized, and lists of magazines, newspapers, publishers, and libraries. Indexed and cross-referenced.

European and World Literature

Columbia Dictionary of Modern European Literature
Bede, Jean-Albert, and Edgerton, William. New York: Columbia University Press, 1980.

Survey articles contributed by 500 scholars on 33 national literatures and 1,853 authors from the 1890s on. Useful brief articles with bibliographies on a wide variety of literary subjects include biographical sketches and critical evaluations.

Encyclopedia of World Literature of the 20th Century
New York: Ungar, 1981–1984. 5 vols. Incl. index.
Five volumes of articles on the entire sweep of world literature. Contains 1,700 articles on national literatures, literary movements, authors, and criticism, with photographs and an index volume.

European Writers
Jackson, William T. H., ed. New York: Scribner's, 1983. 11 vols.
Eleven volumes arranged chronologically with 15,000-word essays on each author or genre. Each essay includes information on the writer's work, life, and personal and professional situation. There is a bibliography after each essay.

Hispanic American Literature

Hispanic Writers Selected from Contemporary Authors
Bryan, Ryan, ed. Detroit: Gale, 1991.
Writings, biographies, critical sources, and periodicals on Hispanic authors.

Literatura Chicana: Critical and Creative Writings
New York: Hispanex, 1985. Incl. indexes.
Poetry, novels, short stories, theater, literary criticism, oral tradition, anthologies, literary periodicals, autobiography, video and sound recordings on Chicano authors; 800 items listed with author, title, and imprint.

Term Paper Guides and Style Manuals (808.02, 808.066)

The Elements of Style
Strunk, William, Jr., with White, E. B. New York: Macmillan, 1979.
This delightfully written little volume provides guidance you on how to write clearly, briefly, and boldly.

A Manual for Writers of Term Papers, Theses and Dissertations
Turabian, Kate L. Chicago: University of Chicago Press, 1987.
This useful manual includes sections on parts of the paper, foot-

notes, bibliography, and punctuation. It is an abridgment of *The Chicago Manual of Style*. Chicago: University of Chicago Press, 1993. 14th ed.

MLA Handbook for Writers of Research Papers
Gibaldi, Josep, and Achtert, Walter S. New York: Modern Language Association, 1988.
This writer's guide has chapters on research, writing, formatting, documenting, and abbreviations.

CHAPTER 12

Medical and Health (610–620)

Drugs (615) / Substance Abuse (362.29)

Health, medical, substance abuse, and anatomy papers and projects can revolve around a variety of issues. Understanding the human body, its organs and systems (611), can also branch into human biology, sexuality, and from there into the practicalities of child rearing and responsibility. Teachers can incorporate the history of medicine and medical care into history projects, through devices such as the Civil War (How were the wounded cared for and treated? How did nursing begin?) or through a review of life a particular time. For example, describe the practice of medicine in colonial America. Who was Hippocrates, and how did he change the practice of medicine? Or discuss the impact of the bubonic plague on the world of the fourteenth century.

Today, some medical questions can be discussed through the pro and con technique: What are the pros and cons of euthanasia or abortion? Cite specific cases that have had an impact on these controversies. AIDS and other sexually transmitted diseases open up a wide variety of debatable positions. Within each, one should understand the medical facts. Similarly, for drug questions, legalization, social impact, and effect on the human body, one should learn the facts. Below are a number of sources to help with research.

STATISTICS (610.2, 312.6, 362.1)

Health United States
Hyattsville, MD: U.S. Department of Health and Human Services. Annual. Incl. index.

All types of statistics, expenditures, and trends in all types of disease, illness, death, and health care are included here.The first stop for statistics.

ENCYCLOPEDIAS AND DICTIONARIES (610.3)

The American Medical Association Encyclopedia of Medicine
Clayman, Charles B., ed. New York: Random House, 1989. Incl. index.

Written in language that's easy to understand, this work is suitable for high school students who need to learn about specific diseases and their symptoms, medical conditions, medical tests and procedures, surgical procedures, medications and new drugs, anatomy, and physiology. There are more than 5,000 entries arranged alphabetically. The work defines medical terminology and is illustrated. Essays cover topics such as prenatal technology and new diseases. An "excellent work," according to *Guide to Reference Books for School Media Centers* (4th ed.).

Black's Medical Dictionary
London: A. & C. Black, 1992. 37th ed.

This source defines 4,500 medical terms. Diseases are often discussed from the patient's point of view, which could help students understand how an illness feels to those who have it.

Marshall Cavendish Encyclopedia of Health
North Bellmore, NY: Marshall Cavendish, 1995. Rev. ed. 14 vols. Incl. index.

This set is written in language suitable for students in fifth or sixth grade through high school. Arranged alphabetically, medical topics, diseases, and mental health problems and treatments are reviewed. The body and how it works, diet, fitness, sports, sex, and substance abuse are also discussed. Articles vary in length and can be several pages long. Illustrations, color photographs, charts, and graphs increase the usefulness of the set. Highly recommended for students.

MEDICAL HISTORY (610.9)

The Age of Miracles: Medicine and Surgery in the Nineteenth Century
Williams, Guy. Chicago: Academy Publishers, 1987.
This text chronicles the great advances of the nineteenth century, including anesthetics, antiseptics, x-rays, and radium. This is a sequel to Williams' *The Age of Agony,* about the practice of medicine in the less-fortunate eighteenth century.

The Cambridge Illustrated History of Medicine
Porter, Roy, ed. Cambridge: Cambridge University Press, 1996. Incl. index.
Illustrations are one of the important values of this text, including paintings and photographs of procedures, equipment, and medical scenes both early and modern. The book helps relate modern developments to the past practices they grew out of. Not only is the history and development of medicine examined, but so is its social and political role.

Medical Discoveries: Medical Breakthroughs and the People Who Developed Them
Travers, Bridget, and Freiman, Fran Locher, eds. Detroit: UXL, 1996. 3 vols. Incl. bibliography and index.
This source, intended for students, is written for easy comprehension. Photographs and boxed information add to the interest level. Medical and dental procedures and equipment—their invention or discovery and development—are discussed in moderate detail. Basic biographical information on the people involved is provided. A time line and glossary are included. Controversies are mentioned or discussed on such issues as breast implants, cloning, abortion, and chlorofluorocarbons.

Note: When using the card or computerized catalog, try the subject heading "Medicine-History."

MEDICAL BIOGRAPHY (610.92)

Biographical Dictionary of Medicine
Bendiner, Jessica, and Bendiner, Elmer. New York: Facts on File, 1990. Incl. bibliography and index.
An alphabetic arrangement of significant people in the history of medicine. A chronology at the back of the book gives name access by year beginning with 2838 B.C. "It includes ancient herbalists, battlefield

surgeons of the Renaissance, alchemists and anatomists . . . and the many people who have participated in the great explosion of biological science and technology in the nineteenth and twentieth centuries," according to the Introduction. Entries vary in length from a couple of paragraphs to a couple of pages, and describe, if known, the individual's upbringing, education, and contributions. "Entries attempt to give the reader at least the flavor of the life and times, difficulties and achievements of each biographical subject." Highly recommended for students seeking biographical and historical information.

Blacks in Science and Medicine
Sammons, Vivian Ovelton. New York: Hemisphere Pub. Corp., 1990. Incl. bibliography and index.
A list of 1,500 individuals in alphabetical order, in a Who's Who style, listing basic birth, death, and other pertinent information (e.g., schools attended, degrees, awards, accomplishments). Unfortunately, there's barely any descriptive narrative. Biographical references, often several, are provided. A large bibliography and thorough index (with headings such as Inventions, Inventors, Mathematicians) help researchers greatly.

Women Physicians of the World: Autobiographies of Medical Pioneers
Hellstedt, Leone McGregor. Washington, DC: Hemisphere, 1978. Incl. index.
This book presents two-to four-page autobiographies of 91 medical women from 27 countries. All were born before 1912. Their backgrounds, education, upbringing, factors influencing their career choice, and obstacles they had to overcome are described. Country of origin is provided in the Table of Contents, increasing the book's usefulness.

HUMAN ANATOMY (611) AND PHYSIOLOGY (612)

Atlas of Human Anatomy
Netter, Frank H. Summit, NJ: CIBA-GEIGY, 1989.
Library Journal (LJ) calls this "a book of outstanding artistic and scientific merit that is destined to become a classic both in the field of human anatomy and in artistic portrayal of the human body." Coverage is arranged into sections: head and neck, back and spinal cord, thorax and abdomen, pelvis and perineum, upper limbs, lower limbs. There are 514 color plates—11 for the eye, 103 for the abdomen. Maybe the best available, *LJ* says: "The book clearly outlines the human body and does a better job than any existing atlas."

Gray's Anatomy of the Human Body
Warwick, Roger, and Williams, Peter L. Philadelphia: Lee and Febiger, 1989. 37th ed.

This frequently revised text is the standard, classic reference in the field. Many libraries circulate older editions and keep the latest in the reference collection. Improved over the years to include color illustrations, thorough and comprehensive text, and indexes.

Human Anatomy and Physiology
Hole, John W., and Martin, Terry. Dubuque, IA: Wm. C. Brown, 1995. 7th ed.

High school students will benefit most from this well-put-together source. "Text is easy to read and simple to understand," according to *American Reference Books Annual* (1991). "The approach is direct, practical, and nonspeculative. The use of clinical and technical terms is held to a minimum." Loaded with illustrations, tables, figures, and charts that complement and clarify the text, this standard source is reliable and intended for those who might be thinking of a career in any aspect of the health sciences.

The Human Body on File
Diagram Group. New York: Facts on File, 1983. Looseleaf binder.

These black and white line drawings of the human body and parts are intended for easy removal from the binder for photocopying. Cells and cell structure, DNA, the body as a whole, joints, bones, muscles, nerves, veins, arteries, the lymphatic system, head, spine individual organs, development charts, and more are included. Parts are clearly numbered and labeled at the bottom of the page. Great for illustrating student reports and for studying the body.

REPRODUCTION (612.6)

A Child Is Born
Nilsson, Lennart, and Hamberger, Lars. New York: Delacorte, 1990. Complete new ed.

Originally published in Sweden in 1965, this breakthrough photographic book reveals development of the human fetus from inception through birth in stunning color photographs taken from within the womb. Nilsson developed this photographic technology and has improved on it over the years. Included is male and female anatomy. A necessary reference when studying human conception and fetal development.

GENERAL HEALTH AND HYGIENE (613)

The Columbia University College of Physicians and Surgeons Complete Home Medical Guide
Tapley, Donald, et al., eds. New York: Crown, 1989. Rev. ed.
Disease and body systems are covered in this source written for the general public.

Teenage Health Care
Slap, Gail B., and Jablow, Marth M. New York: Pocket Books, 1994. Incl. bibliographic references and index.
Bodily systems—how to care for them and what can go wrong with them—are covered in this "encyclopedia of the physical changes and problems that affect teenagers," according to the authors. Common teenage ailments and behaviors are reviewed, and forthright discussions of sexual identity, contraception, pregnancy, depression, drug abuse, learning disorders, and other issues are included. Clear, thorough, nonjudgmental, an "excellent, comprehensive guide," according to *Library Journal* (September 1, 1994).

DIET AND NUTRITION (613.2)

The Columbia Encyclopedia of Nutrition
Winick, Myron, et al. New York: Putnam, 1988.
A good source written for general readers covering vitamins, additives, dieting, and disorders affected by nutrition.

Nutritive Value of American Foods in Common Units
Adams, Catherine F. Washington, DC: Agricultural Research Service, 1975.
This source uses generic names for foods and provides nutritive and fatty acid values for household measures and market units of foods.

The Surgeon General's Report on Nutrition and Health
New York: Warren, 1989.
This condensed version, also issued by the U.S. Government Printing Office with the subtitle *Summary and Recommendations*, discusses many specific diseases and how they can be prevented or managed by good diet and nutrition. Diseases discussed include high blood pressure, coronary heart disease, diabetes, obesity, anemia, behavior, neurological disorders, and skeletal, kidney, and gastrointestinal diseases. Dietary fads and their dangers are reviewed. Public health policy is considered, and meal plans are included. "A wealth of material that is

useful for reports," according to *Guide to Reference Books for School Media Centers* (4th ed.).

SEXUALITY (613.9)

Abortion: A Reference Handbook
Costa, Marie. Santa Barbara, CA: ABC-CLIO, 1991. Incl. bibliographic references and index.

This is a great source, including a chronology of events significant to the topic, a glossary, a list of both print and nonprint resources, brief biographies, laws and policies, facts and statistics, abortion techniques, and a list of organizations.

The Anti-Abortion Movement: References and Sources
Blanchard, Dallas A. New York: G. K. Hall/Simon & Schuster, 1996. Incl. index.

This source provides a historical review of the pro-life/anti-abortion movement, lists organizations, outlines politics and tactics, and provides a history of abortion in the United States.

Columbia University College of Physicians and Surgeons Complete Guide to Pregnancy
New York: Crown, 1988. Incl. index.

This source covers everything: labor and delivery, cesarean section, nutrition, the role of the father, the developing fetus with illustrations, trimesters, what is safe or risky for the pregnant woman (smoking, alcohol, drugs, etc.), infertility, abortion, and more. Readable and informative, it includes a glossary.

The Contraceptive Handbook: A Guide to Safe and Effective Choices
Winikoff, Beverly, et al. Mount Vernon, NY: Consumer Reports Books, 1992. Incl. bibliography.

This book discusses basic anatomy and all available methods of contraception, and advantages with disadvantages of each.

Human Sexuality
Spence, Annette. New York: Facts on File, 1989.

Clearly written for middle school students, this book, one volume in *The Encyclopedia of Good Health,* provides the necessary information for young people to understand their bodies and their emotions to help them make sound, healthful choices regarding their own sexuality.

Human Sexuality: Opposing Viewpoints
Bender, David, and Leone, Bruno, eds. San Diego, CA: Greenhaven Press, 1995. Incl. bibliography and index.

This title presents pro and con viewpoints on sexual issues within five broad topics: "What is the purpose of sex?" Reproduction or sensual pleasure? "What sexual norms should society uphold?" Renounce or accept divorce? "How are gender and sexual orientation determined?" Is it determined biologically or not? "What constitutes normal sexual behavior?" Is homosexuality normal or abnormal behavior? "How is society's view of sexuality changing?" Are Americans satisfied or unsatisfied with their sex lives? The author and source for each essay is provided.

The Magic of Sex
Stoppard, Miriam. New York: Dorling Kindersley, 1992.

This title covers all aspects of a sexual relationship from male and female points of view. It includes discussion of sexual problems, sex and aging, sexually transmitted diseases, safe sex, reproduction, and contraception. The text is straightforward and supported by graphs, questionnaires, and 100 photographs and illustrations.

Sex Care: The Complete Guide to Safe and Healthy Sex
Covington, Timothy R., and McClendon, J. Frank. New York: Pocket Books, 1987. Incl. index.

Strongly written, nonjudgmental discussion of male and female anatomy, all contraceptive methods and how to use them, sexually transmitted diseases, AIDS, and sexual health, including hygiene, premenstrual syndrome, toxic shock syndrome, and abortion.

Teenage Sexuality: Opposing Viewpoints
Bender, David, and Leone, Bruno, eds. San Diego, CA: Greenhaven Press, 1994. Incl. bibliography and index.

This title in the Opposing Viewpoints series presents pro and con statements on specific sexual issues: "What causes teen pregnancy?" Family breakdown or cultural influences? "Is sex education necessary?" Should it be taught in schools or is it harmful? "How should teenage homosexuality be treated?" With support from parents and schools, or not? The author and source for each essay is provided.

DRUGS / PHARMACOLOGY (615)

Alternative Health and Medicine Encyclopedia
Marti, James, with Hine, Andrea. Detroit: Gale, 1995. Incl. bibliographic references and index.

Essays on alternative therapies, nutrition, and botanical medicine are presented along with alternative treatments of cancer, heart disease, mental illness, and substance abuse.

The Complete Drug Reference
United State Pharmacopeial Convention, Inc. Mount Vernon, NY: Consumer Reports Books. Annual. Incl. index.

Prescription and nonprescription drugs and remedies are covered by this source, arranged alphabetically by generic name. Brand names are listed and indexed. Under the generic heading, description, precautions, application, dosage, usage, and side effects are discussed in readable, understandable language. Appendixes discuss precautions during pregnancy, breast-feeding, and for athletes, as well as chemotherapy regimens. "Terrific . . . straightforward . . . highly recommended," according to *Library Journal* (June 1, 1991). A first stop for students.

Physician's Desk   Reference
Montvale, NJ: Medical Economics Co. Annual. Incl. indexes.

Probably the most commonly asked-for source on prescription drugs, this title (commonly referred to as *PDR*) is published with the "cooperation of participating manufacturers," according to the Foreword. It covers the necessary information: generic and brand names, description, applications or dosage, warnings and contraindications, drug interactions, and adverse reactions. Its language can be difficult. Also available on CD-ROM.

Physician's Desk Reference for Nonprescription Drugs
Montvale, NJ: Medical Economics. Annual. Incl. indexes.

Reports on more than 700 over-the-counter remedies in the same way as *PDR* (see the above entry).

DISEASES (616)

AIDS
Flanders, Stephen A., and Flanders, Carl N. New York: Facts on File, 1991. Incl. index.

This title serves as a basic handbook and introduction to the disease. It is thorough in reviewing the history of AIDS and bringing the reader up to date on current research and other developments. A chronology is included, as are extensive bibliographic references.

AIDS Information Sourcebook
Malinowsky, H. Robert, and Perry, Gerald J., eds. Phoenix, AZ: Oryx, 1991–1992. 3d ed. Incl. bibliography and index.

This useful title, updated regularly, provides a thorough background review of the disease, a chronology of key events, support organizations, statistics, and a bibliography.

The American Cancer Society Cancer Book
Holleb, Arthur, ed. New York: Doubleday, 1986. Incl. index.

A comprehensive and authoritative reference source that discusses "prevention, detection, diagnosis, treatment, rehabilitation and cure," according to the subtitle. Treatment therapies and associated problems with them are discussed in separate chapters in Part I, as are smoking and cancer. In Part II, a chapter is devoted to each specific type of cancer, with anatomical line drawings illustrating areas affected, surgeries, or other treatments. A directory of resources and glossary is appended. A *Library Journal* Outstanding Reference Book of 1986, this is an excellent source.

The American Medical Association Handbook of First Aid and Emergency Care
Zydlo, Stanley M., Jr., and Hill, James A., eds. New York: Random House, 1990. Rev. ed.

Alphabetical entries on diseases and injuries provide background, symptoms, checklists of actions. to take, emergency actions and subsequent care.

The Cambridge World History of Human Disease
Kiple, Kenneth F., ed. Cambridge: Cambridge University Press, 1993. Incl. bibliography and index.

Disease—its history, its spread over geography and through populations—is studied in the first half of this book. The second half looks at 158 diseases, from AIDS to yellow fever, reviewing their history, how widespread during history, how and why they spread, plus providing information on distribution, cause, and treatment. An ideal source for answering questions and writing papers, according to *Library Journal* (November 15, 1992).

Cancer Facts and Figures
Atlanta, GA: American Cancer Society. Annual.
The best source for statistics on all types of cancer, including a brief text explanation and analysis for each group of statistics.

Eating Disorders: The Facts
Abraham, Suzanne, and Llewellyn-Jones, Derek. New York: Oxford University Press, 1992. 3d ed. Incl. bibliographic references.
This title discusses diagnosis and treatment of anorexia nervosa, bulimia, and obesity.

The Encyclopedia of Obesity and Eating Disorders
Cassell, Dana K. New York: Facts on File, 1994. Incl. bibliography and index.
Alphabetic entries in this encyclopedia-style book cover diseases, treatments, problems, and behaviors related to eating in order to help the student, parent, medical practitioner, and consumer. Appendixes include referrals and other sources of information.

The Encyclopedia of Phobias, Fears and Anxieties
Doctor, Ronald M., and Kahn, Ada P. New York: Facts on File, 1989. Incl. bibliography and index.
Alphabetical entries are written in language for all to understand in this authoritative source. Diagnosis and various treatments are reviewed.

The Encyclopedia of Sleep and Sleep Disorders
Thorpy, Michael J. and Yager, Jan. New York: Facts on File, 1990. Incl. bibliography and index.
800 popularly and well-written, alphabetically arranged entries cover customs, disorders, research and organizations. Introductory essays on the history and psychology of sleep are included.

The Family Mental Health Encyclopedia
Bruno, Frank J. New York: Wiley, 1989. Incl. index.
This book includes 700 alphabetically arranged entries that vary in length from a paragraph to short articles. Topics covered include terms and concepts (stress), drugs, persons who made significant contributions to the field, schools of thought, and movements. Clearly written; excellent for high school students.

HIV/AIDS Surveillance Report
Atlanta, GA: Centers for Disease Control and Prevention. Semiannual.

Best source for complete, up-to-date statistics, by sex, race, age, city, and more.

Mayo Clinic Heart Book
McGoon, Michael D., ed. New York: Morrow, 1993. Incl. bibliographic references.

This source discusses cardiovascular disease, prevention, treatment, medical and surgical procedures, and the role in it of alcohol, caffeine, and fish oil.

Merck Manual of Diagnosis and Therapy
Berkow, Robert, ed. Rahway, NJ: Merck, 1992. 16th ed. Incl. index.

Intended for practicing medical professionals, this is a one-volume reference that nevertheless is readable and understandable. According to the Foreword, the book "covers all but the most obscure disorders of mankind." It is organized by type of disease or medical specialty and for each disease or disorder includes etiology and pathology, symptoms and signs, diagnosis, and treatment.

Professional Guide to Diseases
Springhouse, PA: Springhouse Corp., 1991. 4th ed. Incl. index.

This is possibly the best source for brief, to-the-point descriptions of 600 diseases, disorders, ailments, and injuries. Each disease is headed by its scientific name with common names listed underneath. A clear and concise definition is provided, along with incidence and prognosis. The following two to three pages (on average) describe causes, signs and symptoms, diagnosis, treatment, and special considerations in boldheaded sections. The text is clear and understandable.

The Sexually Transmitted Diseases
Rinear, Charles. Jefferson, NC: MacFarland, 1986. Incl. bibliography and index.

AIDS, gonorrhea, herpes, scabies, syphilis, and many more STDs are discussed in detail. Each chapter covers history, occurrences, population at risk, communicability, signs and symptoms, diagnosis, disease patterns, and treatment.

Two books on viruses—their history, how they work, the destruction they cause, and their current role in AIDS, cancer, flu, hepatitis, and other diseases:

The Invisible Invaders: The Story of the Emerging Age of Viruses
Radetsky, Peter. Boston: Little, Brown, 1991. Incl. bibliography.

Viruses: Agents of Change
Fettner, Ann Giudici. New York: McGraw-Hill, 1990.

SUBSTANCE ABUSE (616.86, 362.29)

Chemical Dependency: Opposing Viewpoints
Debner, Claudia, ed. St. Paul, MN: Greenhaven, 1985. Opposing
Viewpoint Series. Incl. bibliography and index.
This volume includes pro and con essays on the broad topics of drug
abuse, alcoholism, tobacco smoking, drug addiction, treatment, and drug
laws. Examples include "Marijuana Should Be Legalized" and
"Marijuana Should Not Be Legalized"; "Alcoholism Is Hereditary"
and "Alcoholism Is Caused by Child Neglect."

Drug Abuse: Opposing Viewpoints
Swisher, Karin, ed. San Diego: Greenhaven, 1994. Opposing
Viewpoints Series. Incl. bibliography and index.
The Opposing Viewpoints series is excellent for students because
each title in the series presents pro and con arguments on specific aspects of the general topic. Viewpoints are written by experts whose
opinions have been published elsewhere. The articles are signed, and
the original source is given. Examples in this title include: "The War on
Drugs Should Be Prosecuted More Vigorously," by Joseph D. Douglass,
Jr., "The War on Drugs Should Be Abandoned," by Daniel K. Benjamin
and Roger Leroy Miller. "Legalization Would Reduce the Drug
Problem," by Ethan A. Nadelmann, "Legalization Would Not Reduce
the Drug Problem," by Mitchell S. Rosenthal.

The Encyclopedia of Drug Abuse
O'Brien, Robert, et al. New York: Facts on File, 1992. 2d ed. Incl.
bibliography and index.
All aspects (medical, legal, social, and psychological) of drug
abuse and its impact on individuals and society are discussed in 500 alphabetic entries. Specific drugs, organizations, laws, treatment programs, medical terms, and psychosocial concepts receive treatment.
"The History of Drugs and Man" opens the book. Street terms, statistics,
and other information are appended. An excellent starting place on the
topic for middle and high school students.

Encyclopedia of Drugs and Alcohol
Jaffe, Jerome H., ed. New York: Macmillan, 1995. 4 vols. Incl. bibliography and index.

More comprehensive than the Facts on File titles, this source, according to *Booklist* (October 1, 1995), covers "all aspects, physiological and sociological, of legal and illegal drug and alcohol use and abuse worldwide." It is written to be accessible to nonprofessionals and contains a wealth of information that high school and college students, as well as professionals, will find useful. It discusses, for example, "the history of the use of various substances, specific substances and their chemical properties, treatment programs and activist groups, and the societal impact of such phenomena as addicted babies, drugs in the workplace, substance abuse and AIDS, and drunken driving . . . advertising and its effects on drug and alcohol consumption and drug and alcohol use among specific ethnic groups." The first three volumes are alphabetically arranged; every article includes a bibliography for more information. The last volume contains the master index plus appendixes listing substance programs, poison control centers, U.S. drug control operations, and a list of controlled substances. A master source on the topic for students.

The Encyclopedia of Psychoactive Drugs
New York: Chelsea House. 25 vols. Incl. bibliography and index.

This is the title for a series of 25 books written expressly for young people. Each book is written about a specific drug or group of drugs and answers questions young people are likely to ask. Some titles include: *Heroin: The Street Narcotic; Marijuana: Its Effects on Mind and Body; Over-the-Counter Drugs: Harmless or Hazardous? Cocaine: A New Epidemic;* and *Nicotine: An Old Fashioned Addiction.* These books are extremely useful for reports. They're well and interestingly written. Illustrations increase the interest level, as well as add information. Questions these books answer include: Who takes drugs? Why, when, and how? How do drugs affect mood? What does being "hooked" mean? What happens physically to the body? What signs does a drug user exhibit? How does a drug abuser get off drugs? Also covered in each book are history, culture, efforts to eradicate drugs or drug use, and the effects of political and economic forces.

Smoking: Current Controversies
Wekesser, Carol, ed. San Diego, CA: Greenhaven, 1997. Current Controversies Series. Incl. bibliography and index.

Pro and con essays on smoking discuss such issues as "Are Increased Measures Needed to Combat Teen Smoking?" "Should Government Regulation of Smoking Be Increased?" "Is the Tobacco Industry to Blame for Leading People to Smoke?" "Are the Health Risks of Smoking Exaggerated?"

Taking Sides: Clashing Views on Controversial Issues in Health and Society
Daniel, Eileen, ed. Guilford, CT: Dushkin Publishing, 1993. Incl. index.

This volume in the series provides pro and con essays on substance abuse, smoking, alcoholism, and drug legalization, but also includes health issues such as sex education, teen pregnancy, abortion, nutrition (cholesterol, vitamins), and doctor-assisted suicide for the terminally ill.

SURGERY (617)

The Surgery Book: An Illustrated Guide to 73 of the Most Common Operations
Youngson, Robert M., with the Diagram Group. New York: St. Martin's Press, 1993.

This book explains so everyone can understand why a specific operation is necessary, what it will accomplish, how it's performed, expected recovery time, pain, and side effects; 350 drawings accompany the text and clarify surgical procedure. Root canals, tonsillectomy, cataract surgery, and coronary artery bypass typify the operations covered. Many medical tests, such as biopsies and MRI scans, are also explained. Clear and readable.

CD-ROM MAGAZINE INDEX

Health Reference Center on InfoTrac
Foser City, CA: Information Access Co. Monthly.

Health Reference Center concentrates on medical and health periodicals, pamphlets and reference books. Much of the information presented is full text, especially pamphlets, and medical reference books. About 130 health journal publications are full text, while another 25 are abstracted, and many more are indexed. Disks are updated monthly, each disk containing the past three years of articles and publications, making this source one of the best for the latest in medical and health research. Searching can be done by subject, keyword, or publication title and date. Truly a great source.

INTERNET GUIDES

Health   Online
Ferguson, Tom. Reading, MA: Addison-Wesley, 1996. Incl. index.
Though similar to the title above, this book focuses on discussion groups, self-help, and self-care.

Your Personal NetDoctor: Your Guide to Health and Medical Advice on the Internet and Online Services
New York: Wolff New Media, 1996. Incl. index.
A guide to over 2,000 health sites on the Internet on all kinds of topics, including nutrition, fitness, diabetes, eating disorders, women's health, and cancer.

CHAPTER 13

Politics (320) and Government (350)

"Compare and contrast the governments of two or more nations." This is a common question put to students. What type of government do they have? Do they have constitutions? What do those constitutions say? How well, or poorly, do the people of each nation live under their form of government? Where does the government get its money, and how does it spend it? How are their laws interpreted and enforced? These questions pertain for all nations throughout history.

How do the governmental officers become officers in the government? Are they elected or appointed? Are their positions inherited? What are the methods through which decisions are made? How is influence gained? Government may be the act of governing through decision making, but politics is the method of gaining access to the people in the position to make the decisions or to the positions themselves. These are the topics that students explore in papers on the intriguing world of politics and government. You can use the following resources to answer questions about politics and government.

ENCYCLOPEDIAS AND DICTIONARIES (320.03)

The Encyclopedic Dictionary of American Government
Wellek, Alex, ed. Guilford, CT: Dushkin Publishing, 1991. 4th ed.
Alphabetically arranged, this dictionary defines terms taken from throughout American history such as *featherbedding, Know-Nothings, Democratic party,* and *gross national product.* It also has several indexes: to biographies, acronyms, Supreme Court decisions, presidents, and acts of Congress. Topic guides are boxed insets within large articles that serve as references to related material elsewhere in the book. Useful to students for understanding the legislative process, constitutional law, Congress, presidential elections, and much more. Includes illustrations.

Oxford Companion to Politics of the World
Krieger, Joel, et al., ed. New York: Oxford University Press, 1993. Incl. bibliographies and index.
Students will find this an excellent resource for information on world conflicts and issues, such as the conflict in Yugoslavia, up to 1992, with emphasis on events after World War II. Biographies of 100 significant people in world politics are included. Broad topics such as international relations and foreign policy are discussed at length.

World Government
Taylor, Peter J, ed. New York: Oxford University Press, 1990. Incl. bibliography and index.
Opening chapters explain what makes a state, how they're created, what gives them power, how governments are formed, and how they work. Remaining chapters review countries of the world, organized by region. Forms of government, history, wars, and affiliations are discussed. Maps and diagrams illustrate a readable text. This volume is part of the *Illustrated Encyclopedia of World Geography.*

POLITICAL BIOGRAPHY (320.092)

American Political Leaders from Colonial Times to the Present
O'Brien, Steven G. Santa Barbara, CA: ABC-CLIO, 1991.
Accurate, clearly written biographies of more than 400 important political figures in U.S. history are given in this dictionary source. Beyond the facts, the book imparts the meaning and significance of the political lives and contributions of the people profiled. The more important the person discussed, the longer the biography. "It includes all major party presidential candidates as well as significant third party candidates, all vice presidents, speakers of the house, chief justices of

the supreme court, and secretaries of state. In addition, it profiles many revolutionary and colonial figures, as well as important congressional representatives, senators, presidential advisors, and a few individuals who do not fit easily into any of those categories but who influenced national affairs, such as Jefferson Davis and Eleanor Roosevelt," according to *Booklist* (November 15, 1991). An excellent resource for students.

Black Americans in Congress, 1870–1989
Ragsdale, Bruce A., and Treese, Joel D. Washington, DC: Government Printing Office, 1990.
This source provides biographies plus a portrait of the 66 black Americans to serve in Congress to 1989. Included are Adam Clayton Powell, Barbara Jordan, and Harold Washington.

The Columbia Dictionary of Political Biography
New York: Columbia University Press, 1991. Incl. index.
Profiled in this international alphabetic dictionary are heads of state from all nations, as well as prominent political figures: elected and appointed office-holders at local, state, regional, and national levels; lobbyists; dissidents; and influential opinion makers. Although the focus is on political careers, the biographic write-ups analyze political positions of individuals. Brief and informative.

Current Leaders of Nations
Lansdale, PA: Current Leaders, 1990. Looseleaf. Incl. bibliography.
Arranged by country, this source is updated annually. "Leaders" are considered to be those with power, not heads of state. Data on the country are provided, including a map with location, political history, and biographical and political information about each individual, including rise to power and leadership style and domestic and foreign policies.

Great Political Thinkers: Plato to the Present
Ebenstein, William, and Ebenstein, Alan O. New York: Harcourt Brace, 1991. 5th ed. Incl. index.
This is not biography but an introduction to and discussion of the ideas of major political thinkers throughout history, followed by their significant writings. Plato, Aristotle, Cicero, Machiavelli, Locke, Rousseau, de Tocqueville, Marx, Lenin, Freud, and many others are included.

Women in Congress, 1917–1990
Commission of the Bicentenary of the U.S. House of Representatives. Washington, DC: Government Printing Office, 1991.

A portrait or photo and brief personal and political biography is provided for each of the 129 women who served in Congress during the years listed.

GOVERNMENT ORGANIZATION AND FUNCTION (320.4)

The American Federal Government
Ferguson, John H., and McHenry, Dean E. New York: McGraw-Hill, 1981. 14th ed. Incl. bibliographies and index.

This text strives to "explain and document the American political system as authoritatively, briefly, clearly, and readably as possible," according to the Preface, in order to help the reader "become an informed and functioning citizen." Governmental and political history is traced from colonial times, the political process explained, the organization and functioning of government made clear. Very useful for students seeking to understand the American government and the development of its basic tenets and documents.

Congressional Quarterly's Desk Reference on American Government
Wetterau, Bruce. Washington, DC: Congressional Quarterly, 1995. Incl. bibliographic references and index.

This source uses a question-and-answer format to provide information on the federal government; the presidency; presidents, first ladies, vice presidents, cabinet members, and their personal lives; Congress; the Supreme Court; and campaigns and elections. Some sample questions: How did the bald eagle become the national symbol? What is separation of powers? Which incumbent presidents were defeated? Which Supreme Court justices' nominations were defeated? A solid, quick source for students.

CQ's Guide to Current American Government
Washington, DC: Congressional Quarterly. Semiannual.

This source is most useful to students because it takes the best articles from *CQ Weekly* (see *Congressional Quarterly's Almanac,* below) that examine specific, significant issues facing Congress, the president, and the nation. The underlying principles and processes are demonstrated to aid in understanding the political process. Major controversies and conflicts are identified, and key people in political battles are profiled.

POLITICAL GROUPS (322)

The Ku Klux Klan: An Encyclopedia
Newton, Michael, and Newton, Judy. New York: Garland, 1991. Incl. bibliography.

Every student encounters this organization when studying the history of the American South. This alphabetically arranged source will aid student understanding of the Klan role in significant events; it provides background on prominent members and opponents and summarizes activity through the United States up to 1990. Several subject-arranged lists of entries help provide access to terms, events, factions, places, victims, and members.

CIVIL RIGHTS (323)

The ABC-CLIO Companion to the Civil Rights Movement
Grossman, Mark. Santa Barbara, CA: ABC-CLIO, 1993. Incl. bibliography and index.

Brief, alphabetically arranged entries provide quick reference information on key individuals, martyrs, institutions, court decisions, concepts, events, heroes, and opponents of the civil rights movement. A chronology is included.

Encyclopedia of African-American Civil Rights: From Emancipation to Present
Lowery, Charles D., and Marszalek, John F., eds. Westport, CT: Greenwood Press, 1992. Incl. bibliography and index.

Similar to the previous title, this source is more comprehensive, with better bibliographic information. Alphabetically arranged, it provides biographies and defines and explains court cases, movements, events, terms, laws, and more. In brief, readable paragraphs, it supplies an overview as well as insight into the civil rights movement, describing, for example, the effects of landmark court decisions. A chronology, 1861–1990, is included.

The Eyes on the Prize Civil Rights Reader: Documents, Speeches, and Firsthand Accounts from the Black Freedom Struggle, 1954–1990
Carson, Clayborne, et al. eds. New York: Viking/Penguin, 1991. Incl. bibliographic references.

This book collects in one place the most significant primary source material from the civil rights movement, 1954–1965. Court cases, such as the text of *Brown v. Board of Education*, Nelson Mandela's speech in Atlanta in 1990, and Martin Luther King's "Letter from Birmingham City Jail" are examples of the material provided.

Sources of Our Liberties: Documentary Origins of Individual Liberties in the United States Constitution and Bill of Rights

Perry, Richard L., and Cooper, John C., eds. Chicago: American Bar Association, 1959. Incl. bibliography and index.

The texts of documents that predate the Constitution but form the underlying basis of the Constitution: the Magna Carta, the first Charter of Virginia, the Mayflower Compact, Fundamental Orders of Connecticut, the Habeas Corpus Act, the Bill of Rights, 1689, the Resolutions of the Stamp Act Congress, the constitutions of several of the original thirteen colonies, the Declaration of Independence, and the Constitution of the United States and the first ten amendments.

World Human Rights Guide

Humana, Charles. New York: Oxford University Press, 1992. 3d ed.

A country-by-country survey that provides charts of yes or no answers to various questions on specific freedoms or freedoms from (torture, for example). Brief comments on each are provided. Each country is given an overall human rights rating. France, Germany, and all the Scandinavian countries rate over 94 percent, for example, while the United States rates 90 percent, Israel 76 percent, and Iraq 17 percent. A useful compilation and assessment for students looking to compare countries on specific rights issues.

THE POLITICAL PROCESS (324)

Political Handbook of the World

New York: CSA Publications. Annual. Incl. index.

For each country, identifies and provides data on government operation, offices, officials, politics and parties, and news media.

The Statesman's Year-Book

New York: St. Martin's Press. Annual. Incl. bibliographic references and index.

Subtitled *Statistical and Historical Annual of the States of the World,* this source provides much useful information for students in one handy, slightly-larger-than-pocket-size volume. For each country, as well as political regions or states within countries, basic information is summarized: history, area and population, climate, head of state, government, military, economy, religions, foreign relations, communications, education, energy, welfare, natural resources, industry, and more. Statistics, dates, diplomatic representatives, and references for further reading are given. Surprising depth in brief summary format.

ELECTIONS (324.6)

Almanac of American Politics
Barone, Michael, and Ujifusa, Grant. Washington, DC: National
Journal. Biennial. Incl. index.

This source works state by state, providing a political and election
overview of each, and then for each state, a look at the governor and
senators, election results, and key votes. It then provides an overview
for each voting district in the state and a look at each representative,
election results, and key votes. The book concludes with Senate and
House committee listings and campaign finance figures and sources for
each congressperson, by state.

America Votes: A Handbook of American Election Statistics
Governmental Affairs Institute. Washington, DC: Congressional
Quarterly. Biennial.

This source provides election results by state for all major elections
since 1945—president, governor, senator, and congressman—plus other
statistics and district maps.

Congressional Quarterly's Guide to U.S. Elections
Moore, John L., ed. Washington, DC: Congressional Quarterly,
1994. 3d ed. Incl. index.

Updated election results to 1993, including state and federal elections, are provided in this source. Essays cover politics and issues of congressional and gubernatorial elections from 1945 to 1992, and the issue of
term limits. Keynote speakers at party conventions are listed.

Congressional Quarterly's Politics in America
Washington, DC: Congressional Quarterly. Biennial. Incl. index.

Statistics and biography make up this work, which concentrates
on the people who serve in Congress. Organized by state, the work looks
at the governor, senators, and representatives; it provides biographical
information and political information for each individual, such as activities and assignments in Congress, voting records, election results,
key votes, and interest group ratings. This source concentrates more on
the individual, whereas *Almanac of American Politics,* a similar work,
offers more state and voting district information.

IMMIGRATION AND EMIGRATION (325)

Dictionary of American Immigration History
Cordasco, Francesco, ed. Metuchen, NJ: Scarecrow, 1990. Incl. bibliography.

The alphabetical source defines terms, provides brief biographies of significant people, and examines each immigrant group. Essays on ethnic groups describe the conditions left behind, how the immigration occurred, settlement in the United States, and conditions upon settlement. A handy volume covering all the basics, including laws of immigration.

INTERNATIONAL RELATIONS (327)

Dictionary of American Foreign Affairs
Flanders, Stephen A., and Flanders, Carl N. New York: Macmillan, 1993.

This alphabetical source discusses events and agreements and diplomatic, military, economic, environmental, and technological matters that influence U.S. foreign relations. Coverage is from 1776 through 1992. Immigration policy and relationships with Native American tribes are included. There are biographies of key international figures: heads of state, military leaders, and diplomats, for example. Relations of the United States with specific countries are reviewed. In an easy-to-read format, "this will be a valuable research tool for students," according to *School Library Journal* (November 1993).

The Encyclopedia of the United Nations and International Agreements
Osmanczyk, Edmund. London: Taylor & Francis: 1990. 2d ed. Incl. index.

This source explains the organization, structure, and operation of the UN and its affiliated agencies and provides the text of nearly 3,000 agreements, conventions and treaties.

Everyone's United Nations
Department of Public Information. New York: United Nations, 1986. 10th ed.

This source covers the history of the UN, its role in major events such as the Falklands War, its organization and structure, and its role in world peace. The texts of important documents, such as the UN Charter and the Universal Declaration of Human Rights, are included.

Yearbook of the United Nations
New York: United Nations. Annual. Incl. index.

The UN's record of activities year by year, including review of political and security questions, regional problems, and economic and social problems. Texts of UN resolutions, reports from organizations affiliated with the UN, such as the World Health Organization, data on members, background, dates of admission, votes, discussions, and details on UN agencies are included.

LEGISLATION (328)

American Congressional Dictionary
Kravitz, Robert. Washington, DC: Congressional Quarterly, 1993.

This source explains terms in use in the U.S. Congress today. Procedural terms, legislative terms, and insider terms are illustrated with historical comparisons where possible. Differences between the Senate and the House of Representatives are also pointed out when appropriate.

Congressional Quarterly (CQ) Almanac and Weekly Report
Washington, DC: Congressional Quarterly.

The *Weekly Report* is a magazine that covers the activities of Congress and its legislative acts in detail, with news and analysis. The president's legislative proposals, statements, and major speeches are covered. Political activities and Supreme Court rulings and actions are discussed and analyzed. The magazine is indexed by itself and other sources, such as InfoAccess's *Magazine Index.* The year's *Weekly Report* articles are edited, summarized, and otherwise reduced to fit into one large annual volume, called *CQ Almanac.*

Congressional Quarterly's Guide to Congress
Washington, DC: Congressional Quarterly, 1991. 4th ed.

This extensive source provides biographies of everyone to serve a term in Congress, complete text of important documents on which the governance of the United States is based, including historic documents prior to the Constitution, definitions of terms, and essays on current issues such as lobbying and benefits.

Congressional Record
Washington, DC: U.S. Government Printing Office, 1873– .

This periodical is issued daily while Congress is in session and is the record of congressional speeches and debated, in full, record of votes, presidential messages, and often texts of bills.

Encyclopedia of the American Legislative System
Silbey, Joel H., ed. New York: Scribner, 1994. Incl. bibliography and index.

Ninety-one articles in this set discuss legislative processes in the United States from colonial times to the present. Articles may be up to 30 pages long. Specific topics include "Congress, the Executive, and War Powers," "Pressure Groups and Lobbies," "Legislative Ethics," "Legislative Work Load," and "Women in Legislatures." Comprehensive yet readable, this source is suitable for students needing in-depth information on legislative functioning at any level. "Students will find essays addressing civil liberties, civil rights, the environment, gender issues, corruption, minorities in Congress, and the budget process of particular interest," according to *School Library Journal* (February 1995). Recent topics include the Clarence Thomas hearings, hate speech, gun control, and the policies of Bill Clinton.

Encyclopedia of the United States Congress
Bacon, Donald C., et al., eds. New York: Simon & Schuster, 1995. 4 vols. Incl. bibliographies and index.

The definitive yet readable source on the U.S. Congress, this set reviews the inner workings of Congress—its procedures, how committees function, court cases, even Congress's buildings. It includes biographies of significant past members, as well as hotly debated issues, such as abortion and the balanced budget amendment. Articles can range up to 10 pages or more. Each president has a separate entry emphasizing his relationship with Congress. Each state's congressional representation is reviewed. Important events, legislation, and constitutional amendments are covered. Comprehensive information for the student.

How Federal Laws Are Made
Washington, DC: WANT Publishing, 1994.

An easy-to-read and -understand outline tracing the federal law-making process from idea to statute to subsequent rules and regulations. The federal budget process is similarly outlined. Also included are sections on how to find U.S. statutes and how to use the *Federal Register* and the *Code of Federal Regulations.*

The Young Oxford Companion to the Congress of the United States
Ritchie, Donald A. New York: Oxford University Press, 1993. Incl. bibliographies and index.

An alphabetical, dictionary-format book that provides brief, interesting, and readable explanations of terms, and practices, biographies of significant congresspersons, and events. Examples include "executive privilege," "impeachment," "Fulbright, J. William,"

"Great Compromise, 1787." There are articles on minorities in Congress and interesting explanations for practices such as "bean soup," which is made daily for Congress dining rooms.

THE CONSTITUTION (342.73)

The American Heritage History of the Bill of Rights
Englewood Cliffs, NJ: Silver Burdett, 1990. 10 vols. Incl. bibliographies and index.

Each volume in this series discusses at length one of the first ten amendments to the Constitution. The background under which the amendment was formed, Supreme Court interpretations of the amendment, and challenges to it are all reviewed to the present.

Constitutions of the World
Maddex, Robert L. Washington DC: Congressional Quarterly, 1995. Incl. bibliographical references and index.

This source, arranged by country (there are 80), summarizes each country's constitution, compares and contrasts them, and provides an overview of the country's constitutional history, type of government, fundamental rights, and division of powers. One of a kind.

CQ's Guide to the U.S. Constitution: History, Text, Index, Glossary
Mitchell, Ralph. Washington, DC: Congressional Quarterly, 1986.

This source includes the text of the Constitution and amendments, and a history of the writing of the Constitution. It explains the structure and powers of Congress, the executive and judicial branches as established by the Constitution, and the process of amending the Constitution and ratifying amendments.

Encyclopedia of Constitutional Amendments, Proposed Amendments and Amending Issues, 1789–1995
Vile, John R. Santa Barbara, CA: ABC-CLIO, 1996. Incl. bibliographical references and index.

Arranged alphabetically, this source explains the background of every existing and proposed amendment with terms and brief biographies (e.g., "affirmative action," "balanced budget amendment," "Emancipation Proclamation," "English-language amendment," "Twenty-Seventh Amendment"). A super source for students.

SUPREME COURT (347.7326)

Although the Supreme Court and its decisions are considered "law" in the Dewey Decimal system (347), it is also the third major component of government.

The Oxford Companion to the Supreme Court
Hall, Kermit, ed. New York: Oxford University Press, 1992. Incl. index.
A one-volume dictionary-style encyclopedia that provides brief to substantial articles on cases, people, issues (such as slavery, affirmative action, and privacy), legal terms, amendments to the Constitution; and an extensive article on the history of the Court. An appendix provides the text of the Constitution, another lists Supreme Court nominations, appointments by presidents, and a chronology of judges' succession; and a third appendix lists trivia and traditions. A case index is included. An excellent source for researching constitutional amendments and significant Supreme Court cases.

The Supreme Court A to Z
Witt, Elder, ed. Washington, DC: Congressional Quarterly, 1993. Incl. bibliography and index.
A dictionary format, ready reference, quick answer source, this title gives more attention to major issues faced by the Court, such as abortion. It adequately covers history, procedures, and traditions of the Court, demonstrating how cases come to the Court, and how they are argued and decided. It includes brief biographies of Supreme Court justices with photographs.

Supreme Court Cases

The Evolving Constitution: How the Supreme Court Has Ruled on Issues from Abortion to Zoning
Lieberman, Jethro K. New York: Random House, 1992. Incl. bibliographical references.
This source reveals in easy-to-understand essays how the Supreme Court has interpreted the Constitution through over 2,000 cases covering 200 years.

Great American Trials
Knappman, Edward W., ed. Detroit: Visible Ink/Gale, 1994. Incl. index.
This handy volume covers all the major trials arranged chronologically, from the Salem witch trials to Oliver North.

Historic U.S. Court Cases, 1690–1990: An Encyclopedia
Johnson, John W. New York: Garland, 1992. Incl. bibliography and indexes.

This source presents easily understood reviews of significant cases on a variety of topics, such as labor, discrimination, and due process. Several cases are offered on each topic. Differing viewpoints are given and social implications discussed.

Landmark Decisions of the United States Supreme Court
Harrison, Maureen, and Gilbert, Steve, eds. Beverly Hills, CA: Excellent Books, 1991– . Incl. bibliography and index.

Each volume reviews significant cases in American history, covering school prayer, affirmative action, censorship, flag burning, and many more.

Leading Constitutional Decisions
Cushman, Robert F. Englewood Cliffs, NJ: Prentice-Hall, 1991. 18th ed. Incl. index.

Classic cases, such as *Roe v. Wade* and *Brown v. Board of Education of Topeka,* are presented and explained. Historical context is provided. More recent cases bring the reader up to 1990.

U.S. FEDERAL AND STATE GOVERNMENT (353)

Encyclopedia of the American Presidency
Levy, Leonard, and Fisher, Louis, eds. New York: Simon & Schuster, 1994. 4 vols. Incl. bibliography and index.

This set delves deeply into every aspect of the presidency—its powers, the men who have served as president, and those who have served them. Presidential policies, events during their administrations, cabinet members, first ladies, and even pets are detailed here. Election results—their impact, issues, parties, and also-rans—are included. Thorough, with an excellent index. "A readable, interdisciplinary presentation of the people, events, processes and concepts necessary to understand the American presidency," according to *Booklist* (January 1, 1994).

The Presidency A to Z: A Ready Reference Encyclopedia
Nelson, Michael, ed. Washington, DC: Congressional Quarterly, 1992. Incl. bibliographies and index.

Quick, short answers to questions on the presidency is how this source advertises itself. Well written, it's most useful to high school students. It includes biographies of presidents, vice presidents, first ladies, and also-rans. It lists cabinet members for each president, election summaries, and entries such as "Interest Groups and the Presidency" and "Public Opinion and the Presidency." Campaign financing, White House departments, presidential powers and pay are also covered. This title serves as a companion to the more comprehensive *Congressional Quarterly's Guide to the Presidency*.

Vital Statistics on the Presidency: Washington to Clinton
Ragsdale, Lyn. Washington, DC: Congressional Quarterly, 1996. Incl. bibliography and index.
   Tons of statistics and charts are organized into chapters. Each chapter is introduced by a probing essay on such topics as presidential elections, public appearances, public opinion, and congressional relations. The focus is more on the office than on individuals, yet the statistics allow for closer comparison between presidents and for tracing changes in official behavior over time.

PRESIDENTIAL BIOGRAPHY (973.0992)

Several books provide good biographical and historical information about the presidents.

The Complete Book of Presidents
DeGregorio, William A. New York: Dembner. Incl. bibliographies and index.
   Each edition profiles each president while updating information that may have come to the light since the previous edition and including a new president if one has been elected. A full-page portrait of each president is included, plus descriptive paragraphs on name origin, physical description, personality, ancestors, parents, siblings, children, birth, childhood, education, religion, recreation, romances, marriage, career, political and presidential life, retirement, death, and finally, critical analysis by others. A bibliography follows each chapter.

Facts About the Presidents
Kane, Joseph Nathan. New York: H. W. Wilson. Incl. index.
   This title emphasizes facts, data, statistics, election results, voting records, and chronologies of significant actions and events. It provides only brief narrative paragraphs under highlighted headlines, such as "Roosevelt on Television." Short bibliographies follow each chapter. Much information is reorganized in the last section of the book, titled "Comparative Data," with sections such as presidential nicknames and colleges attended by presidents.

The First Ladies

Klapthor, Margaret Brown. Washington, DC: White House Historical Association, 1994. 7th ed.

Similar to the Frank Freidel's *The Presidents of the United States of America,* also published by the White House Historical Association, this title provides a color portrait and a page of political and personal biography. Longer biographical essays can be found in *America's First Ladies,* by Diana D. Healy (New York: Atheneum, 1988).

Our Vice-Presidents and Second Ladies

Dunlap, Leslie W. Metuchen, NJ: Scarecrow, 1988. Incl. bibliographies and index.

This source provides biographies, emphasizing time of office and recounting the biography and activities of the vice president's wife, of each vice president up through George Bush, Reagan's vice president.

The Presidents Speak: The Inaugural Addresses of the American Presidents, from Washington to Clinton

Lott, Davis Newton. New York: Holt, 1994. Incl. index.

For each president, this source includes a brief biography plus a brief summary of national and world situations at the time. In addition to the text of the speeches, margin notes explain references, comments, audience reactions, even the weather if it influenced a particular part of the speech. Appendixes include list of presidents and vice presidents, biographies of presidents not inaugurated, plus the text of the Declaration of Independence, the Act of Confederation of the United States, and the Constitution of the United States.

Speeches of the American Presidents

Podell, Janet, and Anzovin, Steven, eds. New York: H. W. Wilson, 1988. Incl. index.

Contains 180 major speeches from Washington to Reagan, including many inaugural addresses, Lincoln's Gettysburg Address, Andrew Jackson's "The Removal of the Indians," Theodore Roosevelt's "Westward Expansion," Kennedy's "The New Frontier" and "Ich Bin ein Berliner," Nixon's resignation speech, and many more. Portraits included.

OTHER GOVERNMENT FUNCTIONS

Government Agencies
Whitnah, Donald R., ed. Westport, CT: Greenwood Press, 1983. Incl. index.

An alphabetical listing of federal agencies with brief, and often substantial, essays on the most significant agencies. The Rural Electrification Agency article is seven pages, as is the article on the Peace Corps. The Department of State article is more than eight pages. History, origin, development, function, and problems of each agency are reviewed.

CHAPTER 14

Psychology (150)

The theories of the major psychologists, especially Sigmund Freud, B. F. Skinner, and Carl Jung, come up regularly in student assignments, as in, "Compare and contrast the theories of . . . with those of . . ." These theories are adequately outlined in most of the encyclopedic sources below, along with biographical information about each psychologist. Psychological ailments, such as depression, may also need exploring in student papers. Teachers may assign student research on many topics in psychology—for example, the relationship between parent and child or between siblings; or emotions, their outer manifestations and inner workings. This chapter explores useful resources for psychology projects.

PSYCHOLOGY INDEXES (150.16)

Psychological Abstracts
Lancaster, PA: American Psychological Association, 1927–   .
Monthly.

Also available online (PsychINFO) and on CD-ROM (PsychLIT), this source indexes more than 1,200 English-language journals, books, and dissertations on the subject of psychology and describes the content of the article or report. Coverage is strong on abnormal, clinical, social, and experimental psychology and on human and animal development, according to *Guide to Reference Books*. This source is commonly available in college libraries, less often in large public libraries, and rarely in small public or school libraries. Worth locating for the student with a strong interest in the topic.

ENCYCLOPEDIAS AND DICTIONARIES (150.3)

The ABC of Psychology
Kristal, Leonard, ed. New York: Facts on File, 1982.

A dictionary of terms, theories, and people, this source is interesting because the explanations are brief and readable yet cover the basics and are illustrated with photos and drawings that effectively complement the text. Though a bit dated now, popular terms from the 1960s and 1970s, like "encounter groups" and "transcendental meditation," add to the interest. A good starting point.

Encyclopedia of Psychology
Corsini, Raymond, ed. New York: Wiley, 1994. 2d ed. 4 vols. Incl. bibliography and index.

This encyclopedia has become the standard reference for the subject, covering all aspects, theories, terms, and people. Arranged alphabetically, articles can go on at length, depending on the topic discussed. As comprehensive as can be hoped, this encyclopedia will answer most students' questions.

The Encyclopedic Dictionary of Psychology
Pettijohn, Terry F., ed. Guilford, CT: Dushkin Publishing, 1991. 4th ed.

Brief definitions and explanations, psychological terms and theories, and biographies of people are presented in this source. Alphabetically arranged, it's a good place for students to start before moving on to the longer articles and essays in encyclopedias. A master list of biographies, topics guides, and subjects maps opens the book.

The Gale Encyclopedia of Psychology
Gall, Susan, ed. Detroit: Gale, 1996. Incl. bibliography and index.

This is probably the best overall encyclopedia source for students. It's also the newest. The editor was advised by a college professor and a high school teacher of psychology. While covering the full range of psychology topics, 400 topics studied in high school and college are given entries. "Biographies of significant people in psychology; theories; terms; landmark case studies and experiments; applications of psychology in advertising, medicine, and sports; psychological tests; and career information," are given emphasis, according to *Booklist* (December 15, 1996). Erich Fromm, B. F. Skinner, Jean Piaget, and their theories are examples of significant psychologists covered. Clearly written articles, plus charts and graphs, make this a prime source for students.

A Student's Dictionary of Psychology
Stratton, Peter, and Hayes, Nicky. London: Edward Arnold, 1993.
2d ed.

This is an adequate introductory dictionary covering the basics of
the topic.

Survey of Social Science: Psychology Series
Magill, Frank, ed. Pasadena, CA: Salem Press, 1993. 6 vols. Incl.
index.

This source is an excellent first stop for students, offering understandable six-page essays on major topics in psychology. Each essay
"defines vocabulary, provides an overview of the concept, tells how it
is applied, summarizes research, provides a selective annotated bibliography, and lists related articles," according to *Wilson Library Bulletin* (May 1994). This source serves as a fine introduction and supplement
to Corsini's *Encyclopedia of Psychology* (see above). Corsini offers more
depth but may take more effort to understand. Magill's covers some topics, such as group decision making, that Corsini does not. Magill's weak
point is biography, though theories associated with individuals are
thoroughly discussed. Corsini is stronger on biography, as are other
sources.

PSYCHOLOGY HISTORY (150.9)

History of Psychology
Hothersall, David. Philadelphia: Temple University Press, 1984.
Incl. bibliography and indexes.

This text begins with "psychology and the ancients" and proceeds
through William James to the twentieth century. Along the way, many
types of psychology are explained, and the lives and careers of psychologists are examined.

The Story of Psychology
Hunt, Morton. New York: Doubleday, 1993. Incl. bibliographical
references and index.

The author begins with the early Greeks when psychology was a
branch of philosophy and follows it through time to the 1800s, when
psychology broke from philosophy, and continues to Freud and William
James and then to the present. Readable and interesting, the author
makes clear the different schools of psychological thought, with an
emphasis on the individuals who developed them. The book also
serves as a collection of biographies.

PSYCHOLOGY-BIOGRAPHY (150.92)

The Great Psychologists: A History of Psychological Thought
Waton, Robert I., and Evans, Rand B. New York: HarperCollins, 1991. 5th ed. Incl. indexes.

Students will find this source useful and readable. It discusses the lives and theories of 50 major psychologists and the impact their work has had. Developments in the field are traced to the present.

A Guide to Psychologists and Their Concepts
Nordby, Vernon J., and Hall, Calvin S. San Francisco: Freeman, 1974. Incl. bibliographic references and indexes.

This source is useful for its brief reviews of the theories of 42 major psychologists. Sketched portraits accompany biographies.

The Women of Psychology
Stevens, Gwendolyn, and Gardner, Sheldon. Cambridge, MA: Schenkman, 1982. 2 vols.

Volume 1 covers women pioneers in the field and discusses the role of women at psychology's moment of birth. Volume 2 provides 100 entries on women up to the present.

EMOTIONS (152.4)

Emotions
New York: Time-Life Books, 1994.

Exactly what the title says, this book examines the full range of human emotions, from love to laughter. Time-Life Books are well illustrated and easy to understand.

Encyclopedia of Violence: Origins, Attitudes, Consequences
DiCanio, Margaret. New York: Facts on File, 1993. Incl. bibliography and index.

This A to Z reference source carries substantial articles on child abuse, battered women, gangs, rape, suicide, vandalism, and much more. Articles are thorough and offer clearly written analysis, citing sources in the text. Students will find this most useful.

MEMORY AND LEARNING (153.1)

The Encyclopedia of Memory and Memory Disorders
Noll, Richard, and Turkington, Carol. New York: Facts on File, 1994. Incl. bibliographies and index.

Alphabetically arranged entries in this source focus on memory research and what is currently known about this aspect of the mind. Suitable for general readers and students, this source introduces readers to "medical, historical, social, and scientific aspects of memory function and failure," according to *Library Journal* (March 15, 1995). Definitions, concepts, diseases and disorders, treatments and therapies, as well as profiles of noted researchers, are included.

INTELLIGENCE (153.9)

Encyclopedia of Human Intelligence
Sternberg, Robert J., ed. New York: Macmillan, 1994. 2 vols. Incl. bibliographies and index.

Sample topics covered by this source include "genius, illiteracy, intuition, reasoning, schooling and intelligence, test-taking strategies, underachievement, and wisdom," according to the publisher. Abilities and aptitude, achievement testing, changes with age, effects of birth order, parenting, and socioeconomic status are also included. Alphabetical arrangement of articles is complemented by drawings, charts, and photographs that help explain the functioning of the brain and nervous system. A unique source.

SLEEP PHENOMENA (154.6)

The Encyclopedia of Dreams: Symbols and Interpretations
Guiley, Rosemary Ellen. New York: Crossroad, 1993. Incl. bibliography.

The first part of this book discusses dreams, nightmares, cross-cultural beliefs about dreams, and dream research. Part II alphabetically lists things dreamed about and provides at least a paragraph of possible meaning for each.

The Encyclopedia of Sleep and Dreaming
Carsakadon, Mary A., ed. New York: Macmillan, 1993. Incl. bibliographies and index.

Useful for students, this source reports the results of research into the medical, biological, and psychological aspects of sleep and dreaming. It does not focus on disorders or interpret dreams. The emphasis is on humans, but some animal research is included, especially when it may benefit humans. Entries generally cover up to four pages. Charts, diagrams, and illustrations add interest and aid understanding. Entries vary in length, up to eight pages.

GENETIC PSYCHOLOGY (155)

Encyclopedia of Adolescence
Lerner, Richard, et al. New York: Garland, 1991. 2 vols. Incl. bibliographies and index.

Coverage goes beyond the psychological in this set but is well worth a look no matter what the specific topic. Health concerns such as scoliosis, eating disorders, and drug dependency; teenage parenting; moodiness; puberty; and developmental theories of major psychologists such as Erickson and Freud; even a review of adolescence from colonial times to the present—all this and more can be found in this set. Entries are alphabetically arranged and can be as long as ten pages. A great source for students to use when seeking information on teenage suicide, drug and alcohol use, teenage pregnancies, teenagers in different cultures, and other topics relating to the adolescent experience.

CHAPTER 15

Religion (200) and Philosophy (100)

Student assignments on religion and associated topics can include comparing and contrasting specific religions such as Islam and Catholicism, or religious figures such as Buddha and Jesus, or religious texts, such as the Koran and the Bible. Teachers may want broad questions answered, such as, Why are religions so important in tribal cultures? Or, What changes were effected by missionaries, the Crusades, or the rapid spread of Islam on cultures and nations unexpecting and ill prepared to receive them? Or, How does one explain the moral justifications for violence in religion, as in the Salem witch trials? Why is religious belief so often persecuted?

When using the library to find information on religion in the online public access catalog computer terminals, keep in mind that you can look under both "religion" as a subject heading and "religious life and customs." These headings are subdivided by geography, history, and ethnic groups.

Teachers often want specific philosophies contrasted or explained. How did a specific philosopher develop his or her philosophy? Where do ethics fit into philosophy and/or religion?

A useful starting place when looking for resources is:

The Reader's Adviser, a Layman's Guide to Literature
Sader, Marie, series ed., and Ellwood, Robert S., vol. 4 ed. New York: Bowker, 1994. 14th ed. Vol. 4 of a 5-volume set listing basic titles in each field. Incl. bibliographies and indexes.

This set is a guide to the best books on most topics. Volume 4 is titled *The Best in Philosophy and Religion.* The fourteenth edition adds books on contemporary issues to the historical perspective emphasized in the 13th edition. Books on ancient through modern philosophers and religions are included. Many authors are profiled.

RELIGION (200)

General Reference Works on Religion

Abingdon Dictionary of Living Religions
Crim, Keith, ed. Nashville, TN: Abingdon, 1981.
Guide to historical developments, beliefs, and practices of contemporary religions. Bibliographies, cross-references, and illustrations.

Dictionary of Comparative Religion
Brandon, S.G.F. New York: Macmillan, 1988.
Beliefs, rituals, sacred texts, and other aspects of world religions. Synoptic index, name and subject index, and bibliographies.

Encyclopedia of BioEthics
Reich, Warren Thomas, ed. New York: Macmillan, 1995. Rev. ed. 5 vols. Incl. bibliographic references and index.
This is one of the best sources for detailed discussion of the most controversial issues. Scientific facts, political implications, societal impact, and opinion on every possible side of an issue are presented thoroughly and objectively. Nearly every issue is explored in this set, from abortion, to drug use, to doctor-assisted suicide, to animal rights.

The Encyclopedia of Religion
Eliade, Mircea, editor in chief. New York: Macmillan, 1993. 16 vols. Incl. index.
A recent monumental encyclopedia, this is the standard work on religion with over 2,700 entries from 1,400 scholars. It includes primitive religions, alchemy (16 pages), animism, architecture (10 pages), and a fascinating discussion of the religious meanings of alphabetical symbols. Volume 16 includes an alphabetic list of entries, a synoptic outline of contents, and an extensive general index.

The New Schaff-Herzog Encyclopedia of Religious Knowledge
Hauck, Albert, and Jackson, S. M., ed. New York: Funk and Wagnalls, 1908–1912. 13 vols. Incl. index.

An old but extensive reference on biblical and historical theology, including separate articles on various sects, denominations and churches, organizations, societies, missions, doctrines, and controversies. A general bibliography in the preface and bibliographies for each article. In 1955 a 2-volume supplement was published by Baker Book.

Religion Indexes
American Theological Association, comp. New York: H. W. Wilson. CD-ROM.

This CD-ROM database includes over 600,000 citations and abstracts of articles in 200 journals and books. It covers many different religions and beliefs.

Religious Information Sources: A Worldwide Guide
Melton, J. Gordon, and Koszegi, Michael A. New York: Garland. 1992.

Lists 2,500 sources of religious information, including world religions, occult, and new age material. Print, microform, electronic, associations, research centers, and archival resources are included.

World Spirituality: An Encyclopedic History of the Religious Quest
Cousin, Ewert, gen. ed. New York: Crossroad, 1985–   . Incl. bibliographies and index.

This monumental work will eventually include 25 volumes. A scholar or team of scholars edits each volume, which records the historical development of the religion. In addition to several volumes on Christianity, there is a volume on Egyptian, Greek, and Roman religions and one on South and Meso-American Native spirituality.

The Bible (220)

The Anchor Bible Dictionary
Freedman, David Noel, ed. New York: Anchor Books, 1992. Incl. bibliographies.

Articles reflecting current theological doctrine. Includes illustrations and maps.

Illustrated Guide to the Bible
Porter, J. R. New York: Oxford University Press, 1995. Incl. bibliographic references and index.

Arranged according to the sequence of books in the Bible. Photos, etchings, manuscripts, and historical accounts of Bible stories, the Dead Sea Scrolls, and Roman rule.

The Interpreter's Bible
New York: Abingdon-Cokesbury, 1951–1957. 11 vols.

A monumental interpretation of biblical topics. Maps and introductory and topical articles.

The Layman's Parallel Bible
Grand Rapids, MI: Zondervan, 1991.

This source briefly explains and compares side by side *The King James Version, The New International Version, The Living Bible,* and *The New Revised Standard Version* of the Bible. It's a great tool for noting the differences and similarities between versions.

New Bible Commentary
Grove, IL: Intervarsity Press, 1994. Incl. bibliography.

This source, based on the New International Version (NIV) of the Bible, includes commentary on each book of the Bible, as well as maps, time lines, and family trees.

New Interpreter's Bible
Nashville, TN: Abingdon, 1994.

This revised version began coming out in 1994. It will eventually include 12 volumes. It is based on modern English versions of the Bible and is arranged in the sequence of the books of the Bible. A green-tinted section quotes from both the New International and the New Revised Standard versions of the Bible side by side.

Reference Resources on Prominent Religions

The Book of Saints: A Dictionary of Servants of God
Benedictine Monks of St. Augustine's Abbey, comp. Harrisburg, PA: Morehouse, 1989. 6th ed., rev. 1st American ed. Incl. bibliography and index.

An update of the 1966 version, this source provides nearly 10,000 biographical entries with name, appellation, dates, and other information, and includes an index of emblems.

Concise Encyclopedia of Islam
Glasse, G. New York: HarperCollins, 1989. Incl. bibliography
Useful brief articles on rituals, law, culture, beliefs, and leaders.
Includes illustrations, maps, and chronology.

Encyclopedia of Eastern Philosophy and Religion: Buddhism, Hinduism, Taoism and Zen
Fischer-Schreiber, Ingrid, et al. Boston: Shambhala, 1989. Incl. bibliography.
The cultural and historical traditions of each of these powerful faiths is discussed in this source which includes definitions of terms and the lives of important religious leaders.

Encyclopedia Judaica
New York: Macmillan, 1971–1972. 16 vols. Incl. illustrations, bibliographies, and index.
Comprehensive view of world Jewry. Includes 25,000 articles and an index with 200,00 entries. A decennial supplement covers 1971–1981. Many biographies.

Encyclopedia of Judaism
Wigoder, Geoffrey, ed. New York: Macmillan 1989.
Brief articles on Jewish religious life and development. Reform, conservative, and orthodox Judaism movements are explored in this volume.

New Catholic Encyclopedia
New York: McGraw-Hill, 1967–1989. 16 vols. with two supplements. Incl. bibliographies and index.
Illustrations, maps, and 17,000 signed articles on religions, philosophies, and scientific and cultural developments. No biographies for living persons.

PHILOSOPHY (100)

Dictionary of Philosophy and Religion
Reese, William L. Atlantic Heights, NJ: Humanities Press, 1980.
Dictionary of terms, with articles on the thought and works of major religious and philosophical leaders.

Encyclopedia of Philosophy
Edwards, Paul, ed. New York: Macmillan, 1967. 8 vols. in 4. Incl. bibliographies and index.

This multivolume reference master work includes articles on such unusual philosophical topics as the history of the communist idea and the philosophical idea of energy. Both Western and Eastern philosophies are discussed in nearly 1,500 articles.

Great Thinkers of the Eastern World: The Major Thinkers and the Philosophical and Religious Classics of China, India, Japan, Korea and the World of Islam
McGreal, Ian P., ed. New York: Harper, 1995.
Arranged by country, this source provides essays on philosophical and religious thinkers, including their own writings, as well as religious classics such as the Upanishad (whose authorship remains unclear). The geographical arrangement is subarranged chronologically.

Oxford History of Western Philosophy
Kenny, Anthony, ed. New York: Oxford University Press, 1994. Incl. bibliography and index.
Five essays discuss Western philosophy from ancient beginnings in Greece through current thought on the topic. The last chapter discusses political thought from Plato to the present. Illustrations, some in color, are included. Not for beginners.

Philosopher's Index: 1940–1994
Bowling Green, OH: Bowling Green State University, 1994. CD-ROM.
Indexes monographs and 300 magazines. Allows searching with Boolean operators (and, or, not—see "Boolean Logic" in Glossary). Over 155,000 records, indexed by word/phrase, subject, title, author, publication, and year.

World Philosophy: Essays-Reviews of 225 Major Works
Magill, Frank, ed. Englewood Cliffs, NJ: Salem Press, 1982. 5 vols. Incl. index.
Includes brief summaries of philosophical ideas such as Aristotle's Politics arranged chronologically, with Volume 1 containing works written from the sixth to the third centuries B.C. There is an alphabetical list of titles at the beginning of the first volume. A glossary of philosophical terms and a chronological list of titles are included.

CHAPTER 16

Science (500)

Science may be a student's most important subject of study. It encompasses math, physics, biology, geology, chemistry, plants, animals, earth, weather, astronomy, and much more. Every student will need to perform an experiment; produce a science project; write about a scientist; study plants, animals, and weather phenomena; learn mathematics; study chemical elements; learn the structures of cells and atoms; and understand the basics of physics, as well as the planets and solar system.

INDEXES TO SCIENCE PERIODICALS (501.6, 016.5)

General Science Index
New York: H. W. Wilson, 1978–   .
More specialized than *Reader's Guide to Periodical Literature or InfoTrac's Magazine Index*, this annual indexes well over 100 scientific, medical, and mathematics periodicals of both popular and specialized nature. Because of the spectrum of magazines covered and because of increased emphasis on health, chemistry, math, and medicine, this book is useful in all libraries to students and professionals.

SIRS: Science
Boca Raton, FL: SIRS. 5 vols.
This publisher reprints newspaper and magazine articles and groups them in a single volume by general topic. There's a volume each for earth sciences, physical sciences, life, medical, and applied sciences.

SCIENTIFIC DICTIONARIES (503)

McGraw-Hill Dictionary of Scientific and Technical Terms
Parker, Sybil P., editor in chief. New York: McGraw-Hill, 1993.
5th ed.

This sets the standard for dictionaries of science. The fifth edition includes definitions and pronunciations for 105,100 terms. Abbreviations, drawings, and 3,000 black and white photographs are included, as well as charts, tables, and biographies of past and present scientists. Nearly 2,200 pages make it heavy to handle, yet it's thumb-indexed and lies flat when open.

SCIENTIFIC ENCYCLOPEDIAS (503)

The Addison-Wesley Science Handbook
Coleman, Gordon J., and Dewar, David. Reading, MA: Addison-Wesley, 1997.

This handbook contains all the vital information needed in one volume. Chapters on units and conversion, biology, chemistry, geology, physics, and math contain formulas, charts, drawings of cells and human anatomy, animal classifications, the periodic table, and many more essential facts. This is an extremely useful reference source.

McGraw-Hill Encyclopedia of Science and Technology
New York: McGraw-Hill, 1992. 7th ed. 20 vols. Incl. bibliographic references and index.

Sometimes difficult to understand, this is still the most likely source to answer any scientific question. Currently in its seventh edition, this comprehensive work is technical and is aimed at the serious layperson, student, and nonscientific professional. While offering only three paragraphs on the word "atom," it can lose you right off: "A form of matter consisting of z negatively charged electrons bound predominantly by the Coulomb force to a tiny, positively charged nucleus consisting of Z protons and (A minus Z) neutrons." What's "Coulomb force"? Coulomb's law "is the basic quantitative law of electrostatics." McGraw-Hill was the only source common to public and school libraries found attempting an explanation, and it was complicated. Nevertheless, its 20 volumes plus annual yearbook summarizing the year's scientific and technologic developments are indispensable. In many libraries it may be the only source available to answer certain questions, especially after all the circulating materials have been checked out for a class assignment. A useful and thorough index locates multiple entries throughout the set. No biographies or history.

Van Nostrand's Scientific Encyclopedia
New York: Van Nostrand & Reinhold, 1995. 8th ed. 2 vols.
A huge (nearly 3,500 pages) two-volume work, the most recent edition of this encyclopedia puts in alphabetical arrangement terms from every branch of science and technology. It provides a useful, quick reference for both scientists and informed laypeople. It does not include biographies. Entries vary in length with broad topics given greater length, and specific topics brief entries. As up-to-date as possible, recent developments such as 1993 corrections to the Hubble space telescope and high-definition television are included. Photographs and illustrations are improved over the seventh edition.

SCIENCE EXPERIMENTS AND SCIENCE PROJECTS (507)

The Complete Handbook of Science Fair Projects
Bochinski, Julianne Blair. New York: Wiley, 1996. Rev. ed. Incl. index.
This title explains how to put together a project, outlines 50 award-winning projects, and provides ideas for more.

Science Experiments and Projects Index
Holonitch, Lisa, ed. Atkinson, WI: Highsmith Press, 1994.
This source provides access to 8,400 experiments and projects described in 424, books nearly all published since 1980. Arranged alphabetically under subject headings also used in the rival *Science Fair Project Index* series published by Scarecrow Press, some features in this title make it easier to use. It was compiled by staff at the Columbus, Ohio, Metropolitan Library. Each entry is briefly annotated and identifies the book indexed by title, author, and page number rather than by a letter code. Letter codes have to be inconveniently translated by flipping to a key provided in the front or back of the book. A bibliography in the back of this title lists all books indexed by main entry, and space is provided for a library to write in its own call numbers and other notes. There's only about 15 percent overlap between this and similar titles described below. While designed for students in grades K–12, the lack of grade-level appropriateness for each experiment or project indexed is a sometimes serious oversight.

Science Experiments on File
New York: Facts on File, 1989

More Science Experiments on File
New York: Facts on File, 1991

Where the science experiments indexes listed above lead the user to experiments described in many books, these titles save time by providing all the details needed for 164 experiments. The publisher's "on file" looseleaf series, of which this is one, are ready-made for copyright-free photocopying. In the 1989 volume, intended for middle school and high school students, 84 experiments are arranged in four groupings: earth science, biology, physical science/chemistry, and physics. The 1991 volume separates physical science and chemistry into two sections, and its 80 experiments are intended for grades 3–12.

Both volumes are otherwise identical in format. Within each section, the experiments proceed from the simple to the more complex. Experiments are complete and self-contained, listing topic, introduction, time and materials needed, safety precautions, procedure, and analysis. Nearly all materials needed can be found in the home or inexpensively purchased. Some require equipment found in school labs. Appendixes identify experiments by grade level, appropriateness for home or school, time needed (less or more than one hour), whether adult supervision is required, and whether an experiment can be done alone or with a partner or group. An appendix also lists expected findings or results for each experiment, so a student can compare results after completing the experiment. Master teachers (named by the National Science Foundation for excellence in teaching science) submitted the experiments, and a panel of teachers selected those published and suggested editorial changes.

NATURAL HISTORY (508)

Natural history encompasses all the natural sciences: environmental, atmospheric, geologic, biologic, ecologic—all the scientific studies that delve into the living and natural world from deep within the earth to beyond the solar system.

Cambridge Illustrated Dictionary of Natural History
Lincoln, R. J., and Boxshall, G. A. New York: Cambridge University Press, 1987.

Intending to address the needs of a popular audience whose interest has been stimulated by television nature shows, this book successfully straddles the scientific and the popular need. Scientific and technical terms may complicate understanding for the amateur, yet definitions strive for brevity while adequately conveying the meaning of a term. Plant and animal definitions are found under their Latin names, with cross-references from popular names. More than 700 line illustrations supplement definitions and help readers visualize "small, rare forms" of life, according to the Preface. "The major taxonomic groups of all living organisms . . . are included down to the level of order. For flowering plants, vertebrate animals and the economically more important insect groups, the coverage extends . . . to include families," the Preface states.

Compton's Dictionary of the Natural Sciences
Ford, Charles A., ed. Chicago: Compton, 1966. 2 vols. Incl. index.
This title retains its usefulness after 30 years due to its simple, understandable language and emphasis on plants, animals, and insects. Scientific and Latin names are given with cross-references in the index. Terms from 11 relevant scientific fields are included, and the work provides "broad coverage of the natural sciences as a whole." In the main text, 2,360 articles identify, define, describe, and illustrate terms from the life and earth sciences, according to *Booklist* (July 15, 1996). Alphabetically arranged and illustrated, this is a work of continued value to students and nonspecialists.

World Nature Encyclopedia
Milwaukee: Raintree Publishers, 1989. 24 vols. Incl. Index.
Students from fifth grade up will benefit from this encyclopedia of the world's ecosystems. Oceans, mountains, deserts, savannas, jungles, rain forests, and continental zones are clearly discussed with attention paid to the plants and animals and their habitats within each zone. Numerous charts, maps, and color illustrations complement the text. Each volume includes an index with a master index to the entire set provided. Common and scientific names of plants and animals are given. A glossary explains scientific terms, which are also explained in the text. Students will find this set useful for reports on plants, animals, and geographic and ecological topics.

Natural History Magazines

Natural History
New York: American Museum of Natural History, 1900– .
This monthly "takes a popular approach to specialized subjects," according to Katz's *Magazines for Libraries.* Loaded with beautiful photographs, it "contains authoritative articles in the biological, natural, and earth sciences as well as reports in cultural and physical anthropology." Indexed by *Reader's Guide to Periodical Literature* and InfoTrac's *Magazine Index.*

Nature
London: Macmillan Magazines Ltd., 1869– .
Indexed by *Biology Abstracts* and *Chemical Abstracts,* "*Nature* is

an international journal covering all the sciences." It publishes original research and reports of scientific breakthroughs. It is truly one of the major scientific magazines.

CHRONOLOGIES (509)

Asimov's Chronology of Science and Discovery
Asimov, Isaac. New York: HarperCollins, 1994. Rev. ed.
This book details scientific, medical, and technical discoveries and achievements in a year-by-year format from when humans first stood on two feet (bipedality) to 1988 (first ed.) and to 1993 (rev. ed.). It places events in historical context. Students will appreciate the readable prose by prolific writer Isaac Asimov, himself a scientist and science fiction author.

A Chronology of the History of Science, 1450–1900
Gasgoigne, Robert. New York: Garland, 1987. Incl. index.
Gasgoigne's book differs from similar titles like *Breakthroughs: a Chronology of Great Achievements in Science and Mathematics 1200–1930,* by Claire L. Parkinson (Boston: G. K. Hall, 1985), because Gasgoigne divides his book into two parts, the first describing the "cognitive dimension," the second its "social dimension." The cognitive, he says in his introduction, "deals with discoveries and new ideas and theories, and in general with the growth of scientific knowledge. . . . The social history of science . . . is concerned with persons—the many scientists who, over the centuries, have built up the great edifice of scientific knowledge." He describes their impact on the development of the "scientific community which began to take shape after the introduction of printing in the fifteenth century, and through the following centuries gradually increased in cohesion and internal organization as well as in size."

The Timetables of Science: A Chronology of the Most Important People and Events of the History of Science
Hellemans, Alexander, and Bunch, Bryan. New York: Simon & Schuster, 1988.
This work presents chronologic tables recording major events, discoveries, and inventions to 1988 organized under subject headings for major scientific disciplines. The tables make it easy to compare simultaneous events on the same page, but difficult to provide much information about each event.

SCIENTIFIC BIOGRAPHY (509.2)

Asimov's Biographical Encyclopedia of Science and Technology
Garden City, New York: Doubleday, 1982. 2d rev. ed.

Popularly written, as are most of Asimov's other works, this volume covers 1,510 significant figures from all periods arranged chronologically. Biographies of 150 modern scientists were added to this edition. Entries vary in length from a long paragraph to a couple of pages for an important scientist. Brief, valuable discussions.

Blacks in Science and Medicine
Sammons, Vivian Ovelton. New York: Hemisphere Pub. Corp., 1990. Incl. bibliography and index.

A list of 1,500 individuals in alphabetical order, in a Who's Who style, listing basic birth, death, and other pertinent information (e.g., schools attended, degrees, awards, accomplishments). Unfortunately, there's barely any descriptive narrative. Biographical references, often several, are provided. A large bibliography and thorough index (with headings such as Inventions, Inventors, Mathematicians) help researchers greatly.

Dictionary of Scientific Biography
Gillispie, Charles Coulston, ed. New York: Charles Scribner's Sons, 1970–1980. 16 vols.

This set should be a researcher's first stop because of its thorough coverage throughout time, its excellent index, which references more than the main biographical entry but also mentions the scientist or his or her work throughout the set, and because it usually provides two or more pages on each scientist (more depending on the significance of the person's accomplishments). The lengthy narratives are extremely useful. In some cases, this source provides the first biographical information published. International in scope and covering all history, this work omits living scientists and for the most part excludes figures who worked in technology, medicine, behavioral sciences, or philosophy. It emphasizes scientists in astronomy, biology, chemistry, earth sciences, mathematics, and physics, and provides indexes and bibliographies. Supplemental volumes for this set are issued at undetermined intervals.

Distinguished African American Scientists of the 20th Century
Kidd, Renee A., et al. Phoenix, AZ: Oryx, 1995.

Good for middle and high school students is this volume, which discusses the lives and contributions of 100 African American scientists, medical workers, and mathematicians. About 20 are women. Many are alive and working, and information about them is not readily available elsewhere. In addition to vital statistics and three to five pages of narrative, a black and white photograph of each subject is reproduced. Vocabulary control aims to the middle school student, but the older reader will value the information (*Booklist,* February 15, 1996).

Larousse Dictionary of Scientists
Muir, Hazel, ed. Edinburgh, Scotland; New York: Larousse, 1994.
Alphabetically arranged, *Larousse* aims for comprehensive international coverage of 2,200 scientists "from the pioneers of science to the innovators of modern research." It emphasizes the natural sciences, with a healthy sampling of mathematicians included. Numerous living scientists are listed.

Women in Science: Antiquity Through the Nineteenth Century
Ogilvie, Marilyn Bailey. Cambridge, MA: MIT Press, 1986. Incl. bibliographic references and index.
This volume describes the lives and accomplishments of nearly 200 women scientists, alphabetically arranged. Subjects selected for inclusion were born before 1885, with their important contributions made before 1910. Entries vary in length, depending on the significance of contributions and/or amount of information discovered. Thorough bibliographic information is provided, along with a name chart listing time period, field, and nationality.

MATHEMATICS (510)

Biographical Dictionary of Mathematicians: Reference Biographies from the Dictionary of Scientific Biography
New York: Scribner, 1991. 4 vols. Incl. indexes.
A subject outtake from the finest source of scientific biography, this set provides 1,023 essays on mathematicians and a few outside the profession who made significant contributions to it.

Everyday Math Made Simple
Davidson, Peter. New York: McGraw-Hill, 1984.
A great review source for middle school and high school students, this book applies basic math, percentages, and other calculations to everyday situations. Real estate, budget and investments, energy consumption, building and decorating, measurements, and conversions are discussed in individual chapters. Calculating loan payments, the amount of paint needed for a room, and the kilowatt usage for an appliance are examples of the mysteries the author clarifies.

Mathematics Dictionary
James, Glenn, and James, Robert C. New York: Van Nostrand Reinhold, 1992. 5th ed.

This title fulfills the needs of the more advanced "students, scientists, engineers, and others interested in the meaning of mathematical terms and concepts," according to the Preface. Includes brief biographies.

Prentice-Hall Encyclopedia of Mathematics
West, Beverly H., et al. Englewood, NJ: Prentice-Hall, 1982. Incl. bibliographic references and index.

This excellent compilation of explanatory material on every specific aspect of mathematics is written for high school and college students. It's written by one high school and three college teachers in a readable and interesting style. It's organized under 80 broad topics, such as algebra, probability, and rational and irrational numbers, and provides formulas, definitions, and applications, demonstrates mathematical principles, and provides some history and background. It uses examples from everyday life throughout, and it is well illustrated and cross-referenced, showing the relationship of one mathematical discipline to another. A biographical index connects the user with information on about 200 mathematicians. Appendixes provide the necessary charts and tables.

ASTRONOMY (520)

Atlas of the Universe
Moore, Patrick. New York: Rand McNally, 1994.

More for the amateur than the serious student of astronomy, this volume begins with a short history of the exploration of the universe. It's strong on explanation; heavily illustrated with photographs, charts, graphs, and star maps; and discusses astronomy, space research, cosmology, the planets, solar system, stars, and galaxies. Popularly written, it's perfect for high school students.

Burnham's Celestial Handbook
Burnham, Robert. New York: Dover, 1978. Rev. and enl. 3 vols. Incl. index.

This title is "unsurpassed in value as an adjunct to astronomical texts and atlases," according to a review in *Sky and Telescope* (December 1983). It provides detail for sky objects beyond our solar system to a depth in space reachable by 12-inch telescopes. Burnham "gives lengthy descriptions and data for thousands of objects . . . along with facts, theories and principles associated with them," according to reviewer George Lovi.

A Field Guide to the Stars and Planets
Menzel, Donald H. Boston: Houghton Mifflin, 1983. Rev. ed.

An easy-to-use identification manual for the uninitiated using the naked eye, binoculars, or telescope. New star charts by the renowned Wil Tirion improved this revised edition significantly. The book provides background and history and teaches how to follow from one sky object to another.

The International Encyclopedia of Astronomy
Moore, Patrick, ed. New York: Orion Books, 1987.

The *Booklist* reviewer preferred this title to the previous one as "larger (464 pages to 199), more authoritative, easier to comprehend, and nearly as current." More than 2,500 articles, alphabetically arranged, are well illustrated with charts, diagrams, and photographs. Biographies often include portraits. Seven major essays provide a general introduction and cover the big bang theory, space exploration, interstellar matter, moons of the solar system, pulsars, and superclusters, according to *Wilson Library Bulletin*, (December 1987). *Guide to Reference Books* calls it "useful as a general reference to both historic and contemporary developments in astronomy and astrophysics." Written for a broad audience, this volume should be useful for students from high school through college and should be found in public libraries.

Isaac Asimov's Guide to Earth and Space
Asimov, Isaac. New York: Random House, 1991.

Another of Asimov's popularly written science guides, this one covers the solar system and the objects in it, ancient history and new discoveries, and the universe in general. It does this through two- and three-page chapters, each answering a question, such as "What Are Stars?" and "How Old Is the Universe?"

McGraw-Hill Encyclopedia of Astronomy
Parker, Sybil and Jay Pasachoff, eds. New York: McGraw-Hill, 1993. 2d ed. Incl. bibliographies and index.

Pertinent articles on astronomy have been taken from the parent *McGraw-Hill Encyclopedia of Science and Technology* for this volume. The text is complete, updated somewhat, and written to the level of the serious undergraduate. The topical articles are easier to locate and use in this subject volume rather than in the larger 20-volume set.

Oxford Illustrated Encyclopedia of the Universe
Roy, Archie, ed. New York: Oxford University Press, 1993.

Excellent color photographs and diagrams enhance the value of this encyclopedia. First published in Great Britain in 1992, the "contents emphasize biography, history, observatories and general astronomy," according to *Booklist* (December 1, 1993). Good cross-references from common terms to technical terms and from specific to general terms.

Space Almanac
Curtis, Anthony R., ed. Houston: Gulf Publishing, 1992. 2d ed. Incl. index.

This volume collects all the basic facts about space exploration—its history and science bringing readers up to fall 1991. It claims "thousands of facts, figures, names, dates, and places that cover space from earth to the edge of the universe." Chapter headings indicate coverage: Astronauts and Cosmonauts; Space Stations; Space Shuttles; Space Rockets; Space Satellites; Solar System; Deep Space. The book includes a complete list of astronauts, cosmonauts, space flights, and even a description of the development of spaceship toilets. Details of planetary exploration and the scientific results are listed.

Astronomy Magazines

Astronomy
Milwaukee, WI: Kalmbach Publishing, 1973– .

Indexed by most general periodical indexes including *InfoTrac* and *Reader's Guide to Periodical Literature*, as well as by science and astronomical indexes, *Astronomy* has the highest circulation in the field. It's readable and contains articles of interest to high school and college students, hobbyists, and general readers. Visual attractiveness, use of color and superb photography, clear detail on the sky map, and sky almanac plus informative, well-written articles and news, and hobby features make this one of two major stops for students needing information on sky science.

Sky and Telescope
Belmont, MA: Sky Publishing, 1941– .

The other major stop for students, this magazine tends to be a bit more technical, geared more to serious sky students and professional astronomers. The title provides long features developments on sky science, and it publishes sky maps and "descriptions of astronomical objects to observe in the coming month," according to *Magazines for Libraries*.

Sky Calendar
Victor, Robert C. East Lansing, MI: Abrams Planetarium. Michigan State University, 1968–   .

Published quarterly, this is an inexpensive publication for dedicated sky observers. It provides sky maps for the coming three or four months. It locates constellations, star clusters, nebulae, galaxies, and planets, and gives a brief description of the month's important events. A great tool for student enthusiasts and teachers.

PHYSICS (530)

Encyclopedia of Physics
Lerner, Rita G., and Trigg, George L., eds. New York: VCH, 1991. 2d ed. Incl. bibliographies and index.

Alphabetically arranged, this source is comprehensive yet introductory. While written at an advanced undergraduate level, it still may find use among high school students. It covers every branch of physics, as well as newer topics like superconductivity. Articles range in length from 1 page to 20 pages and are written by recognized authorities in the field, including several Nobel laureates.

Magill's Survey of Science, Physical Science Series
Magill, Frank, ed. Pasadena, CA: Salem Press, 1992. 6 vols. Incl. bibliographies and indexes.

This set covers mathematics, physics, physical chemistry, computational sciences, astronomy, and astrophysics. While intended for a general audience by providing solid background and presentation of up-to-date research, upper-level high school and college undergraduates will benefit most from this series. Essays of about seven pages in length discuss background, related fields of study, context, summary, and practical applications and include a glossary and annotated bibliography.

McGraw-Hill Dictionary of Physics
Parker, Sybil P., ed. New York: McGraw-Hill, 1985.

The work defines 11,200 terms taken from the *McGraw-Hill Dictionary of Scientific and Technical Terms*. Terms from the classical areas of physics (acoustic, electricity, mechanics) and the newer fields of particle physics, quantum mechanics, and solid state physics are given. Definitions vary in length and complexity, with abbreviations indicating in which specific field the term is commonly used. Numerous cross-references help locate definitions.

McGraw-Hill Encyclopedia of Physics
Parker, Sybil P., ed. New York: McGraw-Hill, 1993. 2d ed. Incl. index.

An outtake of 828 articles from the parent *McGraw-Hill Encyclopedia of Science and Technology,* this volume, according to the first edition, "focuses on those subjects concerned with physics' original aim of understanding the structure of the natural world and explaining natural phenomena." It is intended to answer questions pertaining to "all major branches of physics, including acoustics, atomic physics, particle physics, molecular physics, nuclear physics, classical mechanics, electricity, electromagnetism, fluid mechanics, heat and thermodynamics, low-temperature physics, optics, relativity, and solid-state physics." It's authoritative, up-to-date, thoroughly illustrated, and written in a narrative style with a minimum of mathematical detail, according to *American Reference Books Annual.* Like its parent, the text is demanding, written for advanced college undergraduates.

A Physicist's Desk Reference
Anderson, Herbert L., ed. New York: American Institute of Physics, 1989.

Tables, references, formulas, fundamental constants, units, and conversion factors are provided in 22 chapters.

Physics Abstracts
Piscataway, NJ: Institute of Electrical and Electronics Engineers, 1898– . Updated biweekly.

This comprehensive index abstracts 142,000 articles, covering all aspects of physics from all over the world. Other than periodicals, it also covers books, dissertations, and conference papers. The standard in its field, it is found primarily in college and corporate libraries and is most useful to professional and serious students.

CHEMISTRY (540)

Chemical Abstracts
Columbus, OH: American Chemical Society. 1907– . Weekly.

This service abstracts 14,000 scientific and technical periodicals published in 150 countries. It tracks patents, proceedings of conferences, dissertations, government reports, and books, according to Katz's *Magazines for Libraries.* Abstracts are organized into 80 subject sections, spread among five basic groupings: biochemistry, organic chemistry, macromolecular chemistry, applied chemistry and chemical engineering, and physical, inorganic, and analytical chemistry. This excellent resource, available in many formats, is found primarily in college and corporate libraries and is most useful for professional and serious students.

Concise Encyclopedia Chemistry
Eagleson, Mary, tr. and ed. Berlin, NY: W. de Gruyler, 1994.
Clearly written and useful, this 1,201-page volume contains a lot of information on elements, compounds, chemical concepts, experimental techniques and hazards. No bibliographic references. (See also *Magill's Survey of Science, Physical Science Series,* p. 210.)

CRC Handbook of Chemistry and Physics: A Ready-Reference Book of Chemical and Physical Data
Lide, David R., and Frederikse, H.P.R., eds. Boca Raton, FL: CRC Press, 1994. 75th ed. Incl. bibliographic references and index.
A constant source of referral for scientists and engineers, this compendium of tables, formulas, constants, elements, compounds, and laboratory information emphasizes commonly used properties. Published for nearly 80 years, it is regularly updated. At 2,500 pages, it provides added value by complementing other data sources and refers to other collections.

Great Chemists
Farber, Eduard. New York: Interscience, 1961. Incl. bibliographies.
Essays about the lives of more than 100 important chemists from ancient times to the twentieth century collected for this volume from the writings of scholars since the 1800s.

A Guide to the Elements
Stwertka, Albert. New York: Oxford University Press, 1996, Incl. bibliography and index.
A great source for students having to write brief papers on chemical elements. It opens with the periodic table and an essay that explains the atom, radioactivity, and isotopes. Two-page explanations of each element are provided, along with atomic number, chemical symbol, and group, and a photo illustrating the element in use. Includes a glossary and chronology.

Hawley's Condensed Chemical Dictionary
Lewis, Richard J., Sr., ed. New York: Van Nostrand Reinhold, 1993. 12th ed.
This volume concisely defines chemical terms. It "describes industrial and scientific chemicals, terms, processes, reactions, and related terminology, and phenomena," according to the *New York Public Library Book of How and Where to Look It Up.* "Charts chemical struc-

tures, gives uses and trademarked products that employ these chemicals. Some emphasis is on environment and energy sources." Brief biographies of notable chemists are included. Appendixes provide the origins of chemical names and list significant events in the history of chemistry.

McGraw-Hill Dictionary of Chemistry
Parker, Sybil P., ed. New York: McGraw-Hill, 1993. 2d ed.
An outtake from the parent *McGraw-Hill Dictionary of Scientific and Technical Terms,* which can be used instead.

McGraw-Hill Encyclopedia of Chemistry
Parker, Sybil, ed. New York: McGraw-Hill, 1993. 2d ed. Incl. bibliographic references and index.
Mainly drawn from *McGraw-Hill Encyclopedia of Science and Technology,* some topics in this comprehensive text have been updated. Coverage includes some areas of physics that pertain to chemistry. Diagrams and structural formulas are used liberally. Valuable to those with some chemistry background.

Women in Chemistry and Physics: A Biobibliographic Sourcebook
Grinstein, Louise S., Rose, Rose K., and Rafailovich, Miriam H., eds. Westport, CT: Greenwood, 1993. Incl. index.
This book provides biographic information on 75 women over three centuries, all deceased or born before 1933. Personal history, scientific contributions, and a bibliography of publications are given for each woman in about five pages. Arrangement is alphabetical, with additional access provided through appended lists of subjects by date, place of birth, and scientific field of interest.

MINERALOGY (549)

The Encyclopedia of Gemstones and Minerals
Holden, Martin. New York: Facts on File, 1991. Incl. bibliography and index.
Designed for student use rather than a field guide for the collector or a compendium for the specialist, this book identifies rocks, minerals, and gems; describes their uses, where they can be found and processes involved in extracting them; and relates them to geologic processes, formations and time periods and to chemical elements, properties and compounds. The alphabetic arrangement of 225 entries from "actinolite" to "zircon" suits student study. According to *Booklist* (March 15, 1992), "Highlighted information includes classification, composition, crystal system, hardness, and specific gravity. Within the text can be found

the description of physical properties, where the mineral occurs in the world, how it forms, its uses and values, and simulated and synthetic forms and how to recognize them." Superb color photographs accompany the text. An appendix provides a map of mineral deposits and mining areas around the world and a time line of geologic periods. This 303-page book should be found in most libraries.

Mineral Resources A–Z
Hillside, NJ: Enslow, 1991. Incl. bibliography.
　　This book, geared to middle and high school students, defines 300 terms, with an emphasis on commercial use. "Seismic prospecting" is included because it is used to locate oil, "nickel" because it is used to produce stainless steel.

EARTH SCIENCES: GEOLOGY, METEOROLOGY (WEATHER), HYDROLOGY (WATER) (550)

Audubon Society Field Guide to North American Weather
Ludlum, David M. New York: Knopf, 1991.
　　This book provides a lot of information for middle and high school students, making it an excellent resource. The opening essay explains in depth basic weather phenomena (clouds, snowstorms, floods, etc.) in readable text. Photographs, charts, diagrams, maps, and illustrations comprise half the book. "The third section gives description, environment, season, range, and significance of each type of weather," according to *School Library Journal* (March 1992). A glossary is also included.

Climatological Data
Publishing body varies. 1914–
　　Monthly summaries of government-compiled weather statistics from every state and designated areas.

Dictionary of Global Climate Change
Maunder, John W., comp. New York: Routledge, Chapman & Hall, 1992.
　　A small one-volume encyclopedia that reports climactic studies for both general readers and researchers. An "'informed perspective on environmental matters of profound importance to us all,' summarizes its purpose," according to *American Reference Books Annual 1994*. It covers "volcanic eruptions and their effects, chlorofluorocarbons, ozone, methane, the carbon cycle, sunspots, the pH scale, and the `slow climate system: oceans and glaciers.'"

Encyclopedia of Earthquakes and Volcanoes
Ritchie, David. New York: Facts on File, 1994. Incl. bibliography and index.

Volcanoes, eruptions, earthquakes and faults, geological terms and concepts, and a few short biographies are alphabetically arranged in this volume suitable for middle school students and up. Maps, diagrams, and photographs enhance the text. A chronology lists earthquakes and eruptions from 1470 B.C. to December 10, 1992. Entries provide date and place, casualties, and Richter scale measurements if available. This book also describes the geology of the event, which increases the reader's understanding significantly.

A Field Guide to the Atmosphere
Shaefer, Vincent J., and Day, John A. Boston: Houghton Mifflin, 1981. A Peterson Field Guide.

Middle school and high school students will find this useful. Studied, discussed, and interpreted are atmospheric phenomena such as clouds, rainbows, pollution, particles, storms, hailstones, dust, fog, haze, and snow. Numeric data are tabulated or graphed. Fifteen simple experiments are outlined, and tips on photographing atmospheric events are provided. The books includes a glossary and 358 photographs of interesting and unusual atmospheric phenomena.

Macmillan Encyclopedia of Earth Sciences
Dasch, E. Julius, ed. New York: Macmillan, 1996. 2 vols. Incl. bibliography and index.

Essays in this set attempt to cover the sciences of the earth, oceans, and the atmosphere, plus biological science and the solar system. Fifty short biographies of notable scientists in the field are included.

Magill's Survey of Science, Earth Science Series
Magill, Frank N., ed. Pasadena, CA: Salem Press, 1990. 5 vols. Incl.bibliographies and index.

This entry in the Magill's series covers geology, oceanography, meteorology, astronomy, geophysics, geochemistry, paleontology, hydrology, seismology and soil science, and environmental issues. (These topics are also known as oceans, weather, climate, water, earthquakes, and so on.) The text is aimed at the college undergraduate level. The book contains 377 well-written articles that explore these topics in about seven pages each. The set provides a thorough study and overview of the sciences listed. Reviewers noted some weaknesses in the indexes, such as the omission of "ozone" without a cross reference to "atmospheric ozone."

McGraw-Hill Dictionary of Earth Sciences
Parker, Sybil, ed. New York: McGraw-Hill, 1984.

The Guide to Reference Books, 11th ed., finds this dictionary of value to secondary school students and general readers. It briefly defines 15,000 terms from 18 disciplines within earth sciences. Terms are drawn from the parent *McGraw-Hill Dictionary of Scientific and Technical Terms*. Though it lacks illustrations, *Booklist* (January 15, 1985) says this dictionary is "very practical" for those "desiring short, clear and succinct definitions of terms in the literature of earth sciences."

McGraw-Hill Encyclopedia of the Geological Sciences
Parker, Sybil, ed. New York: McGraw-Hill, 1988. 2d ed. Inc. bibliographies and index.

This source provides a comprehensive look at all aspects of geology and the earth sciences in 520 articles. The book follows the same standard as other titles in this series; all are drawn from the parent *McGraw-Hill Encyclopedia of Science and Technology* and are written by experts in the field, with numerous illustrations, charts, tables, and so on provided. The text is aimed at an educated audience—serious high school students and above.

McGraw-Hill Encyclopedia of Ocean and Atmospheric Sciences
Parker, Sybil, ed. New York: McGraw-Hill, 1980. Incl. bibliographies and index.

Another spin-off from the parent *McGraw-Hill Encyclopedia of Science and Technology*, this volume offers 236 alphabetically arranged articles aimed at general readers, but as with the parent volume, upper-level educational background will aid understanding. Coverage includes "the marine and atmospheric aspects of geology, chemistry, biology, weather, energy ar l other topics," according to *Wilson Library Bulletin* (March 1980). Five hundred illustrations enliven the text.

Standard Encyclopedia of the World's Mountains
Huxley, Anthony J. New York: Putnam, 1962.

Standard Encyclopedia of the World's Oceans and Islands
Huxley, Anthony J. New York: Putnam, 1962.

Standard Encyclopedia of the World's Rivers and Lakes
Gresswell, R. Kay, and Huxley, Anthony J. New York: Putnam, 1965.

Each of these companion volumes is arranged alphabetically and describes each earth feature by name, size, location, and history. Text descriptions are written in popular style. The books include illustrations, photographs, maps, and indexes.

The Times Atlas and Encyclopedia of the Sea
Couper, Alastair, ed. New York: Harper & Row, 1989. 2d ed. Incl. bibliography and index.
This volume examines the world's oceans from the perspectives of natural resources, their commercial use, geography, and environmental condition. It includes photographs, charts, tables, and maps.

Times Books World Weather Guide
Pearce, E. A., and Smith, Gordon. New York: Times Books, 1990. Upd. ed. Incl. geographic index.
Seasonal weather conditions for 500 cities worldwide are provided in this 480-page resource. Arrangement is by continent, nation, and city, providing an overview of the country's climate, followed by tables of data (precipitation, temperature, humidity, etc.) for the cities. Introductory matter explains weather phenomena, charts outline data such as the wind-chill index, and a glossary defines terms.

Weather Almanac
Bair, Frank E., ed. Detroit: Gale, 1992. 6th ed. Incl. index.
This valuable resource for students and laypeople provides 30 years of month-by-month statistical data, such as precipitation and temperature, for 109 U.S. cities. Similar but older data are provided for 550 worldwide locations. Weather phenomena are explained, as are environmental concerns (e.g., global warming) and related events such as earthquakes and volcanic activity. The book discusses the effects of changing climate on agriculture, economics, and health. It gives background on the National Weather Service and describes the equipment it uses.

PALEONTOLOGY (FOSSILS, DINOSAURS) (560)

The Dinosaur Society's Dinosaur Encyclopedia
Lessem, Don, and Glut, Donald F. New York: Random House, 1993. Incl. index.
Wilson Library Bulletin called it "the best popular dictionary of dinosaurs available today." *Booklist* called it "an important contribution to dinosauria literature." It's suitable for both fifth graders and adults. It identifies in 533 pages more than 600 species of known dinosaurs. They're arranged alphabetically by genus, and for each the book provides pronunciation, species, order, suborder, family, name origin, size, period, place, diet, and often year of discovery. Explanatory text

and 400 drawings complement it. There are a geological time line and a discussion of the classification of dinosaurs. The authors seeks to dispel myths about dinosaurs and to contradict misleading information. Definitely the first stop for dinosaur projects.

Macmillan Illustrated Encyclopedia of Dinosaurs and Prehistoric Animals: A Visual Who's Who of Prehistoric Life
Dixon, Dougal, et al. New York: Macmillan, 1988. Incl. bibliography and index.

This resource, suitable for general readers and students, profiles over 600 species of dinosaurs and other prehistoric animals. Each is depicted with a color illustration. Included are prehistoric fish, birds, reptiles, and mammals. How each animal moved and behaved and what it ate are described. Comparison are made with today's animals. The text discusses fossilization, the discovery of fossils, and how scientists interpret them, along with changes in the earth over time. An evolution chart for each type of animal is also provided.

Simon and Schuster's Guide to Fossils
Arduini, Paolo, and Teruzzi, Giogio. New York: Simon & Schuster, 1986.

This guide describes 260 genera of plant and animal fossils and provides locations of where they can be found. Well illustrated with color photographs, *Library Journal* (June 1, 1987) said, "The book is interesting and attractive." It also said, "The genera used here are only representatives of a group and the information is of a very general nature. . . . More than is offered here is needed to really identify almost any of the organisms mentioned." *Best Science and Technology Reference Books for Young People,* however, called it "an excellent field guide to identifying collecting fossils."

LIFE SCIENCES (HUMANS, ANTHROPOLOGY, BIOLOGY) (570)

The Biographical Dictionary of Scientists: Biologists
Abbott, David, ed. New York: Peter Bedrick Books, 1983. Incl. index.

This 182-page source covers about 180 significant biologists from ancient times to the present. Biographies, arranged alphabetically, are one page in length, clear and informative, and include black and white photos. The text concentrates on the scientist's work and its significance. The opening chapters review the history of the science. A good source for high schoolers.

Biological Abstracts
Philadelphia: BioSciences Information Service (BIOSIS), 1926–
Semimonthly.

For serious researchers and professionals, this source abstracts 9,200 journals and serial publications worldwide. Coverage is broad, extending into agronomy, biomedicine, horticulture, nutrition, pest control, and veterinary medicine. Access is provided through multiple indexes, and this source is available online, on CD-ROM, and in print. One of the best ways to keep abreast of current research.

Biology Digest
Tailored to the needs and subject interests of high school and college students, this source, available in recent years on full-text CD-ROM, provides lengthy abstracts of articles from over 200 journals—some highly specific and technical, others more general. Broad coverage ranges from natural history, animals, diseases, to environment, ecology, and the human body. An excellent source for students. For more information, see also p. 47.

The Cambridge Encyclopedia of Human Evolution
Jones, Steve, et al., eds. Cambridge: Cambridge University Press, 1992. Incl. bibliography and index.

Library Journal (June 1, 1993) calls this "unquestionably the best reference work dedicated to human evolution yet published." The reviewer (Eric Hinsdale) thought the book "an absolutely essential source for all libraries." *Booklist*, more reserved, thought the book more appropriate for college and research libraries. Both seemed to agree this title surpasses immediate rivals: Richard Milner's *Encyclopedia of Evolution: Humanity's Search for Its Origins* (Facts on File, 1990. "Too quirky," said Hinsdale.) and *Encyclopedia of Human Evolution and Prehistory* (Garland, 1988. "Solid, if comparatively unspectacular," Hinsdale said). Both of these are arranged alphabetically, while this title, arranged into ten thematic sections, such as "Patterns of Primate Evolution," "The Primate Fossil Record," and "Human Populations, Past and Present," reads more like a textbook. Well illustrated with photographs, drawings, and graphs, a thorough index to text, and captions overcome the organization and make the source easy to use. Liberal cross-references and a glossary also help. An excellent resource for students wishing to trace human development from primates to the present and to determine the distinct and distinguishing elements that make us human.

Encyclopedia of Human Biology
Dulbecco, Renato, ed. San Diego, CA: Academic Press, 1991. 8 vols. Incl. bibliographies and indexes.

The source on the topic but probably available only in college and large public libraries due to its high cost ($1,950). Written primarily for students, researchers, and practitioners, readability of its 600 articles varies. This master reference discusses topics of broad relation, such as the history of addiction in the United States, dreaming, and reading comprehension, as well as body systems and diseases. Coverage includes anthropology, behavior, biochemistry, biophysics, cytology, ecology, evolution, genetics, immunology, neurosciences, pharmacology, physiology, and toxicology. Thoroughly up-to-date, it presents the latest research accessible through a master index and an index of related articles. Information on hard-to-research topics, such as space flight health care, are readily found here. This source provides invaluable assistance to student researchers.

Grzimek's Encyclopedia of Evolution
Grzimek, Bernhard, ed. New York: Van Nostrand Reinhold, 1976. Incl. bibliography and index.

Twenty-three essays, translated from the 1972 German edition, discuss human evolution, evolutionary theory, the origin of life and history of the earth, paleontology, paleobotany, paleogeology, genetics, and the origin of mammals. Grzimek's reputation for detail and scientific accuracy ensures the lasting value of this title. Illustrated with many color photographs, charts, and drawings and black and white line drawings.

Henderson's Dictionary of Biological Terms
Lawrence, Eleanor. New York: Wiley, 1989. 10th ed.

This, with 22,000 definitions, is the most complete dictionary in the field.

Life Sciences on File
Diagram Group. New York: Facts on File, 1986.

Reproducible drawings of plant, animal, and biologic structures.

Magill's Survey of Science, Life Sciences Series
Magill, Frank, ed. Pasadena, CA: Salem Press, 1991. 6 vols. Incl. bibliographies and indexes.

Intended for general readers, this survey, covering biology, genetics, ecology, biochemistry, and evolution, as well as plant and animal anatomy and physiology and cell biology, is best understood with some background coursework in biology. The 370 articles are arranged alphabetically and composed in a standard format of about seven pages, including a glossary, summary, related fields of study, background information, and an annotated bibliography. A serious drawback is a lack of illustrations. High school students will benefit from this set.

The World of the Cell
Becker, Wayne M., et al., eds. Menlo Park, CA: Benjamin/ Cummings, 1996. 3d ed. Incl. bibliographical references and index.

Though a college-level textbook, this source explains everything about cell biology and includes many color and black and white photographs and illustrations. Emphasis is not only on what is known about cells, but on how it was learned.

ECOLOGY (574.5)

The Dictionary of Ecology and Environmental Science
Art, Henry W., ed. New York: Holt, 1993.

Eight thousand terms are defined succinctly in this 632-page reference. Many come from environmental biology, chemistry, geology, and physics, making background in these fields helpful to the user. The book aims to provide "a complete collection of all the terms and key ideas that are central to understanding the environment," with students and professionals the intended audience. There are few illustrations, but they are helpful. No index.

The Encyclopedia of the Environment
Eblen, Ruth A., and Eblen, William R., eds. Boston: Houghton Mifflin, 1994. Incl. bibliographies and index.

Intended to help people make informed decisions, 550 alphabetically arranged entries in this source stress the impact of environmental concerns on human and societal well-being. Articles from acid rain to zoning reflect this concern. The effects of humans on nature are discussed. Articles on the Clean Water Act, Clean Air Act, and other environmental legislation are included. A few biographies, maps, charts, and illustrations are also provided.

Endangered Wildlife of the World
New York: Marshall Cavendish, 1993. 11 vols. Incl. bibliographies and indexes.

This important and attractive resource, designed for students in middle school through high school, provides current status and other information on 1,200 species found on national and international lists of endangered species. Arrangement is alphabetical by common name. Entries are one to three pages in length. Scientific name is provided along with classification and status in the wild (possibly extinct, endangered, threatened, in captivity, or rare). Physical description, behavior, diet, and habitat are discussed, along with reasons that the animal is threatened. Conservation efforts are discussed. Color photographs, illustrations, maps, good indexing, and cross-referencing all add up to a student's dream for such a topic.

Grzimek's Encyclopedia of Ecology
Grzimek, Bernhad, ed. New York: Van Nostrand Reinhold, 1976. Incl. bibliography and index.

A master reference studying the relationship of all life to its environment and of the effects of people on the environment and life. Forty-three experts wrote 33 essays divided into two parts: the environment of animals and the human environment. Part I includes chapters with titles like "The Influence of Temperature and Humidity" and "Acidity and Salinity." Other chapters study adaptations such as camouflage, and the relationships between animals, insects, and plants. Habitats (e.g., steppes and savannas, tropical rain forest, and the ocean) are discussed. In Part II the effects of humans are reviewed with chapters on the waste explosion, air pollution, pesticides and fertilizers, changes in the natural landscape, and the seas. Excellent color plates and black and white line drawings add to the lasting value of this source.

The Official World Wildlife Fund Guide to Endangered Species of North America
Osprey, FL: Beacham Publishing, 1990–   . 4 vols. Incl. bibliography and cumulative index.

Volume 1 in this set describes plants, birds, and insects that are considered threatened or endangered by the Office of Endangered Species. Volume 2 describes mammals, reptiles, amphibians, fish, shellfish, and crustaceans. Volumes 3 and 4 update the original volumes, covering 1989–1991 and 1991–1994, respectively. Species described come from the 50 states and Puerto Rico. A black and white photo is provided for most species and color plates illustrate selected species. Outline maps show the range of each species. Its appearance, habitat, environment, and distribution are described, along with the threats it faces. Conservation efforts and plans are also discussed. An appendix provides geographic access to species. Another lists conservation agencies and other sources of information. A great source for students and those with environmental concerns.

BOTANY (580s)

The Audubon Society Field Guide to North American Wildflowers, Eastern Region
Spellenberg, Richard. New York: Knopf, 1979.

The Audubon Society Field Guide to North American Wildflowers, Western Region
Niering, William A., and Olmstead, Nancy C. New York: Knopf, 1979.
Roughly speaking, "eastern" means east of the Rockies and "western" California through Alaska. Identification is via color, so the hundreds of color photos are useful and important. Six hundred wildflowers are described in each volume, with notes on hundreds of other wildflowers. Great for student field trips and identification projects.

Common Poisonous Plants and Mushrooms of North America
Turner, Nancy J., and Szczawinski, Adam F. Portland, OR: Timber Press, 1991. Incl. bibliography and index.
This source describes 150 of the most common poisonous wild, household, garden, and crop plants and plant products. Toxicity, symptoms, and treatment are included, as are history and use of each plant. Each plant is illustrated with a color photograph in the text.

The Complete Trees of North America: Field Guide and Natural History
Elias, Thomas. New York: Van Nostrand Reinhold, 1980. Incl index.
An excellent and comprehensive source providing detailed descriptions of 652 native and 100 common introduced trees. Range maps are provided. Drawings show leaves, branches, and often spring, summer, and fall appearance.

Concise Oxford Dictionary of Botany
Allaby, Michael, ed. New York: Oxford University Press, 1992.
This title defines 5,000 terms from plant physiology and related sciences. Some entries are brief; others are succinct yet explanatory. About a third "describe taxonomic groups of seeds plants, ferns, algae, mosses and liverworts, and also fungi, bacteria, and slime molds," according to the Preface.

The Encyclopedia of Flowers
Fell, Derek. New York: Smithmark, 1992. Incl. index.

For gardeners, this book is selective, not encyclopedic. Plants were included depending on their impact and availability. It's divided into perennials, annuals, bulbs, shrubs, and small trees. Good color photographs and a hardiness zone map are included.

The Facts on File Dictionary of Botany
Tootill, Elizabeth, ed. New York: Facts on File, 1984.

Three thousand entries define technical terms common to plant science and related sciences such as horticulture. Definitions are aimed at undergraduates but are written simply enough for younger students. Major plants groups are listed and defined.

The Oxford Encyclopedia of Trees of the World
Bayard, Hora, ed. New York: Oxford University Press, 1981. Incl. bibliography and indexes.

Five hundred species are described and illustrated with drawings and color photographs. Leaves, bark, and distinguishing features are depicted. There are chapters on trees of tropical Asia, Africa, and the Americas. Description, distribution, history, characteristics, uses, ecology, cultivation, diseases, and varieties are discussed. An excellent source for going beyond America.

Popular Encyclopedia of Plants
Heywood, Vernon H., ed. New York: Cambridge University Press, 1982. Incl. indexes.

Written for students and general readers, this resource describes 2,000 plants of economic importance to humans, such as food crops, trees, herbs, spices, and medicines. Alphabetically arranged with color illustrations, indexes of common names and scientific names provide quick access. Plant products are discussed in articles, as is the biology of some plant groups.

The Visual Dictionary of Plants
New York: Dorling Kindersley, 1992. Incl. index.

A graphic supplement to the dictionaries listed above, this is more of visual text. Twenty-five topics, such as leaves, plant types, and plant processes, are illustrated on two pages each. Lavish, close-up color photographs and color diagrams with detailed labels make this book most useful for student projects.

ZOOLOGY (MAMMALS, BIRDS, INVERTEBRATES, INSECTS) (590s)

Animal Anatomy on File
Diagram Group. New York: Facts on File, 1990.
Like others in the On File series, this binder holds easily remov-
able looseleaf pages with thousands of line illustrations suitable for
photocopying. Drawings are arranged from simple animals to mammals
and include skeletons, muscle and organs, embryos, stages of development, and so on.

Atlas of Animal Migration
Jarman, Cathy. New York: Crowell, 1972.
This book provides maps and describes migratory routes of many
animals and answers questions about why animals migrate.

A Field Guide to Animal Tracks
Murie, Olaus J. Boston: Houghton Mifflin, 1975. 2d ed.
This interesting and well-illustrated text depicts and describes
tracks, droppings, and marks left on bones and leaves by all kinds of
wild animals.

Grzimek's Animal Life Encyclopedia
Grzimek, Bernhard. New York: Van Nostrand Reinhold,
1972–1975. 13 vols.
A prime source that covers all classes of animal life in separate
volumes. Authoritative, scientific, and well illustrated. "The single
most complete source on the animal kingdom," according to *Reference
Quarterly*.

Illustrated Encyclopedia of Wildlife
Lakeville, CT: Grey Castle Press, 1991. 15 vols. Incl. index.
Thoroughly illustrated with 4,000 color photographs and 1,400
color illustrations, this set is suitable for all age groups. A master index
by common and scientific name and by subject makes access easy. Color-
coded boxes distinguish, for example, animal behavior (yellow) from
endangered species (pink). Numerous maps, charts, and diagrams support the text, which is readable and covers the entire animal kingdom.
Volumes 1–5 cover mammals, 6–8 birds, 9 reptiles and amphibians, 10
fishes, 11–15 invertebrates.

Macmillan Illustrated Animal Encyclopedia
Whitfield, Philip, ed. New York: Macmillan, 1984. Incl. index.
This one-volume source covers mammals, birds, reptiles, amphibi-
ans, and fishes. It provides brief and basic information for thousands of

animals with lots of color illustrations. Access is by common or scientific name. Descriptions give range, habitat, size and physical characteristics, habits and mating behavior, gestation period, size of litter, and weaning period. Excellent background source for students.

The Visual Dictionary of Animals
New York: Dorling Kindersley, 1991. Eyewitness Visual Dictionaries. Incl. index.
Color photographs and illustrations depict animals and their parts, with each part clearly labeled. For example, all the external parts and internal anatomy of a crayfish are given in a two-page spread on crustaceans.

INVERTEBRATES (592)

The Audubon Society Field Guide to North American Seashore Creatures
Meinkoth, Norman A. New York: Random House, 1981.
In this guide, 850 marine invertebrates are depicted and discussed, including sponges, corals, anemones, sea squirts, stars, and urchins. Physical description, habitat, range, and common and scientific names are provided.

INSECTS (595)

The Encyclopedia of Butterflies
Feltwell, John. Englewood Cliffs, NJ: Prentice-Hall, 1993.
This source identifies 1,000 species. Color photographs depict individual butterflies, and the text provides common and scientific name, physical characteristics, range, and other details. Life cycles, biology, migration, conservation, collection, and study are discussed in the opening chapters.

Encyclopedia of Insects
O'Toole, Christopher. New York: Facts on File, 1986. Incl. bibliography and index.
Like other titles by this publisher, quality color photographs and highlight boxes make this source attractive and interesting. Twenty-eight orders of insects are discussed in an engaging writing style, with each group's characteristics and natural history provided. Common name, family name, and scientific name are given. Arachnids (spiders, scorpions, ticks, and lice) are included. An excellent source for habitat, life cycle, and behavior of insect families.

FISH (597)

The Audubon Society Field Guide to North American Fishes, Whales and Dolphins
Boschung, Herbert, et al. New York: Knopf, 1983.

Brief descriptions and photographs of freshwater and marine species found north of Mexico. Descriptions include physical characteristics, range, and habitat.

Encyclopedia of Aquatic Life
Campbell, Andrew, and Bannister, Keith. New York: Facts on File, 1985. Incl. bibliography and index.

This unique one-volume reference covers fish, marine mammals, and invertebrates, especially crustaceans and mollusks. Emphasis is on the best-known animal families, and common names are used as much as possible. Color photographs and illustrations abound. Information provided includes physical description, evolution, reproduction, and behavior. A fine source for students.

Fish
Bailey, Jill. New York: Facts on File, 1990. Encyclopedia of the Animal World Series. Incl. bibliography and index.

Color photographs and illustrations highlight this 96-page volume arranged by species. Two to six pages are given to each species or group of closely related species, with text discussing unique characteristics, physical traits, behavior, feeding habits, general lifestyle, conservation, and relationships with people. Color boxes highlight details of size, distribution, habitat, and so on. Attractive layout, detailed photographs and drawings, and readable text make this suitable for younger students as well as interested adults. Other volumes in the series cover mammals, birds, reptiles and amphibians, insects and spiders, simple animals, pets, and farm animals.

AMPHIBIANS (597.6) AND REPTILES (597.9)

The Encyclopedia of Reptiles and Amphibians
Halliday, Tim R., and Adler, Kraig, eds. New York: Facts on File, 1986. Incl. bibliography and index.

A good source for students, covering all families in each class, with representative species. Excellent illustrations and informative text. Information panels list numbers, distribution, habitat, color, size, reproduction, and longevity.

Reptiles and Amphibians
Cogger, Harold G., and Zweifel, Richard G., eds. New York: Smithmark, 1992. Incl. bibliographic references and index.

In Part I, the opening chapter discusses diversity, body temperature and metabolism, body components, senses, reproduction, and life cycles. Classification, natural history, habitat and adaptations, behavior, and conservation are discussed in subsequent chapters. Part II discusses amphibians and their various orders. Part III discusses reptiles. Color photographs are superb, with many color drawings included. A readable text discusses families, common characteristics, behavior, physical traits, range, and evolution.

BIRDS (598)

Birds of North America
Robbins, Chandler S., and Zim, Herbert S. New York: Golden Press, 1983. Rev. ed. Incl. index.

Comprehensive full-color illustrations make this inexpensive pocket guide popular. It includes brief descriptions of range, habitats and habits, and "sonograms" of songs or calls.

The Encyclopedia of Birds
Perrins, Christopher and Middleton, Alex, eds. New York: Facts on File, 1985. Incl. bibliography and index.

This source describes 180 families and 8,800 species of birds, including physical characteristics, voice, behavior, distribution, habitat, plumage, nests, eggs, and diet. Four hundred color photographs accompany a well-organized, readable, and authoritative text.

The Illustrated Encyclopedia of Birds
Perrins, Christopher, consultant-in-chief. Englewood Cliffs, NJ: Prentice-Hall, 1990.

Subtitled *The Definitive Reference to Birds of the World,* this source lists 9,300 species and describes and illustrates many in a similar manner to *The Encyclopedia of Birds* (the previous entry).

MAMMALS (599)

Grzimek's Encyclopedia of Mammals
New York: McGraw-Hill, 1989. 2d ed. 5 vols. Incl. bibliography and index.

This set provides more information about mammals than *Grzimek's Animal Life Encyclopedia,* covers more species, is more current, yet maintains the same high-quality and readable style. "Entries pro-

vide common and scientific names, size, distinguishing features, reproduction, life cycle, diet, enemies, habitat and behaviors," according to
a review. Though each volume is indexed, a master index is lacking.
This means readers must figure out which volume is likely to list a particular mammal.

Mammals of the World: A Multimedia Encyclopedia
National Geographic, 1990. CD-ROM
More than 200 animals are covered with text, fact boxes, range
maps, 700 photographs, 155 animal sounds, and 45 full-motion video
clips.

Walker's Mammals of the World
Nowak, Ronald M. Baltimore: Johns Hopkins Press, 1991. 2 vols.
5th ed. Incl. bibliographic references and index.
This standard reference, completely revised since its 1983 edition,
provides much information that students require for both little-known
and well-known mammals. In addition to a photograph, "scientific and
common name, number and distribution of species, measurements, physical description, habitat, locomotion, daily and seasonal activity, diet,
population dynamics, home range, social life, reproduction, longevity
and relationships with people," are provided, according to the Preface.

CETACEANS (599.5)

Whales, Dolphins and Porpoises
Harrison, Richard, et al., eds. New York: Facts on File, 1988. Incl.
bibliography.
Clear writing and fine illustrations characterize this source,
which "covers the distribution, ecology, evolution, and kinds of whales
along with their anatomy, adaptations to aquatic environments, reproduction and development, behavior, intelligence, relations with humans in captivity and in the wild, whales in art and in literature," according to *Science Books and Films*.

CHAPTER 17

Sports (796)

Teachers tend to be more interested in the social and historical effects of sports than in what team is winning this year in basketball or football. Issues such as use of anabolic steroids or other drugs in sports, whether a gifted college athlete should complete his or her education or go for the big money in professional sports, gambling and cheating, and sport as one component of a healthy, balanced life or as the only component in a narrow life are worthy of exploration. Determining what sports were played in ancient Greece or during the Middle Ages requires research. Researching the history of the Olympics and tracing the development of Olympic performances over time can be interesting. Teachers may also ask students to research the biography of a favorite or past athletic performer. If you need to do research on sports, go first to the 796 section of the library. There you may find many of the resources profiled in this chapter.

BIBLIOGRAPHY (796.016, 016.796)

The Reader's Catalog
O'Brien, Geoffrey, ed. New York: Reader's Catalog, 1997. 2d ed. Incl. indexes.

This unusual publishing venture is 1,968 pages long and contains descriptions of 40,000 best books in 15 categories and 208 subcategories. It has an index and illustrations, and you can order the books directly from the catalog. The section on sports is 14 pages long.

ENCYCLOPEDIAS AND DICTIONARIES (796.03)

The Encyclopedia of North American Sports History
Hickok, Ralph. New York: Facts on File, 1992. Incl. bibliography
and index.

There is much valuable information for students in this source of
1,600 alphabetically arranged entries that cover major and minor
North American sports; historical items and current concerns, such as
colonial sports, women and blacks in sports, and anabolic steroids; biographies of people of enduring importance in sports; rules, professional
teams, and stadiums, halls of fame and sports museums; major sporting
events and results; and major awards.

The Encyclopedia of Sports
Menke, Frank G. Cranbury, NJ: A. S. Barnes, 1978. 6th rev. ed. Incl.
index.

In 1,125 pages Menke includes 68 major sports in alphabetical order. The section on baseball is 120 pages long and includes a history of
baseball year by year starting in 1800, an executive history, champions,
basic rules, and a section on the Cobb/Ruth rivalry.

Encyclopedia of World Sport: From Ancient Times to the Present
Levinson, David, and Christensen, Karen, eds. Santa Barbara, CA:
ABC-CLIO, 1996. 3 vols. Incl. bibliography and index.

Arranged alphabetically from acrobatics to yachting, this major
new source, covers 300 major and minor sports plus major issues. Emphasis is on history, culture, and the global nature of sport and on sports in
society. A sampling of entries includes cricket, drugs and drug testing,
football (Gaelic), luge, Olympic Games (ancient), skateboarding, and
women's sports. Articles range in length from 500 to 8,000 words. Illustrations add interest and value. Biographies are not included, though
major players are mentioned. Statistics are left to almanacs and other
sources, though records are mentioned, as are overviews of rules, equipment, and playing surfaces.

Guinness Book of Sports Records
Young, Mark, ed. Stamford, CT: Guinness Media, 1997. 18th ed.

Sixty-six chapters cover the major sports plus aviation sports,
equestrian sports, extreme sports, games and pastimes, greyhound racing, martial arts and the Olympics. Action photographs and comments
from athletes are included.

Historical Dictionary of the Modern Olympic Movement
Findling, John E., and Pelle, Kimberly D. Westport, CT: Greenwood, 1996.

Information on the historical context of the modern games; sites and how they are chosen; political influence and occasional confrontations; and many related events, with less stress on the winners and losers. A valuable background for anyone studying the overall story of the Olympic Games. Good photos.

The Language of Sport
Considine, Tom. New York: Facts on File, 1982. Incl. index.

This book looks at baseball, basketball, bowling, boxing, football, golf, ice hockey, soccer, and tennis. It covers history, basic rules, notable people, and firsts; gives definitions with background and anecdotes; and is illustrated.

The 1997 Information Please Sports Almanac
Hassan, John. Boston: Houghton Mifflin, 1997.

This book has it all: college and professional sports, Hall of Fame, ballparks, and arenas. It covers all major sports and athletes, with detailed biographies written by some of America's best sports writers.

Rules of the Game: The Complete Illustrated Encyclopedia of All the Major Sports of the World
New York: Diagram Group/St. Martin's, 1990.

Rules, history, playing area, equipment, and descriptions of players and officials, with 2,000 illustrations.

Social Issues in Contemporary Sports
Wise, Suzanne. Hamden, CT: Garland, 1994.

An annotated bibliography that documents over 2,000 resources, including books, magazine articles, and government documents. Chapters are arranged by subject matter, and entries are alphabetical.

Sports Rules Encyclopedia
White, Jess R., ed. Champagne, IL: Leisure, 1990.

A comprehensive source in one volume of rules for 51 sports, arranged alphabetically, from archery to wrestling. Useful for those administering multiple sports activities, as well as any sports enthusiast needing detailed information on how they are played.

World Sports Record Atlas
Emery, David, and Greenberg, Stan. New York: Facts on File, 1986. Incl. color pictures.

It covers athletics, ball games, winter sports, racing, and other sports.

SPORTS BIOGRAPHY (796.092)

African-American Sports Greats: A Biographical Dictionary
Porter, David L., ed. Westport, CT: Greenwood, 1995.

This is useful in providing the background and current status of all distinguished African American sports figures in alphabetical order, including cross-references for married women athletes.

Biographical Dictionary of American Sports
Porter, David L., ed. Westport, CT: Greenwood, 1987– . Incl. bibliographical references and index.

Volumes in this series cover football, baseball, basketball, and other indoor sports, and outdoor sports. A supplement to these volumes covers 1992–1995. Overall, more than 2,000 sports figures are profiled, often with extensive bibliographies for each. Each volume covers about 500 sports figures. Biographies average a page to a page and a half in length. Entries are arranged alphabetically and include athletes, managers, coaches, officials, owners, and others back to the Revolutionary War, with most living in the twentieth century.

A Hard Road to Glory
Ashe, Arthur. New York: Warner, 1988. 3 vols.

A history of African American athletes told in biographical form.

The Lincoln Library of Sports Champions
Columbus, OH: Frontier Press, 1993. 6th ed. 14 vols.

This set of 14 illustrated volumes contains biographical information on sport stars, arranged alphabetically by athlete's names.

Outstanding Women Athletes: Who They Are and How They Influenced Sports in America
Woolum, Janet. Phoenix, AZ: Oryx, 1992.

Biographies of the leading women in sports, covering how their entry into what was a man's domain has altered and in some cases improved the sports world. With statistics and photographs.

A Who's Who of Sports Champions: Their Stories and Records
Hickok, Ralph. Boston: Houghton Mifflin, 1995. Incl. bibliography and index.

This source includes 2,200 brief (quarter- to half-page) biographies of significant North American athletes. Important coaches and managers are also included, as are major non–North American champions, such as Steffi Graf and Gary Player. Coverage includes 50 sports at all organized levels. Birth and death dates and birthplace are listed, along with major records, awards, and achievements. No illustrations or portraits. Organized alphabetically by name; the index is by sport played.

The Womansport Directory
Stauffer, Kathleen, and Cylkowskil, Gray. Little Canada, MN: Athletic Achievements, 1995. Incl. index.

A complete guide to women athletes in the marketplace. Biographies contain records and news stories, with action photographs.

INDIVIDUAL SPORTS

Baseball (796.357)
The Baseball Encyclopedia
Reichler, Joseph. New York: Macmillan, 1990.

A complete statistical record, chronological listings, alphabetical register of players, pitchers, managers, history, rules, awards, and lifetime team rosters.

The Baseball Timeline: The Day to Day History of Baseball from Valley Forge to the Present Day
Solomon, Burt. New York: Avon Books 1997.

Early literary references and how it all began; the first teams, the formation of leagues, and yearly summaries of games and players. Fully illustrated.

Basketball (796.323)

The Official NBA Basketball Encyclopedia
Sachare, Alex, ed. New York: Villard, 1994. 2d ed. Incl. index.

A history of the league, Hall of Fame list, rules, coaches, records, and all-time player directory.

Boxing (796.83)

The Boxing Register
Roberts, James B., and Skutt, Alexander G. Ithaca, NY: McBooks, 1997.
Beginning with early pioneers and listed chronologically, it gives full biographies and statistics covering all aspects of the sport, its rules, and early radio and TV coverage. It also reveals the occasional tragic, seamy side of boxing. Many photos.

Football   (796.332)

Pro Football Guide
Carter, Craig, and Sloan, Dave, eds. St. Louis, MO: Sporting News, 1996.
Includes the National Football League directory, with names and biographies of individual teams and sections. Reviews, statistics, and sport history.

Sports Encyclopedia: Pro Football, the Modern Era, 1960–1995
Neft, Davis S., Cohen, Richard M., and Korch, Rick. New York: St. Martin's Press, 1996. 14th ed., rev. and upd.
Short summaries of the teams and players, but mainly this is a book of football statistics compiled from 1960 to 1995: yards run, goals scored, passes completed, and so on, covering all the major professional leagues. For quick reference.

Golf (796.352)

International Encyclopedia of Golf
Campbell, Malcolm. New York, Random House, 1991.
The whole story of golf, from its misty origins, possibly going back to ancient Rome, to the present day, with biographies of the all-time greats, tournaments, and prizes, with a foreword by Tom Watson. Good illustrations and maps.

Ice Hockey (796.962)

Illustrated Hockey Encyclopedia
Ronberg, Gary. New York: Balsam, 1984.
Teams, players, and statistical tables.

Ice Skating (796.91)

Inside Edge: A Revealing Journey into the Secret World of Figure Skating
Brennan, Christine. New York: Scribner, 1996.
A *Washington Post* sports writer chronicles a season on the skating circuit with current stars and backward glances at earlier skaters—how they decided to enter this competitive field and what it did to them all. Descriptions of a skater's training and routines and which skaters succeeded and why. A good book for those considering a skating career.

Skiing (796.93)

From Skiport to Skiing: 100 Years of an American Sport, 1840 to 1940
Allen, John B. Boston: University of Massachusetts, 1994.
The first full-length study of skiing in the United States, from its origins as a means of transport and travel to a competitive Olympian sport. An excellent source of information on how skiing became the giant industry it is today and how to become part of it. A good introduction into other winter sports research.

Soccer (796.334)

1996 NCAA Soccer
Brown, Gary T., ed. Overland Park, KS: National Collegiate Athletic Association, 1996.
A short directory to the members of the Men's and Women's Soccer Rules Committee and a complete update of the recent changes in the game.

The World Encyclopedia of Soccer
LaBlanc, Michael L., and Henshaw, Richard. Detroit: Gale, 1994.
This large book presents the game in all its facets—its history, spread of popularity around the world, and special features on stars, in alphabetical order. Fully illustrated.

Tennis (796.342)

Bud Collins' Modern Encyclopedia of Tennis
Collins, Bud, and Hollander, Zander, eds. Detroit: Gale, 1994.
A comprehensive book that traces the history of the game in the United States from 1876, when there were only two courts in the country, to modern times, with over 30 million players. Descriptions of

matches, tennis greats, locations, with many pictures. A good overall view.

1996 Tennis Yearbook
Zimman, H. O. Lynn, MA: U.S. Tennis Association, 1996.
Gives all current rankings of men and women players, biographies of the important players in tennis history, championship rules, international results and records, by-laws, and official rules.

PART III

Assignment Index to Reference Sources

CHAPTER 18

Guide to Homework Questions

The intent of this index is to connect student researchers with information resources that will help them complete their homework, term paper, and other research assignments. This index works first by subject keyword, and then suggests topic questions for the student to consider.

Page references in this section refer to the bibliographic information and annotation found in this book in Part II. Other books on the same topic may also be listed on the given page or on pages preceding or following, so for best results, users should browse the pages for additional sources. As a time-saving option, a student may check the library's catalog for a title listed in this index, record the call number, and go directly to the shelf. General Dewey Decimal numbers are also provided here, so that that student may go directly to the suggested shelf area in the library for books on the topic.

ABORTION (363.46, 613.9)—Chapter 12, pp. 161–162—I need to find information on both sides of the abortion debate. I also need statistics.

In addition to finding pro and con information in the Taking Sides and Opposing Viewpoints series, the following sources offer a lot of information:

> *Abortion: A Reference Handbook,* p. 161
> *The Anti-Abortion Movement,* p. 161
> *The Encyclopedia of BioEthics,* p. 194
> Abortion statistics can be found in:
> *Health United States,* p. 156
> *Statistical Abstract of the United States,* p. 32

Many newspaper and magazine articles have been written on this issue. They can be found using standard periodical indexes (see Chapter 4).

Articles on medical aspects can be found in:

Health Reference Center on InfoTrac, p. 169, or other medical and health databases

ADOLESCENCE (155)—See TEENAGERS

AFFIRMATIVE ACTION (323.1, 331.1, 342)—Chapter 13, pp. 182–183—I need information on the pros and cons of affirmative action.

Arguments on both sides can be found in the Taking Sides and Opposing Viewpoints series.

Information on Supreme Court rulings on this issue can be found in:

The Evolving Constitution, p. 182

Leading Constitutional Decisions, p. 183

Newspaper and magazine articles can be found using standard periodical indexes (see Chapter 4).

AFRICA (916, 960)—Chapter 10, p. 127—See also COUNTRIES—I need to write a paper about the war in Rwanda.

This event has occurred so recently that magazine and newspaper articles may be your best bet. They can be found using standard periodical indexes (see Chapter 4).

Historical, statistical, and other factual background on the country can be found in:

Cambridge Encyclopedia of Africa, p. 127

Country Studies (Area Handbook Series), p. 127

Political Handbook of the World, p. 176

Statesman's Yearbook, pp. 32, 176

Worldmark Encyclopedia of the Nations, p. 127

AFRICAN AMERICANS (305.8, 973)—I need to find information on the civil rights movement of the 1950s and 1960s. **See CIVIL RIGHTS.**

AFRICAN AMERICANS—BIOGRAPHY (305.8, 920)—Chapter 10, pp. 138–139—See also BLACK DOCTORS; BLACK SCIENTISTS AND INVENTORS—I need biographical information on Rosa Parks, Medgar Evers, and other famous black Americans.

There are numerous biographical sources about black Americans. Try:

Dictionary of American Negro Biography, p. 139

AIDS (362.1, 616.97)—Chapter 12, pp. 163–166—Where can I get statistics on AIDS?

For the most up-to-date statistics on AIDS, see:
HIV/AIDS Surveillance Report, p. 166
Also try:
Health United States, p. 156
For other information on AIDS, see:
AIDS, p. 163

ALCOHOL, ALCOHOLISM (362.292, 616.861)—Chapter 12, pp. 167–169—I need information on teenagers and alcohol.

For information on the pros and cons of alcohol use and abuse by teenagers, see:
Chemical Dependency (Opposing Viewpoints series), p. 167
Also covering this and other problems of teenagers is:
The Encyclopedia of Adolescence, p. 192
The following source covers alcoholism as it affects individuals, families, and society overall:
Encyclopedia of Drugs and Alcohol, p. 168

AMENDMENTS—See CONSTITUTIONAL AMENDMENTS

AMERICAN HISTORY—See UNITED STATES HISTORY

AMERICAN REVOLUTION (973.3)—Chapter 10, pp. 137–138—See also COLONIAL LIFE AND TIMES—I need to identify some significant people in the American Revolution. I have a list of names my teacher gave me.

The following source includes biographies:
Encyclopedia of the American Revolution, p. 137

ANATOMY, HUMAN (611, 612)—Chapter 12, pp. 158–159—I need to write a paper about the heart.

There are many books to help you with this assignment. Try starting with:
Atlas of Human Anatomy, p. 158

ANCIENT HISTORY—See HISTORY, ANCIENT

ANIMALS (590)—Chapter 16, pp. 221–222, 225–229—See also ENDANGERED SPECIES, MAMMALS—I need to write a report on grizzly bears [or any other animal or mammal].

Information on mammals can be found in many sources. See:

Illustrated Encyclopedia of Wildlife, p. 225
Macmillan Illustrated Animal Encyclopedia, p. 225

ANOREXIA NERVOSA (616.85)—Chapter 12, p. 165—How can I find out about people who won't eat because they want to stay thin?

For information on this health problem and for information on bulimia, see:

Eating Disorders, p. 165
The Encyclopedia of Obesity and Eating Disorders, p. 165

ARABS (953)—Chapter 10, p. 127—I need to write a paper on the social and religious customs of the Arab people.

One place to start might be:

A History of the Arab Peoples, p. 127

ARCHITECTURE (720)—Chapter 7, pp. 88–89, 91–93—See also HOUSES—Where can I find information on the Paris Opera House?

If you need historical information on architecture in a particular country, see the series of books published by Yale University Press:

Art and Architecture (in or of) (name of country), pp. 88–89

Other good sources include:

Sir Bannister Fletcher's History of Architecture, p. 92
The World Atlas of Architecture, p. 92

ART AND ARTISTS (700, 709.2)—Chapter 7, pp. 86–91—I need to find out some background on American impressionists and who they are.

The Dictionary of Art, p. 86, explains nearly every style of art and art form from any time period or place. It also discusses the lives of significant artists throughout history. You might also try:

A Biographical Dictionary of Artists, p. 90
The Encyclopedia of World Art, p. 86
History of Art, p. 88
World Artists, 2 vols., p. 91

ARTIFICIAL INSEMINATION (613.94)—Chapter 12, pp. 161–162; Chapter 15, p. 194—Where can I find scientific information, and the moral arguments for and against artificial insemination?

Both types of information can be found in:

The Encyclopedia of BioEthics, p. 194

Also try:

Taking Sides, p. 35

Medical information can be found in:

Columbia University College of Physicians and Surgeons Complete Guide to Pregnancy, p. 161

ASIA (915, 950)—Chapter 10, p. 128—See also COUNTRIES—Where can I find information on the Silk Road and trade routes through Asia?
　　You might start with:
　　　Encyclopedia of Asian History, p. 128

ATLASES (912)—Chapter 3, pp. 28–31—I need an atlas that shows the world's natural resources in color and which country they're in.
　　Many general atlases have country and world maps, but they also contain maps that show such things as population distribution, religions, and the distribution of natural resources. Try:
　　　Atlas of the World, p. 28
　　　National Geographic Atlas of the World, p. 29
　　　The Times Atlas of the World, p. 29

ATOMS (539.7)—Chapter 16, pp. 210–211—I need to write a paper on atoms, protons, and neutrons, and I need to draw diagrams.
　　Some good places to begin are:
　　　Encyclopedia of Physics, p. 210
　　　Magill's Survey of Science, Physical Science Series, p. 210

BABIES (612.6)—Chapter 12, pp. 159, 161–162—I need pictures of babies in the stages of development from conception to birth.
　　An excellent and astounding source for this topic is:
　　　A Child Is Born, p. 159

BASEBALL (796.357)—Chapter 17, p. 235—Where can I find Jackie Robinson's career statistics for a report?
　　For Robinson's and other players' and teams' statistics, see:
　　　The Baseball Encyclopedia, p. 235

BIBLE (220)—Chapter 15, pp. 195–196—I need to compare the King James Version of the Bible with any other version. Is there something that will summarize the major differences and similarities for me?
　　This type of information can be found in:
　　　The Layman's Parallel Bible, p. 196

BIOGRAPHY (920)—Chapter 10, pp. 138–141—I need biographical information on a [fill in the blank: scientist, a general in the Civil War, a black inventor, a woman mathematician, an American Indian chief, etc.].
　　Biographical reference sources come in two types: general sources and subject sources. *Current Biography* is a general source issued each year profiling significant persons who made some impact on the world in recent years. *The Discoverers: An Encyclopedia of Explorers and Ex-*

ploration is a specific subject source profiling explorers of the ancient and modern world.

For general biographical sources, see:
Biography and Genealogy Master Index, p. 139
Biography Index, p. 140
Current Biography, pp. 80, 140
Dictionary of American Biography, p. 140
Dictionary of National Biography, p. 140
Webster's New Biographical Dictionary, p. 141
Some subject-specific biographical sources are:
Dictionary of American Negro Biography, p. 139
The Discoverers, p. 140
Great North American Indians, p. 136
Notable American Women, 1607–1950, p. 141

BIRDS (598)—Chapter 16, pp. 221–222, 228—How do birds know where to go when they migrate?

This information, and other fascinating facts about birds, can be found in:
The Encyclopedia of Birds, p. 228
The Illustrated Encyclopedia of Birds, p. 228

BIRTH CONTROL (613.9)—Chapter 12, pp. 161–162—Where can I find arguments for and against birth control?

For information on the pros and cons of this issue, see:
Encyclopedia of BioEthics, p. 194
Human Sexuality: Opposing Viewpoints, p. 162
Taking Sides, p. 35
A review of birth control methods can be found in:
The Contraceptive Handbook, p. 161
Sex Care, p. 162

BLACK DOCTORS (610.92)—Chapter 12, pp. 157–158, 205–206—Where can I find information on the important contributions of black doctors?

Biographical information on black doctors can be found in:
Blacks in Science and Medicine, pp. 158, 205

BLACK SCIENTISTS AND INVENTORS (500.92)—Chapter 16, pp. 205–206—I need to write a paper on a black scientist who has made an important discovery in chemistry.

The following book provides biographical information on black scientists and inventors. It indexes them by scientific field. See:

Distinguished African American Scientists of the 20th Century, p. 206

BOOK REVIEWS (016.8)—Chapter 11, p. 149—I need book reviews of *Catcher in the Rye.*
See:
Book Review Digest, p. 149

BRAND NAMES (650)—Chapter 9, pp. 116–117—How do I find out what company makes a particular product?
Try:
Brands and Their Companies, p. 116
For product information, see:
Encyclopedia of Consumer Brands, p. 117

BULIMIA—See ANOREXIA NERVOSA

CANADA (917,971)—Chapter 10, p. 128—See also COUNTRIES—Is Quebec trying to secede from Canada?
This information and more on Canada is covered in:
The Canadian Encyclopedia, p. 128

CAPITAL PUNISHMENT—See DEATH PENALTY

CAREERS (331.702)—Chapter 9, pp. 113–114—I need to find out what a market analyst [nurse, architect, mechanic, etc.] does, what kind of education and skills the job requires, what the potential earnings are, and what the hiring prospects are for the future.
For the most common source, updated annually, that provides this information, see:
Occupational Outlook Handbook, p. 113

CATHEDRALS (726.6)—Chapter 7, pp. 91–93—I need pictures and descriptions of Gothic cathedrals.
An excellent source with 220 photographs and drawings is:
The Gothic Cathedral, p. 93

CELLS (574.87, 581.87, 591.87)—Chapter 16, pp. 218–221; Chapter 12, pp. 158–159—I need information on cells in the human body.
See:
The Encyclopedia of Human Biology, p. 220
The Human Body on File, p. 159
For information on cells in general, not just human cells, see:
Life Sciences on File, p. 220

Magill's Survey of Science, Life Sciences Series, p. 220
The World of the Cell, p. 221

CFC (363.73)—Chapter 16, pp. 214–217, 221—What are CFCs, and how do they affect the atmosphere?
    For a definition, see:
        The Dictionary of Ecology and Environmental Science, p. 221
    See also:
        Magill's Survey of Science, Earth Science Series, p. 215
        McGraw-Hill Encyclopedia of Ocean and Atmospheric Sciences, p. 216

CHAMBERS OF COMMERCE (380)—Chapter 9, p. 116—Where do I write for information on a town?
    For addresses of chambers of commerce, tourist bureaus, and embassies, see:
        World Chamber of Commerce Directory, p. 116

CHEMICAL ELEMENTS (546)—Chapter 16, p. 212—Where can I find information on hydrogen and other chemical elements?
    The periodic table and information on the chemical elements can be found in:
        A Guide to the Elements, p. 212
        McGraw-Hill Encyclopedia of Science and Technology, p. 200

CHILD ABUSE (362.7, 364.1555)—Chapter 14, p. 190—See also VIOLENCE—I need to write a report on child abuse. Where can I start?
    One good source is:
        Encyclopedia of BioEthics, p. 194
    Also try:
        Taking Sides, p. 35

CHINA (915, 951)—Chapter 10, p. 128—See also COUNTRIES—Should the United States trade with China? What problems does China face, being communist and with such a large population? What role does religion play there? I need to answer these question for a paper I'm working on.
    The following sources may help you get started answering these questions:
        Cambridge Encyclopedia of China, p. 128
        Cambridge Illustrated History of China, p. 128
    You might find answers in newspaper and magazine articles, too. They can be found using standard periodical indexes (see Chapter 4).

CHRISTIANITY (200–289)—Chapter 15, pp. 194–197—I need to write a paper comparing and contrasting a Christian religion with an Eastern or Middle Eastern religion.

This type of information can be gathered from:
Abington Dictionary of Living Religions, p. 194
Dictionary of Comparative Religion, p. 194

CHRONOLOGIES (GENERAL HISTORY) (902.02)—Chapter 3, p. 34; Chapter 10, pp. 122–123, 132–133—I need to find out what other events took place around the world during the Renaissance.

Chronologies are perfect sources for this type of question. Try:
The People's Chronology, p. 122

CIVIL RIGHTS (323.4)—Chapter 13, pp. 175–176—I need information on the civil rights movement of the 1960s.

Three excellent sources are:
The ABC-CLIO Companion to the Civil Rights Movement, p. 175
Encyclopedia of African-American Civil Rights, p. 175
The Eyes on the Prize Civil Rights Reader, p. 175

For a country-by-country comparative guide on civil and human rights issues, see:
World Human Rights Guide, p. 176

CIVIL WAR—UNITED STATES (973.7)—Chapter 10, pp. 133–134—I need an overview of the Civil War, its causes and results, and then I need to expand on a specific topic within the Civil War time period. Can you help me?

An easy overview source that will help with both questions is:
The Civil War Source Book, p. 134

CLIMATE AND CLIMATE CHANGE (363.7, 551.6)—Chapter 16, pp. 214–217—My topic is to explain how cutting down forests affects climate. Where can I get information?

In addition to researching this topic through magazine and newspaper articles (see Chapter 4), *Biology Digest,* pp. 47, 219, is an excellent source for this topic. See also:
The Dictionary of Global Climate Change, p. 214
Magill's Survey of Science, Earth Science Series, p. 215

CLONING (574, 575)—Chapter 16, pp. 218–221—Where can I find information on cloning?

Cloning is part of the study of genetics. See:

Encyclopedia of Human Biology, p. 220
Magill's Survey of Science, Life Science Series, p. 220
For recent articles, see *Biology Digest,* pp. 47, 219

CLOUDS (551.6)—Chapter 16, pp. 214–217—I need to draw the different types of clouds and explain how they form.
Cloud formation and other weather phenomena are explained in:
A Field Guide to the Atmosphere, p. 215

COCAINE (362.29, 616.86)—Chapter 12, pp. 167–169—I need to write a report on crack cocaine.
Cocaine and its related problems are discussed in the following sources:
Chemical Dependency, p. 167
The Encyclopedia of Drug Abuse, p. 167
The Encyclopedia of Drugs and Alcohol, p. 168
The Encyclopedia of Psychoactive Drugs, p. 168

COLONIAL LIFE AND TIMES (973.2)—Chapter 10, pp. 135, 137–138—What did teenagers in colonial times do?
For a discussion of how teenagers lived in colonial America and through the decades up to the present, see:
The Encyclopedia of Adolescence, p. 192
Also try:
Almanacs of American Life, p. 135

COMMODITIES (330.9)—Chapter 9, pp. 111–112—I need prices on commodities, such as oil, copper, soybeans, and coffee. The most helpful source is:
Commodity Prices, p. 111

COMPANIES (CORPORATIONS) (338, 650)—Chapter 9, pp. 116–118—I need information about a company.
If you need background on a company or corporation, such as when the business was founded, what it makes or produces, or financial information, many sources can be used. One of the best is:
Hoover's Handbook, p. 117

COMPUTERS (004, 005)—Chapter 8, pp. 105–108—I need to write a basic description of how a computer works.
Probably the best source is:
Encyclopedia of Computer Science, p. 106
Since computer science is such a rapidly changing topic, you may

also want to consider magazine and newspaper articles (see Chapter 4), CD-ROM and online sources such as *Computer Select* (Chapter 8, p. 106), and the Internet (Chapter 5).

CONGRESS (U.S.) (328)—Chapter 13, pp. 179–180—I need to find out what a congressional committee is, how someone gets on one and what they do.

    One good source to start with is:

        Encyclopedia of the United States Congress, p. 180

CONSTITUTION (U.S.) (342.73)—Chapter 13, p. 181—I need to write a paper that tells how the Constitution came to be written.

    A great source is:

        CQ's Guide to the U.S. Constitution, p. 181

    Also see:

        Encyclopedia of the American Constitution, p. 134

CONSTITUTIONAL AMENDMENTS (342.73)—Chapter 13, p. 181—I need to find out what was going on in the country that led to the Fourteenth Amendment.

    Political and historical background on each amendment can be found in:

        Encyclopedia of Constitutional Amendments, Proposed Amendments and Amending Issues, 1789–1995, p. 181

    For good background on the first ten amendments, the Bill of Rights, see:

        The American Heritage History of the Bill of Rights, p. 181

    You may also want to consult:

        CQ's Guide to the U.S. Constitution, p. 181

CONSTITUTIONS (328)—Chapter 13, p. 181—I need to find the constitution of a country other than the United States.

    To find it, see:

        Constitutions of the World, p. 181

CONSUMER INFORMATION AND PRODUCT REVIEWS—Chapter 4, pp. 37–43—How do I find information on whether a particular product is good or bad?

    Check these magazines for articles comparing brands of the particular product (such as roller blades, portable stereos, televisions, automobiles, or vacuum cleaners):

        Consumer Guide

        Consumer Reports

Consumer Research
Consumers Digest

All of them are indexed in *Magazine Index, Reader's Guide to Periodical Literature,* and other general magazine indexes. It may be best to start with the index (see Chapter 4).

CONTRACEPTION—See BIRTH CONTROL

COST OF LIVING (330.9)—Chapter 9, pp. 111–112—I need to compare the cost of living in the United States every ten years from 1900 to the present. Where do I start?

"Cost of living" is a common term used interchangeably with "inflation." Inflation, or cost of living, is measured by the government using the Consumer Price Index (CPI). If an assignment or report calls for you to research cost of living, CPI, or inflation during the last few decades or currently, ask for:

American Cost of Living Survey, p. 111
ACCRA Cost of Living Survey, p. 111
CPI Detailed Report, p. 112
Statistical Abstract of the United States, p. 32

COUNTRIES (914-919, 941-999)—Chapter 10, pp. 127–131—How can I find information on a country, such as its population, type of government, monetary unit, head of state, how much it spends on its military, health care, and education?

Many sources provide this type of information. One of the best, and most compact in one-easy-to-handle-and-use volume, is:

Country Studies (Area Handbook Series), p. 127
See also:
The Statesman's Year-Book, pp. 32, 176
Worldmark Encyclopedia of the Nations, p. 127

CRITICISM, LITERARY—See DRAMA; LITERATURE

CULTURES AND CUSTOMS (390)—Chapter 10, p. 123—How can I find out about the cultures of tribes in different countries?

The best source to use is:
Encyclopedia of World Cultures, p. 123

DANCE (792.8)—Chapter 7, p. 103—Where would I find a history and explanation of ballet?

Most aspects of dance are covered in:
The Dance Encyclopedia, p. 103

DEATH PENALTY (364.66)—Chapter 15, p. 194; Chapter 4, p. 35—I need to answer the question, Does the death penalty deter violent crime? For the pros and cons of this issue, see:
> *Encyclopedia of BioEthics*, p. 194
> *Taking Sides*, p. 35

DECADES—See, by decade—for example, **THE TWENTIES (1920s)**

DEFORESTATION (574.5)—Chapter 16, pp. 221–222—I need to write a paper explaining the causes of deforestation and its effects on wildlife and environment.
> One source that might explain human impact on forests, and the effect on environment, is:
> *Grzimek's Encyclopedia of Ecology*, p. 222

DICTIONARIES (403, 423)—Chapter 11, pp. 144–145—I need to find out the history of a word—how it developed, where it came from, how its use changed over time.
> The absolute best, and perhaps only, source for answering this type of question is:
> *The Oxford English Dictionary*, p. 144

DINOSAURS (560)—Chapter 16, pp. 217–218—I need pictures of dinosaurs, and I need to place them on a time scale.
> An excellent source for pictures, bone structure, geologic time periods, and other information is:
> *The Dinosaur Society's Dinosaur Encyclopedia*, p. 217

DISEASE (616)—Chapter 12, pp. 156, 163–167—Where do I find information on disease?
> For general information on disease , see:
> *Marshall Cavendish Encyclopedia of Health*, p. 156
> For information on specific diseases, see:
> *Professional Guide to Diseases*, p. 166
> For historical information, see:
> *The Cambridge World History of Human Disease*, p. 164

DOCTORS (610.92)—Chapter 12, pp. 157–158—Who were some of the famous doctors throughout history? What did they do?
> For medical biography—the description of the lives and activities of famous medical personnel—see:
> *Biographical Dictionary of Medicine*, p. 157
and other sources, pp. 157–158

DRAMA (808.82, 812, 822, etc.)—Chapter 11, pp. 149–150—I need to write a paper on the plays of Eugene O'Neill.

You might want to narrow the topic down a bit, as O'Neill wrote many excellent plays. Perhaps you'll want to focus on a theme that runs through several plays. The following sources may help you determine what themes he used:

> *Critical Survey of Drama,* p. 149
>
> *McGraw-Hill Encyclopedia of World Drama,* p. 149

Also try the CD-ROM sources:

> *DISCovering Authors,* pp. 70, 147
>
> *DiscLit: American Authors,* pp. 70, 147

DREAMS (154.6)—Chapter 14, p. 191—Where do I find out what dreams mean?

> The following book offers dream interpretations and symbols:
>
> *The Encyclopedia of Dreams,* p. 191

DRUGS (615, 616.86, 362.29)—Chapter 12, pp. 163, 167–169—See also ALCOHOL/ALCOHOLISM; MARIJUANA; SUBSTANCE ABUSE; SMOKING; TOBACCO—Where do I find information on drugs?

> For a general discussion of illegal drugs, see:
>
> *The Encyclopedia of Drug Abuse,* p. 167
>
> For a general discussion of prescription drugs, see:
>
> *The Complete Drug Reference,* p. 163
>
> For information on specific illegal drugs, such as marijuana, cocaine, PCP, and others, see:
>
> *Encyclopedia of Drugs and Alcohol,* p. 168
>
> For information on specific nonprescription drugs, see:
>
> *Physician's Desk Reference for Nonprescription Drugs,* p. 163
>
> For information on specific prescription drugs, see:
>
> *Physician's Desk Reference,* p. 163
>
> For pro and con views on drugs, see:
>
> *Drug Abuse,* p. 167
>
> *Taking Sides: Clashing Views on Controversial Issues in Health and Society,* p. 169

EARTH (PLANET) (525)—Chapter 16, pp. 207–210—Where can I find an explanation of how the universe came into being?

> Start with:
>
> *Isaac Asimov's Guide to Earth and Space,* p. 208

EARTH SCIENCES (550)—Chapter 16, p. 215–216—Where can I find out why there's heat within the earth?

The study of the earth includes earthquakes, geology, volcanoes, water, and weather.

For an overall guide, see:

Macmillan Encyclopedia of Earth Sciences, p. 215

EARTHQUAKES (551.22)—Chapter 16, pp. 215–216—Where can I find out what makes the earth move?

Earthquakes are explained in:

Encyclopedia of Earthquakes and Volcanoes, p. 215

See also:

McGraw-Hill Encyclopedia of the Geological Sciences, p. 216

Recent earthquakes—their size, damage inflicted, numbers killed, and so on—can be researched through magazine and newspaper articles. See Chapter 4 for how to do this.

EATING DISORDERS—See ANOREXIA NERVOSA

ECOLOGY (574.5)—Chapter 16, pp. 221–222—See also ENVIRONMENT—Where can I find information on the relationship between wetlands and the ocean?

For topics such as the relationship between prairies and mountains, between rain forests and the greenhouse effect, between swamps forests, see:

Grzimek's Encyclopedia of Ecology, p. 222

ECONOMICS (330)—Chapter 9, pp. 110–111—Most questions can be answered by:

A Field Guide to the U.S. Economy, p. 110
The McGraw-Hill Encyclopedia of Economics, p. 110
The New Palgrave, p. 110

EGYPT, ANCIENT (932)—Chapter 10, pp. 123–124—I need information on the pyramids, Tutankhamen, and the dynasties of ancient Egypt.

Many books have been written on these subjects. One good reference source is:

Cambridge Ancient History, p. 337

THE EIGHTIES (1980s) (902, 973.02)—Chapter 10, pp. 122–123, 132–133—I need books that will tell me about the events, fashions, and pastimes of the 1980s.

Chronologies list significant events and make good starting points for reports on time periods. For lists of events of the 1980s, including fashion, the arts, pastimes, and more, see:

American Decades, p. 133
Chronicle of the Twentieth Century, p. 122
Day by Day: The Eighties, p. 133

ELECTION STATISTICS (324.6)—Chapter 13, p. 177—I need to find out how people voted in the last election.

If you mean the presidential election, see:
The World Almanac and Book of Facts, p. 27

More detailed information on issues, state, and national elections can be found in sources such as:
Almanac of American Politics, p. 177
America Votes, p. 177
Congressional Quarterly's Guide to U.S. Elections, p. 177

ELEMENTS, CHEMICAL —See CHEMICAL ELEMENTS

EMBASSIES (380)—Chapter 9, p. 116—I need to write a foreign embassy for information on a country. Where do I find an address?

For addresses of chambers of commerce, tourist bureaus, and embassies, see:
World Chamber of Commerce Directory, p. 116

EMOTIONS (152.4)—Chapter 14, p. 190; Chapter 11, pp. 149–150—I need to describe a human emotion. Then I need to find a poem and a short story about an emotion.

Human emotions are covered in detail in:
Emotions, p. 190

Two excellent sources that index by subject, such as love or grief, are:
Columbia Granger Index to Poetry, p. 150
Short Story Index, p. 149

ENDANGERED SPECIES (574.5)—Chapter 16, pp. 221–222—Where can I find a list of endangered animals?

These lists are revised every so often as some animals become endangered and others thrive after being protected. Good sources include:
Endangered Wildlife of the World, p. 221
The Official World Wildlife Fund Guide to Endangered Species of North America, p. 222

ENLIGHTENMENT (940.25)—Chapter 10, pp. 123–124—For an overview of this historical period, see:
Encyclopedia of World History, pp. 73, 123

ENVIRONMENT (574.5)—Chapter 16, pp. 202–204, 221–222—See also ECOLOGY—I need to explain why wetlands are an important element in the food chain. I also need to explain why they shouldn't be developed.

Environmental and ecological issues are covered in:
The Dictionary of Ecology and Environmental Science, p. 221
Grzimek's Encyclopedia of Ecology, p. 222
Another good choice is:
World Nature Encyclopedia, p. 203
Pro and con issues are discussed in:
Taking Sides, p. 35

ESSAYS (804)—Chapter 11, p. 149—How can I find an essay on the use of military power as a political tool?

Essays on specific subjects can be located by using:
Essay and General Literature Index, pp. 76, 149

ETHICS (170-179)—Chapter 15, p. 194 —How can I respond to the question, "Should animals be used in medical research?"

Many ethical questions can be answered using:
Encyclopedia of BioEthics, p. 194

EUROPEAN HISTORY (940)—See HISTORY, EUROPEAN

EVOLUTION (573.2, 575)—Chapter 16, pp. 219–221—I need to compare Cro-Magnon and Neanderthal man.

An excellent source on human evolution is:
The Cambridge Encyclopedia of Human Evolution, p. 219
Animal evolution is covered by:
Grzimek's Encyclopedia of Evolution, p. 220
Magill's Survey of Science, Life Sciences Series, p. 220

FEUDALISM (940.14)—See HISTORY, MIDDLE AGES

THE FIFTIES (1950s) (902, 973.02)—Chapter 10, pp. 122–123, 132–133—How can I find a list of important events in the 1950s, so I can decide on one to write about?

Chronologies list significant events and make good starting points for reports on time periods. For lists of events of the 1950s, see:
American Decades, p. 133
Chronicle of the Twentieth Century, p. 122
Day by Day: The Fifties, p. 133

THE FORTIES (1940s) (902, 973.02)—Chapter 10, pp. 122–123, 132–133—Who were some of the significant people in the 1940s and what did they do?

Chronologies list significant events and make good starting points for reports on time periods. Chronologies will also provide the names of people who made the events happen. Start with:

> *American Decades*, p. 133
> *Chronicle of the Twentieth Century*, p. 122
> *Day by Day: The Forties*, p. 133

FRANCE (709.44, 944)—Chapter 7, pp. 86–88; Chapter 10, p. 129—See also COUNTRIES—I need to find information on the architecture of Paris, as well as on the social customs of the people of France, their history and other details, like the type of government, monetary system, population, and so on.

For Parisian architecture, try:

> *Art and Architecture in France, 1500–1700*, p. 88

For history and culture, try:

> *Cambridge Illustrated History of France*, p. 129

Background information can be found in:

> *Country Studies (Area Handbook Series)*, p. 127
> *Worldmark Encyclopedia of the Nations*, p. 127

FRENCH REVOLUTION (944.04)—Chapter 10, p. 129—I need to write about the causes of the French Revolution.

A good source to start with is:

> *Historical Dictionary of the French Revolution*, p. 129

FREUD (150.1952, 150.92)—Chapter 14, pp. 188–190—I need biographical information on Sigmund Freud, and I need to explain his psychoanalytic theories.

Some of the best sources to answer this question, and similar questions about other psychologists, are:

> *Encyclopedia of Psychology*, p. 188
> *The Gale Encyclopedia of Psychology*, p. 188
> *A Guide to Psychologists and Their Concepts*, p. 190
> *The Great Psychologists*, p. 190

GANGS (152.4, 364.106, 364.36)—Chapter 14, p. 190—I need information that explains what needs a gang fulfills for its members.

An excellent source for answering this and other questions on the roots of violence is:

> *Encyclopedia of Violence*, p. 190

GENE RESEARCH, GENES (573.2, 575.1)—Chapter 16, pp. 218–221—I need to write a paper on DNA.

> For an overview, see:
> *Magill's Survey of Science, Life Sciences Series,* p. 220
> For human genes, see:
> *Encyclopedia of Human Biology,* p. 220
> For pro and con information and background on issues, see:
> *Encyclopedia of BioEthics,* p. 194

GENETIC DISORDERS (573.228, 575.28, 591.158, 616.042)—Chapter 16, pp. 219–221; Chapter 12, p. 156)—I need to find examples of genetic disorders in humans and animals.

> For humans, see:
> *Encyclopedia of Human Biology,* p. 220
> For animals, try:
> *Magill's Survey of Science, Life Sciences Series,* p. 220
> For inherited human disease, see medical and health sources such

as:

> *American Medical Association Encyclopedia of Medicine,* p. 156

GEOLOGY (550)—Chapter 16, pp. 214–217—I need to find information on the different strata of rock—how they were formed, when and how they got there.

> Information of this type can be found in:
> *McGraw-Hill Encyclopedia of the Geological Sciences,* p. 216
> You might also try:
> *Macmillan Encyclopedia of Earth Sciences,* p. 215
> *Magill's Survey of Science, Earth Science Series,* p. 215

GERMANY (914.3, 943)—Chapter 10, p. 129—See also COUNTRIES —I need to compare conditions in Germany before World Wars I and II, and now.

> You might try:
> *A History of Germany,* p. 129
> Also consult:
> *Country Studies (Area Handbook Series),* p. 127
> *The Statesman's Year-Book,* pp. 32, 176
> *Worldmark Encyclopedia of the Nations,* p. 127

GLOBE THEATRE—(792, 822.33)—Chapter 7, p. 102; Chapter 11, pp. 149–150—I need pictures of the Globe Theatre and its stage. I need to build a model.

Information on the Globe Theatre, where Shakespeare's plays were originally performed, could be found in the Shakespeare section

(822.33), the theater section (792), or perhaps even architecture (720).
    For starters, try:
        Shakespeare: An Illustrated Stage History, p. 102
        The Shakespeare Handbook, p. 150

GOVERNMENT (320, 350)—Chapter 13, pp. 172, 174—I need to compare and contrast the governments of two countries—one from the East, one from the West.
    For information on governments in general, how they're formed and how they work, see:
        World Government, p. 172
    For information on U.S. government, see:
        CQ's Guide to Current American Government, p. 174
    You may also want to try:
        The Encyclopedic Dictionary of American Government, p. 172
        Worldmark Encyclopedia of the Nations, p. 127

GRAMMAR (400, 808.20, 808.066)—Chapter 11, pp. 146, 153–153
—What books will help me write better term papers?
    Some good sources for understanding grammar are:
        Errors in English and Ways to Correct Them, p. 147
        The Oxford Companion to the English Language, p. 145
    For style manuals, try:
        The Elements of Style, pp. 72, 152
        A Manual for Writers of Term Papers, Theses and Dissertations,
pp. 72, 152

GREAT BRITAIN AND IRELAND (941)—Chapter 10, p. 129—See also COUNTRIES—Is there a book that will help me put in order the kings and queens of England, along with their dates?
    Several sources could help with this. A good one is:
        The Cambridge Historical Encyclopedia of Great Britain and Ireland, p. 129

GREECE, ANCIENT (938)—Chapter 10, pp. 124–125—I need to find out how ancient Greece became such an important civilization.
    Start with:
        Cambridge Ancient History, p. 124
        Oxford History of the Classical World, p. 124

GREENHOUSE EFFECT (550)—Chapter 16, pp. 214–217—I need to write a paper explaining the greenhouse effect.
    Several sources may help. See:

Dictionary of Global Climate Change, p. 214
Macmillan Encyclopedia of Earth Sciences, p. 215
Magill's Survey of Science, Earth Science Series, p. 215

HEALTH (610)—Chapter 12, p. 156—See also specific health issues (e.g., AIDS; MEDICINE)—Where can I find information on health problems of minorities?

A good encyclopedia on general health issues of all types, written for students, is:
Marshall Cavendish Encyclopedia of Health, p. 156

HISTORY (900–909, 930–999)—Chapter 10, pp. 123–127—See also UNITED STATES HISTORY—How can I find background information so I can discuss and relate time periods in world history, such as the Renaissance and the Middle Ages?

You may want to check more specific sources eventually. General sources such as these may serve as good starting points:
Encyclopedia of World History, pp. 73, 123
Larousse Encyclopedia of Ancient and Medieval History, p. 124
New Cambridge Modern History, pp. 73, 124

HISTORY, ANCIENT (930)—Chapter 10, pp. 124–125—I'm supposed to compare and contrast life in ancient Greece and Rome.

The perfect source might be:
Greek and Roman Life, p. 124
These sources may help, too:
Cambridge Ancient History, p. 124
Oxford History of the Classical World, p. 124

HISTORY, EUROPEAN (940–949)—Chapter 10, pp. 123–131—I need to describe how the boundaries of European countries came to be.

You might start your research with:
Encyclopedia of World History, pp. 73, 123
New Cambridge Modern History, pp. 73, 124

HISTORY, MIDDLE AGES (909.07, 940.1)—Chapter 10, pp. 123–125—I need to write a paper on the Middle Ages.

Feudalism, medieval craft guilds, and the Crusades are major topic ideas. The following sources will provide information on these as well as other ideas for topics:
Cambridge Medieval History, p. 125
Dictionary of the Middle Ages, p. 125
The Oxford Illustrated History of Medieval Europe, p. 125

HISTORY, MODERN (940–999)—Chapter 10, pp. 123–127—I need to find a topic for a modern history term paper.

For a good general source, from 1453–1945, see:

New Cambridge Modern History, pp. 73, 124

For the twentieth century, see:

Dictionary of Twentieth Century History: 1914–1990, p. 123

HOLOCAUST (940.5318, 940.5472)—Chapter 10, pp. 125–126—See also WORLD WAR II—How was it that the Holocaust went undiscovered for a while?

Most aspects of this topic are explored in:

Encyclopedia of the Holocaust, p. 125

HOUSES (720)—Chapter 7, pp. 91–93—I need to find illustrations and descriptions of American houses, especially colonial through the nineteenth century.

The best sources to answer this question are:

American Architecture since 1780, p. 91

A Field Guide to American Architecture, p. 91

Identifying American Architecture, p. 91

HUMAN BODY (611, 612)—Chapter 12, pp. 158–159 —Where do I find information on the human organs and systems and how they work?

For information on human anatomy, see:

Human Anatomy and Physiology, p. 159

For individual systems and organs, such as the digestive system, try:

Atlas of Human Anatomy, p. 158

For reproducible diagrams of the body and its organs and systems, see:

The Human Body on File, p. 159

HURRICANES (550)—Chapter 16, pp. 214–217—I need to find out how hurricanes form.

Hurricanes and other weather phenomena are explained in:

Audubon Society Field Guide to North American Weather, p. 214

A Field Guide to the Atmosphere, p. 215

Recent hurricanes—their paths, damage inflicted, and so on—can be researched through newspaper and magazine articles. See Chapter 4 for how to do this.

IMMIGRATION (325)—Chapter 13, p. 178—I need to find out about how Poles immigrated to the United States.

A source that should help is:

Dictionary of American Immigration History, p. 178

INDIA (915.4, 954)—Chapter 10, p. 127–128—See also COUN-TRIES—How did the British come to occupy India?

Most questions on India can be answered by:

Cambridge Encyclopedia of India, Pakistan, Bangladesh, Sri Lanka, Nepal, Bhutan, and the Maldives, p. 128

Governments, population, brief history, culture, and so on can also be found in:

Country Studies (Area Handbook Series), p. 127

The Statesman's Year-Book, pp. 32, 176

Worldmark Encyclopedia of Nations, p. 127

INDIANS—See NATIVE AMERICANS

INDUSTRIAL REVOLUTION (909.81, 940.28)—Chapter 10, pp. 123–126—How did the Industrial Revolution get started? Who were its main contributors? Where did it occur?

The best place to start on this topic is:

The ABC-CLIO World History Companion to the Industrial Revolution, p. 125

For information on the Industrial Revolution in Europe and Great Britain, you might also try:

Cambridge Historical Encyclopedia of Great Britain and Ireland, p. 129

Encyclopedia of World History, pp. 73, 123

For the United States, try:

Encyclopedia of American History, pp. 77, 135

INTELLIGENCE (153.9)—Chapter 14, pp. 188–191—I need to find an example of an idiot savant.

For an explanation of this and other phenomena of the mind, see:

Encyclopedia of Human Intelligence, p. 191

INTERNET (004)—Chapter 5, pp. 51–62; Chapter 8, pp. 106–108—How can I use the Internet to help me with my research?

For a description of what the Internet is, see:

The Whole Internet User's Guide and Catalog, p. 107

For a directory of sites by topic, try:

McKinley Internet Yellow Pages, p. 107

For an overview on using the Internet, see Chapter 5, pp. 51–62

ISLAM (297)—Chapter 15, p. 197—See also MUSLIMS—I need to write a paper comparing the history and beliefs of Islam with the way the religion is practiced now.

You may want to start with:

Concise Encyclopedia of Islam, p. 197

You may want to follow up with newspaper and magazine articles (see Chapter 4) for information on how the religion is currently practiced, and you may want to keep in mind that Islam is practiced all over the world but the practices may vary in different countries.

JAPAN (915.2, 952)—Chapter 10, pp. 127, 130—See also COUNTRIES —Should I write about Japan now, as an economic power, or should I write about Japan's culture and its history?

For the first topic, see:

Kodansha Encyclopedia of Japan, p. 130

For the second, try:

Country Studies (Area Handbook Series), p. 127
Worldmark Encyclopedia of the Nations, p. 127

JOBS—See CAREERS

JUDAISM (296)—Chapter 15, p. 197—Where can I go to find out why the Jewish people don't accept Jesus Christ as the son of God?

Two main sources that delve deeply into the tenets of the Jewish faith are:

Encyclopedia Judaica, p. 197
The Encyclopedia of Judaism, p. 197

KU KLUX KLAN (322)—Chapter 13, p. 175—See also CIVIL RIGHTS; UNITED STATES HISTORY—For a paper on the civil rights movement, I need to know what Ku Klux Klan did during that time.

For a good background source, see:

The Ku Klux Klan: An Encyclopedia, p. 175

LABOR AND UNIONS (331)—Chapter 9, pp. 112–113—Where can I find information on Cesar Chavez and the grape picker's strikes of the late 1960s and 1970s?

Information on strikes can be found in:

Labor Conflict in the United States, p. 113

Two good biographical sources are:

The ABC-CLIO Companion to the American Labor Movement, p. 112
Biographical Dictionary of American Labor, p. 113

LATIN AMERICA (917.2, 918, 972, 980)—Chapter 10, pp. 127, 130—See also COUNTRIES—I need to pick a Latin American country that has had a war in the last 20 or 30 years, and compare it with another Latin American country that hasn't had a war.

A good place to get started might be:

Cambridge Encyclopedia of Latin America and the Caribbean, p. 130

LAWS (328)—Chapter 13, pp. 179–181—I need to trace how an idea gets turned into a law.

A good general outline can be found in:

How Federal Laws Are Made, p. 180

More detailed discussion can be found in:

Encyclopedia of the American Legislative System, p. 180

Encyclopedia of the United States Congress, p. 180

LEARNING—See MEMORY AND LEARNING

LEAVES (580)—Chapter 16, pp. 223–224—I need to identify five leaves that I find in my yard and neighborhood.

Most tree guide books identify leaves. Try:

The Complete Trees of North America, p. 223

The Oxford Encyclopedia of Trees of the World, p. 224

LEGALIZING DRUGS (362.29)—Chapter 12, pp. 167–169—I need to find out about legalizing drugs. Should they be legal or not?

For the pros and cons of this controversial issue, see:

Chemical Dependency: Opposing Viewpoints, p. 167

Drug Abuse: Opposing Viewpoints, p. 167

Encyclopedia of BioEthics, p. 194

Taking Sides: Clashing Views on Controversial Issues in Health and Society, p. 169

LITERARY CRITICISM—See DRAMA; LITERATURE

LITERATURE (800–899)—See Chapter 11, pp. 148–152—Where can I find criticism of *Jane Eyre,* by Charlotte Brontë?

There are several sources to try:

British Writers, pp. 69, 148

The Chelsea House Library of Literary Criticism, pp. 68, 148

Moulton's Library of Literary Criticism Through the Beginning of the Twentieth Century, pp. 68, 148

Nineteenth Century Literature Criticism, pp. 69, 148

The Oxford Companion to English Literature, pp. 67, 151

MAMMALS (599)—Chapter 16, pp. 221–222, 228–229—See also ANI-MALS; ENDANGERED SPECIES—I want to write about tigers.
    A tiger is a mammal. There are many excellent sources on mammals. See:
        Grzimek's Encyclopedia of Mammals, p. 228
        Walker's Mammals of the World, p. 229

MAN AND THE ENVIRONMENT (574.5)—See ECOLOGY; ENVI-RONMENT

MARIJUANA (362.29, 616.86)—Chapter 12, pp. 167–169—I need to find out as much as I can about marijuana.
    For an excellent source on the topic, see:
        Marijuana: Its Effect on Mind and Body, p. 168, a volume in the *Encyclopedia of Psychoactive Drugs* series
        Chemical Dependency, p. 167
        Encyclopedia of Drugs and Alcohol, p. 168

MEDICINE—HISTORY (610.9)—Chapter 12, p. 157—Where can I find information about the practice of medicine during the Middle Ages?
    Historical information on the development and practice of medicine can be found in:
        The Cambridge Illustrated History of Medicine, p. 157

MEMORY AND LEARNING (153.1)—Chapter 14, pp. 188–191—I'm interested in amnesia, especially famous cases.
    Try starting with:
        The Encyclopedia of Memory and Memory Disorders, p. 190

MICROCOMPUTERS (004)—See COMPUTERS

MIDDLE AGES (909.07, 940.1)—See HISTORY—MIDDLE AGES

MIDDLE EAST (915.6, 956)—Chapter 10, pp. 127, 130—See also COUNTRIES —Where can I find background on Middle Eastern conflicts?
    For coverage of Middle Eastern countries, history, and regional conflicts, see:
        Cambridge Encyclopedia of the Middle East and North Africa, p. 130

MIGRATION (590)—Chapter 16, pp. 225–226—Do you have a map showing the route of the wildebeest migration?

Maps of wildebeest and other animal migrations can be found in:
Atlas of Animal Migration, p. 225

MINERALS (549)—Chapter 16, pp. 213–214—I need information on certain minerals: where they are found, what they are used for, their chemical formula.

The following source should help answer these questions:
Mineral Resources A–Z, p. 214

MONEY (330, 332)—Chapter 9, pp. 100, 111–112, 114—I need to find out what a dollar was worth in 1860.

For this information, and for comparative prices, wages, and incomes during the years 1860–1989, see:
The Value of a Dollar, p. 112
Legal and governmental questions can be answered by:
Encyclopedia of Banking and Finance, p. 114
Monetary units and U.S. dollar equivalents can be found in:
World Almanac and Book of Facts, p. 27

MUSIC AND MUSICIANS (780s)—Chapter 7, pp. 95–101—I need to compare and contrast two classical composers, like Beethoven and Mozart.

For the best overall source that will answer most questions on any type of music and most prominent musicians, see:
The New Grove Dictionary of Music and Musicians, p. 95
Another good bet for biographical information is:
Baker's Biographical Dictionary of Musicians, p. 97

MUSLIMS (297, 955, 960s)—Chapter 10, p. 130; Chapter 15, pp. 194–197—See also ISLAM—I need to write a paper showing the influence of Islam on the governments of Muslim countries.

For a good source on Muslim history and culture, see:
Muslim Peoples, p. 130

NATIONAL ANTHEMS (784.71)—Chapter 7, p. 100—I need the words to the national anthem of Belgium.

See:
National Anthems of the World, p. 100

NATIVE AMERICANS (970.00497, 970.1–970.3)—Chapter 10, pp. 136—I need biographical information on Chief Joseph. I need to find out what tribe he led and describe their culture.

A good place to start is:
Encyclopedia of North American Indians, p. 136
A good biographical source is:
Great North American Indians, p. 136

THE NINETIES (1890s) (902, 973.02)—Chapter 10, pp. 122–123, 132–133—Where can I find a list of events showing what went on in different fields such as the arts and science during the 1890s?
Chronologies list significant events and make good starting points for reports on time periods. For lists of events of the 1890s, see:
The People's Chronology, p. 122

THE NINETIES (1990s) (902, 973.02)—Chapter 10, pp. 122–123, 132–133—How can I find significant worldwide events of the 1990s so I can choose some for a report?
Chronologies list significant events and make good starting points for reports on time periods. For lists of events of the 1990s, see the latest edition or supplement to:
Chronicle of the Twentieth Century, p. 122

NUTRITION (613.2)—Chapter 12, pp. 160–161—I need to identify calories, fat content, vitamins, and so forth for several foods.
The following source should help:
Nutritive Value of American Foods in Common Units, p. 160

OCEANS (550)—Chapter 16, pp. 214–217—I need to draw a map of the Mediterranean Sea and write a report about its wildlife, plants, history, and commercial use.
A good source for this information is:
The Times Atlas and Encyclopedia of the Sea, p. 217

OPERA (782)—Chapter 7, p. 98—I need information on the Paris Opera.
The best source on opera is:
New Grove Dictionary of Opera, p. 98

OZONE (550)—Chapter 16, pp. 214–217, 221–222—Does the ozone layer help us or hurt us? I need to find out for a project.
You might gain an answer from:
A Field Guide to the Atmosphere, p. 215
Magill's Survey of Science, Earth Science Series, p. 215

PHILOSOPHY (100)—Chapter 15, pp. 197–198—I need to explain the philosophy of Descartes.
> Major philosophers and their ideas can be found in:
>> *Dictionary of Philosophy and Religion,* p. 197
>> *Encyclopedia of Philosophy,* p. 197
>> *World Philosophy,* p. 198

PLANETS (523.4)—Chapter 16, pp. 207–210—I need to find information on the planets in the solar system, especially Mars.
> General encyclopedias, like *World Book Encyclopedia,* p. 22, give basic information plus a short bibliography. The *McGraw-Hill Encyclopedia of Science and Technology,* p. 200, provides scientific information. Other good reference sources include:
>> *Atlas of the Universe,* p. 207
>> *McGraw-Hill Encyclopedia of Astronomy,* p. 208
>> *Oxford Illustrated Encyclopedia of the Universe,* p. 209

PLATE TECTONICS (550)—Chapter 16, pp. 214–217—Where can I find an explanation of plate tectonics?
> Try:
>> *McGraw-Hill Encyclopedia of the Geological Sciences,* p. 216

PLAYS—See DRAMA

POEMS (808.81, 811, 821)—Chapter 11, p. 150—I need to find a poem whose theme is an emotion.
> For a subject, author, title, first line, and keyword (CD-ROM) index to poems, see:
>> *Columbia Granger Index to Poetry,* p. 150

POETRY (808.81, 811, 821)—Chapter 11, pp. 150—I need to find criticism of the poetry of Matthew Arnold.
> To find criticism of poetry, see:
>> *Critical Survey of Poetry,* p. 150
>> *The Chelsea House Library of Literary Criticism,* pp. 68, 148
>> *Nineteenth Century Literature Criticism,* pp. 69, 148

POLLUTION (574.5)—Chapter 16, pp. 214–217, 221–222—What are the particles in the air that make the air polluted?
> For information on air, water, and land pollution, see:
>> *A Field Guide to the Atmosphere,* p. 215
>> *Grzimek's Encyclopedia of Ecology,* p. 222

PREGNANCY (612.6, 613.9)—Chapter 12, pp. 159, 161–162—Where do I find information on teenage pregnancy?
Statistical information can be found in:
Health United States, p. 156
Statistical Abstract of the United States, p. 32
Discussion of issues can be found in:
Teenage Health Care, p. 160
Teenage Sexuality, p. 162
Many recent **newspaper and magazine articles** can be found. See Chapter 4 on searching indexes.
For discussion of pro and con issues relating to teen pregnancy, see:
Taking Sides, p. 35

PRESIDENTS (353, 973)—Chapter 13, pp. 183–185—Is there a book that tells everything about each president?
"Everything" might be a stretch, but a good biography and summary of each president's term of office can be found in:
The Complete Book of Presidents, p. 184
Facts about the Presidents, p. 184
For famous presidential speeches, such as Lincoln's Gettysburg Address, see:
Speeches of the American Presidents, p. 185
Inaugural addresses can be found in:
The Presidents Speak, p. 185
Information about the presidency itself can be found in:
The Presidency A to Z, p. 183

PRICES (330, 332)—Chapter 9, pp. 111–112—See also MONEY —I need to find out what a haircut cost in 1920.
For this information, and for comparative prices, wages, and incomes during the years 1860–1989, see:
The Value of a Dollar, p. 112
For comparative prices today in different parts of the United States, see:
American Cost of Living Survey, p. 111

PSYCHOLOGISTS (150.92)—Chapter 14, pp. 188–190—I need information on a famous psychologist.
For biographical information and information on individual psychological theories, try:
The Great Psychologists, p. 190
A Guide to Psychologists and Their Concepts, p. 190

PSYCHOLOGY (150)—Chapter 14, pp. 188–190—How can I compare and contrast the theories of two psychologists?

For general information on psychologists and their concepts, see:

The Gale Encyclopedia of Psychology, p. 188

Encyclopedia of Psychology, p. 188

Survey of Social Science: Psychology Series, p. 189

PSYCHOLOGY—HISTORY (150.9)—Chapter 14, p. 189—When did psychology start and how did it develop?

For complete background, from the Greeks on, see:

The Story of Psychology, p. 189

History of Psychology, p. 189

RAIN FORESTS (574.5)—Chapter 16, pp. 221–222—I need to find out how a tropical rain forest affects others parts of the world.

Start with:

Grzimek's Encyclopedia of Ecology, p. 222

REFORMATION (270.6, 909.5, 940.23)—Chapter 10, pp. 123–125; Chapter 15, pp. 194–195—See also HISTORY, MIDDLE AGES—Where can I find information that explains the causes and results of the Reformation?

A lengthy discussion of the Reformation can be found in:

The Encyclopedia of Religion, p. 194

RELIGION (200)—Chapter 15, pp. 194–195—I need to compare an Eastern religion with a Western religion.

You might get started with:

Dictionary of Comparative Religion, p. 194

For more information, go to:

The Encyclopedia of Religion, p. 194

RENAISSANCE (940.21)—Chapter 10, pp. 123–125—See also HISTORY, MIDDLE AGES—I need to write a paper on life during the Renaissance.

For this information, you might try:

The Oxford Illustrated History of Medieval Europe, p. 125

REVOLUTION, AMERICAN—See AMERICAN REVOLUTION

RIVERS (551.345, 574.526)—Chapter 16, pp. 214–217, 221–222—What's the longest river in the world?

Facts like these can be found in almanacs. See:

World Almanac and Book of Facts, p. 27

For information on the formation of rivers, see:
   Magill's Survey of Science, Earth Science Series, p. 215
   Standard Encyclopedia of the World's Rivers and Lakes, p. 216
For the ecology of rivers, see:
   Grzimek's Encyclopedia of Ecology, p. 222

ROCK (550)—See GEOLOGY

ROCK MUSIC (784.54)—Chapter 7, pp. 95–101—Where can I find information about rock groups and rock musicians?
   There are many sources on rock music. See:
   Encyclopedia of Rock Stars, p. 99
   The Harmony Illustrated Encyclopedia of Rock, p. 100
   The New Rolling Stone Encyclopedia of Rock and Roll, p. 99

ROME, ANCIENT (937)—Chapter 10, pp. 123–125—I need to write a paper telling how Rome was founded.
   See:
   Greek and Roman Life, p. 124
   Oxford History of the Classical World, p. 124

RUSSIA (947)—Chapter 10, pp. 130–131—How did Russia become the Soviet Union, then become Russia again?
   Try these sources for background and explanation:
   Cambridge Encyclopedia of Russia and the Soviet Union, p. 130
   A History of Russia, p. 131

SAINTS (200)—Chapter 15, pp. 196–197—I need biographical information on Saint [fill in the blank].
   Biographical information on most saints can be found in:
   The Book of Saints, p. 196
   New Catholic Encyclopedia, p. 197

SCIENCE (500)—Chapter 16, pp. 200–201—I have a list of scientific principles I have to define.
   Most science questions can be answered in detail by:
   McGraw-Hill Encyclopedia of Science and Technology, p. 200
   Another useful, less complicated source, is:
   The Addison-Wesley Science Handbook, p. 200

SCIENCE FAIR PROJECTS (507)—Chapter 16, pp. 201–202—I need to do a science fair project. Do you have any books to get me started?
   There are lots of books providing outlines of experiments. For two of the best, see:

More Science Experiments on File, p. 201
Science Experiments on File, p. 201

For information on how to select, research, and produce a science fair project, see:

The Complete Handbook of Science Fair Projects, p. 201

There are many indexes to science fair projects too. Try this one:

Science Experiments and Project Index, p. 201

SCIENTIFIC DISCOVERIES (509)—Chapter 16, p. 204—My teacher gave us a list of discoveries and inventions important to humanity—planets, electricity, radar, iron, copper—and we're supposed to fill in who made the discovery and when. Where do I look?

There are several great sources that list and explain many scientific discoveries and inventions. See:

Asimov's Chronology of Science and Discovery, p. 204
The Timetables of Science, p. 204

SCIENTISTS (500.92)—Chapter 16, pp. 205–206—I need to find some information on a scientist who's the same nationality I am.

For one of the best sources for this type of information, see:

Dictionary of Scientific Biography, p. 205

THE SEVENTIES (1970s) (902, 973.02)—Chapter 10, p. 133—Where can I find out about the dance crazes, songs, and fashions of the seventies?

Chronologies list significant events and make good starting points for reports on time periods. There are many available. See:

American Decades, p. 133
Chronicle of the Twentieth Century, p. 122
Day by Day: The Seventies, p. 133

SEX (613.9)—Chapter 12, pp. 161–162—Where can I find out about STDs?

Sexually transmitted diseases of all types are discussed in:

The Magic of Sex, p. 162
Sex Care, p. 162
The Sexually Transmitted Diseases, p. 166

Also consult in general sources, such as:

The Columbia University College of Physicians and Surgeons Complete Home Medical Guide, p. 160

SEX EDUCATION (613.9, 372.372)—Chapter 12, pp. 161–162—Where can I find out whether sex education should be allowed in the schools?

Arguments for and against this issue can be found in:

Taking Sides, p. 35
Teenage Sexuality, p. 162

SHAKESPEARE (822.33)—Chapter 11, pp. 149–150—I need to find out about the life and times of Shakespeare. How people dressed, what they ate, what games they played—stuff like that.
　　Some of this information might be found in:
　　The Shakespeare Handbook, p. 150
　　Historical sources may also help, such as:
　　The Cambridge Historical Encyclopedia of Great Britain and Ireland, p. 129

SHARKS (597)—Chapter 16, pp. 227–229—I want to write a report on sharks.
　　For information on sharks, see:
　　Encyclopedia of Aquatic Life, p. 227

SHORT STORIES—Chapter 11, p. 149—I need to find short stories about the quest for truth [the triumph of love, the need for tolerance, etc.].
　　The best source for finding short stories on specific topics is:
　　Short Story Index, p. 149

THE SIXTIES (1960s) (902, 973.02)—Chapter 10, p. 133—My teacher calls them the tumultuous sixties. Where can I find an outline of events that shows why they were the tumultuous?
　　Chronologies list significant events and make good starting points for reports on time periods. For lists of events of the 1960s, see:
　　American Decades, p. 133
　　Chronicle of the Twentieth Century, p. 122
　　Day by Day: The Sixties, p. 133

SKELETON (611.71)—Chapter 12, pp. 158–159—I need a picture of a human skeleton. I need to label the bones.
　　A useful source for diagrams and illustrations of the human body and its parts:
　　The Human Body on File, p. 159

SLEEP (154.6)—Chapter 12, p. 165; Chapter 14, p. 191—How does sleep affect health? I need to know for a report.
　　Two good sources are:
　　The Encyclopedia of Sleep and Dreaming, p. 191
　　The Encyclopedia of Sleep and Sleep Disorders, p. 165

SMOKING (363.19, 613.85, 616.865)—Chapter 12, pp. 167–169—I need statistics on smoking-related deaths and cancer. I need to find out why people smoke and why they shouldn't.

Statistics on smoking, cancer, and deaths related to these causes can be found in:

Cancer Facts and Figures, p. 165

Health United States, p. 156

Statistical Abstract of the United States, p. 32

For discussion of smoking, see:

Smoking, p. 168

Taking Sides: Clashing Views on Controversial Issues in Health and Society, p. 169

SNAKES (597.9)—Chapter 16, pp. 225–228—I need to find out which snakes bear live young and which produce eggs.

A general encyclopedia such as *World Book Encyclopedia* might provide a basic answer to this question. Other sources to check include:

The Encyclopedia of Reptiles and Amphibians, p. 227

Grzimek's Animal Life Encyclopedia, p. 225

SONGS (780)—Chapter 7, pp. 98–99, 100–101—I need to find some of the popular songs from the twenties, thirties, and forties.

For hits of the period, see:

Hit Parade, 1920–1955, p. 101

For words and music to songs of any era, you will probably have to use indexes. There are many—for example,

Song Index, p. 98

For recordings of period music, from Gregorian chant to the American Revolutionary period, and more, ask the information librarian for help.

SPAIN (946)—Chapter 10, p. 131—I need to find out about the Spanish-American War.

For history, see:

Spain, p. 131

SPORTS (796)—Chapter 17, pp. 232–235—I need biographical information on Jesse Owens.

Try:

A Hard Road to Glory, p. 234

For rules of various games and sports, see:

Rules of the Game, p. 233

For sports records, see:

Guinness Book of Sports Records, p. 232

SPORTS AND DRUGS (362.29, 613.71, 615.77)—Chapter 12, pp. 167–169 —See also DRUGS; SUBSTANCE ABUSE—I need information on the risks and benefits of performance-enhancing drug use by athletes.

Drug use by athletes is discussed in:

Encyclopedia of BioEthics, p. 194

Encyclopedia of Drug Abuse, p. 167

Many newspaper and magazine articles on this topic can also be found (see Chapter 4).

STEROIDS (362.29, 615.77)—See SPORTS AND DRUGS

STOCKS (332)—Chapter 9, pp. 114–115—I need to research the value of several stocks over several weeks [or months or years]. How do I do this?

Numerous excellent resources will help you with this research. See:

Moody's Handbook of Common Stocks, p. 115

Moody's Manuals, p. 115

Standard and Poor Stock Reports, p. 115

Value Line Investment Survey, p. 115

Of course, you can always use the *Wall Street Journal, New York Times,* or a local newspaper that carries stock exchange listings.

If you have trouble locating stock symbols or understanding the financial pages in the newspaper, see:

Common Stock Newspaper Abbreviations and Trading Symbols, p. 114

The Dow-Jones Irwin Guide to Using the Wall Street Journal, p. 114

STYLE MANUALS (808.02, 808.066)—See GRAMMAR

SUBSTANCE ABUSE (362.29, 613.8, 616.86)—Chapter 12, pp. 167–169 —See also ALCOHOL/ALCOHOLISM; DRUGS; MARIJUANA; SUBSTANCE ABUSE; SMOKING; TOBACCO—I need to write a paper about substance abuse and its effect on families.

For a useful overview of this problem, see

Chemical Dependency, p. 167

The Encyclopedia of Drug Abuse, p. 167

The Encyclopedia of Drugs and Alcohol, p. 168

Taking Sides: Clashing Views on Controversial Issues in Health and Society, p. 169

SUICIDE (179.7)—Chapter 15, p. 194; Chapter 3, pp. 34–35—Where do I find information on assisted suicide?

A controversial topic always, but more so recently, newspaper and magazine articles can be found using any of the common indexes (see Chapter 4). Also try:

The Encyclopedia of BioEthics, p. 194
Taking Sides, p. 35

SUPREME COURT DECISIONS (347.7326)—Chapter 13, pp. 182–183—Where can I get information on *Roe v. Wade* and other important Supreme Court cases?

There are many sources available. Try:

The Evolving Constitution, p. 182
Historic U.S. Court Cases, 1690–1990, p. 183
Leading Constitutional Decisions, p. 183

SURGERY (610.9, 617)—Chapter 12, pp. 157–169—I need pictures of surgical instruments used during the Civil War

Finding the right picture can be difficult and time-consuming. Try:

The Age of Miracles, p. 157
The Cambridge Illustrated History of Medicine, p. 157

SURROGATE MOTHERHOOD (306.8743)—Chapter 15, p. 194; Chapter 3, p. 34–35—Should people bear babies for other people? I need to write a paper telling why they should and shouldn't, and how this became possible.

Solid information on this controversial topic can be found in:

Encyclopedia of BioEthics, p. 194

TEENAGERS (155)—Chapter 14, p. 192—I need information on the problems of teenagers.

One of the best overall sources for information about teenagers is:

Encyclopedia of Adolescence, p. 192

TELEVISION (791.45)—Chapter 7, p. 101—I need to find pro and con discussions of the effects of television on society.

Good sources for this topic include:

Encyclopedia of BioEthics, p. 194
Taking Sides, p. 35

To research people, shows, networks, and other aspects of television, see:

Les Brown's Encyclopedia of Television, p. 101

THE THIRTIES (1930s) (902, 973.02)—Chapter 10, pp. 122–123, 132–133—Was the Great Depression in the thirties? How do I find out?

Chronologies list significant events and make good starting points for reports on time periods. For lists of events of the 1930s, see:

American Decades, p. 133

Chronicle of the Twentieth Century, p. 122

TOBACCO (613.85, 616.865)—Chapter 12, pp. 167–169—See also SMOKING—I need arguments on the question, "Is tobacco a drug?"

See:

Encyclopedia of Drug Abuse, p. 167

Taking Sides: Clashing Views on Controversial Issues in Health and Society, p. 169

This topic has recently been in the news, so newspaper and magazine articles can also be found. (See Chapter 4.)

TORNADOES (550)—Chapter 16, pp. 214–217—I need to find out how tornadoes form.

Tornadoes and other weather phenomenon are explained in:

Audubon Society Field Guide to North American Weather, p. 214

Recent tornadoes—their paths, damage, inflicted, and so on—can be researched through newspaper and magazine articles. See Chapter 4 for how to do this.

TRACKS (590)—Chapter 16, p. 225—I need pictures of animal tracks for my project.

See:

A Field Guide to Animal Tracks, p. 225

TRAVEL (380, 910s)—Chapter 9, p. 116—I need to write to a state for information about it. Where do I get an address?

For addresses of chambers of commerce, tourist bureaus, and embassies, see:

World Chamber of Commerce Directory, p. 116

TREES (580)—Chapter 16, pp. 223–224—How can I identify trees?

Shape, height, bark, leaves, flowers, and fruit are all characteristics used to identify trees. Information of this type can be found in:

The Oxford Encyclopedia of Trees of the World, p. 224

TV—See TELEVISION

THE TWENTIES (1920s) (902, 973.02)—Chapter 10, pp. 122–123, 132–133—What happened during the twenties other than the stock market crash? I need to write a report on the decade.

Chronologies list significant events and make good starting points for reports on time periods. For lists of events of the 1920s, see:
Chronicle of the Twentieth Century, p. 122

UNITED NATIONS (327)—Chapter 13, pp. 178–179—Where can I find the UN Charter?

For the charter and background on the UN, see:
Everyone's United Nations, p. 178

For the charter and other documents and a detailed summary of UN activities during each year, see:
Yearbook of the United Nations, p. 179

UNITED STATES HISTORY (973)—Chapter 10, pp. 131–138—See also AMERICAN REVOLUTION; COLONIAL LIFE AND TIMES—I need to write a paper on the Cuban missile crisis. Where can I find information?

A lot of information is available on this major event in American and world history. Start with:
America in the 20th Century, pp. 77, 133
Twentieth-Century America, pp. 77, 80, 137

VIETNAM (915.97, 959.7)—Chapter 10, pp. 127–128—See also COUNTRIES —Where can I find information on the history, culture, and government of Vietnam?

Good information can be found in:
Encyclopedia of Asian History, p. 128
Worldmark Encyclopedia of the Nations, p. 127

VIETNAM WAR (959.7043)—Chapter 10, pp. 127–128, 133, 137—I need to write about the conflicts in America during the Vietnam War.

Two good starting points are:
America in the 20th Century, p. 77, 133
Twentieth-Century America, p. 77, 80, 137

VIOLENCE (152.4, 364.1)—Chapter 14, p. 190—Can I find out what the causes of criminal violence are?

Violence in all its forms is discussed in:
Encyclopedia of Violence, p. 190

VOLCANOES (551.21)—Chapter 16, pp. 214–217—I need to find a list of volcanoes: when they erupted, how many people died, how much damage they did.

Modern volcanoes—when they erupted, numbers of people killed and injured, monetary damage—can be researched through newspapers and magazine articles. (See Chapter 4.) A good reference source to try, among others, is:

Encyclopedia of Earthquakes and Volcanoes, p. 215

WATER (551.4)—Chapter 16, pp. 214–217—How do I find out about the relationship between groundwater and water wells used for drinking?

This aspect of hydrology is covered in:

Magill's Survey of Science, Earth Science Series, p. 215

WEATHER (551.5)—Chapter 16, pp. 214–217—I need to compare the weather of Moscow, Paris, and New York.

A book that will help is:

Times Books World Weather Guide, p. 217

WETLANDS (574.526)—Chapter 16, pp. 221–222—I need to answer the question, Why are wetlands important to a healthy environment?

For a good explanation, see:

Grzimek's Encyclopedia of Ecology, p. 222

WHALES (599.5)—Chapter 16, pp. 228–229—How can I find out the different body parts of a whale?

This book illustrates and labels the body parts:

Whales, Dolphins and Porpoises, p. 229

WIFE ABUSE (362.83, 364.1555)—Chapter 14, p. 190; Chapter 15, p. 194
—I need to find the causes of wife abuse and effects on women and children.

Good places to start are:

Encyclopedia of BioEthics, p. 194
Encyclopedia of Violence, p. 190

WOMEN'S BIOGRAPHY (920.72)—Chapter 10, pp. 139–141—I need to write about a woman who made a difference in colonial or Revolutionary days.

To identify such a woman, search in:

Notable American Women, 1607–1975, p. 141

WOMEN'S HISTORY/ISSUES (305.4)—Chapter 3, pp. 34-35—Have women's lives improved due to feminism and the liberation movement of the 1960s?

Pro and con discussions can be found in:
Encyclopedia of BioEthics, p. 194
Taking Sides, p. 35

WORLD HISTORY—See HISTORY

WORLD WAR I (940.3-940.4)—Chapter 10, p. 126—I need to write a paper on whether the balance of power shifted because of World War I.

Excellent coverage of World War I can be found in:
World War One Source Book, p. 126

WORLD WAR II (940.53-940.54)—Chapter 10, p. 126—I need to identify which countries were the Allies and which were the Axis powers.

There are several sources available, but the best one to start with for this question is:
Encyclopedia of the Second World War, p. 126

APPENDIX A

Dewey Decimal Classification

000   GENERALITIES

010 Bibliography
020 Library and Information
    Sciences
030 General Encyclopedia
    Works
040 Unassigned
050 General Serial Publications
060 General Organizations and
    Museology
070 Journalism, Publishing,
    Newspapers
080 General Collections
090 Manuscripts and Book
    Rarities

**100   PHILOSOPHY AND
RELATED DISCIPLINES**

110 Metaphysics
120 Epistemology, Causation,
    Humankind
130 Paranormal Phenomena and
    Arts

140 Specific Philosophical
    Viewpoints
150 Psychology
160 Logic
170 Ethics (Moral Philosophy)
180 Ancient, Medieval,
    Oriental
190 Modern Western
    Philosophy

200   RELIGION

210 Natural Religion
220 Bible
230 Christian Theology
240 Christian Moral and
    Devotional
250 Local Church and Religious
    Orders
260 Social and Ecclesiastical
    Theology
270 History and Geography of
    Church
280 Christian Denominations
    and Sects

290 Other and Comparative
    Religions

300 SOCIAL SCIENCES

310 Statistics
320 Political Science
330 Economics
340 Law
350 Public Administration
360 Social Problems and
    Services
370 Education
380 Commerce (Trade)
390 Customs, Etiquette, Folklore

400 LANGUAGE

410 Linguistics
420 English and Anglo-Saxon
    Languages
430 Germanic Languages,
    German
440 Romance Languages,
    French
450 Italian, Romanian, Rhaeto-
    Romanic
460 Spanish and Portuguese
    Languages
470 Italic Languages,
    Latin
480 Hellenic, Classical Greek
490 Other Languages

500 PURE SCIENCES

510 Mathematics
520 Astronomy and Allied
    Sciences
530 Physics
540 Chemistry and Allied
    Sciences

550 Sciences of Earth and Other
    Worlds
560 Paleontology
570 Life Sciences
580 Botanical Sciences
590 Zoological Sciences

600 TECHNOLOGY
(APPLIED SCIENCES)

610 Medical Sciences
620 Engineering and Allied
    Operations
630 Agriculture and Related
    Technologies
640 Home Economics and Family
    Living
650 Management and Auxiliary
    Services
660 Chemical and Related
    Technologies
670 Manufactures
680 Manufactures for Specific
    Uses
690 Buildings

700 THE ARTS

710 Civic and Landscape Art
720 Architecture
730 Plastic Arts, Sculpture
740 Drawing, Decorative and
    Minor Arts
750 Painting and Paintings
760 Graphic Arts, Prints
770 Photography and
    Photographs
780 Music
790 Recreational and
    Performing Arts

**800 LITERATURE
(BELLES-LETTRES)**

810 American Literature in
English
820 English and Anglo-Saxon
Literatures
830 Literatures of Germanic
Languages
840 Literatures of Romance
Languages
850 Italian, Romanian, Rhaeto-
Romanic
860 Spanish and Portuguese
Literatures
870 Italic Literatures, Latin
880 Hellenic Literatures, Greek
890 Literatures of Other
Languages

**900 GENERAL GEOGRAPHY
AND HISTORY**

910 General Geography, Travel
920 General Biography and
Genealogy
930 General History of Ancient
World
940 General History of Europe
950 General History of Asia
960 General History of Africa
970 General History of North
America
980 General History of South
America
990 General History of Other
Areas

APPENDIX B

Library of Congress Classification System

A: General Works
B: Philosophy and Religion
C: History—Auxiliary Sciences
D: History and Topography (except America)
E–F: American History
G: Geography, Anthropology, Folklore, Manners and Customs,
         Recreation
H: Social Sciences
J: Political Sciences
K: Law of the United States
L: Education
M: Music and Books on Music
N: Fine Arts
P: Language and Literature
Q: Science
R: Medicine
S: Agriculture and Plant and Animal History
T: Technology
U: Military Science
V: Naval Sciences
Z: Bibliography and Library Science

Glossary

Abstract—A brief summary of the full text of a newspaper, magazine, or other published article.

Academic Library—A library affiliated with or belonging to a college or university and supporting that institution's coursework. **See also Public Library; School Library; Special Library.**

Adult Department—The section in a public library housing books, reference sources, magazines, newspapers, and other materials written to adult reading levels.

Adult Fiction—Fiction (stories made up to entertain and instruct) written primarily for adult readers.

Bibliographic Record—A record comprising details about a book, periodical, or audiovisual item that describe the item so it can be distinguished from others: author or authors, editor, or compiler; title; publisher; place and date of publication; edition; number of pages; whether an index, bibliography, or illustrations are included; even physical size.

Bibliography—A list of books, magazine articles, or other nonbook media on a particular subject or a mix of subjects. A bibliography can be arranged alphabetically by subject, author, or title; chronologically by date of publication; or topically by large subject divisions. There are even bibliographies of bibliographies, which are lists of bibliographies. A bibliography at the end of an article, term paper, or book cites sources used to compile the information from which parts of the book or article are written. A bibliography also refers the reader to these sources for more information. **See also Footnotes; Plagiarize.**

Boolean Logic—A form of computer logic based on algebra that reduces the answers to all questions to either true or false, yes or no. Boolean operators refer to the words **and, or, not,** which are used in the question to include or exclude. For example, a computer search could be executed for all BRONTEs **and** CHARLOTTEs. Another search could be executed for all BRONTEs **not** CHARLOTTEs.

Browse—To look casually through library shelves for books or other items of interest.

Call Number—The Dewey Decimal or Library of Congress number on the spine of the book that corresponds to the number given in the card or computerized catalog. This number places the book on the shelves with other books of similar subject matter. It also allows users to find the specific book once it is identified in the library's catalog. In the past, library collections were stored away from the public, which had access only to the catalogs, so the spine number was literally the number used to "call" for the book. A slip of paper was filled out with the call number, and a library staff member went to fetch the book for the person needing it.

Catalog Card—A card on which is typed the bibliographic information for a book. The card was filed alphabetically with cards for other books, creating a catalog or index to the library's collection. Now the same information is listed in computerized catalogs.

CD-ROM (compact disk read-only memory)—A compact disk similar to a musical recording disk that contains information that can be searched using a microcomputer with a CD-ROM drive. These are increasingly sophisticated, with the latest versions containing sound, moving images, and hypermedia links. **See also Multimedia.**

Children's Department—A collection of books and other materials within a public library suitable for children up to about age 12.

Children's Fiction—Stories written especially for children.

Circulation—To the location in a library where materials are returned or checked out, usually near the entrance. The **circulating** collection is that portion of the library's materials that can be borrowed from the building, as distinguished from the reference materials (**noncirculating**), which cannot be checked out of the building. A user who does not find what he or she is looking for in the circulating collection may request it at the circulation or reference desk, and it will then be set aside when it is returned to the library and the user who wants it will be told when it becomes available. In most libraries materials may be renewed and retained for an additional lending period.

Citations—See Footnotes.

College Library—See Academic Library.

Compact Disk Read-Only Memory—See CD-ROM.

Computerized Catalog—See OPAC.

Data—Information.

Database—Data stored on a computer (online) or transferred to and stored on a disk (CD-ROM or floppy). **See also Online Databases; CD-ROM.**

Decimal Point—See Dewey Decimal System.

Dewey Decimal System—The system found in most public libraries that allows a library to sequence materials by subject. There are three numbers to the left of the decimal point, such as 973. The number to the far left, 9, indicates the most general classification. The 9 signifies history. All history materials are grouped together in the 900 section. The next number, 7, indicates the subdivision under history. 970 indicates all materials about the history of the Americas, both North and South. The last number to the left of the decimal point indicates a further subdivision of materials about the history of the Americas. The 3 in 973 indicates materials about the history of the United States. All three numbers together indicate books about the United States. Numbers after the decimal point indicate further chronological or time subdivisions within the category. 973.46, for example, indicates materials about a particular period of United States history—in this case, the Revolutionary period, 1776.

The major Dewey divisions are:

100   General Works
200   Religion

300   Politics and Economics
400   Language
500   Science
600   Applied Science
700   Art and Sports
800   Literature
900   Travel and History

DIALOG—A fee-based online database service. It offers several hundred databases on a variety of topics, (business, science, magazines and newspapers, patents, etc.). Services such as DIALOG enable a library to expand its resources beyond its building, though the cost of using DIALOG can often be high.

Dictionaries—Books or databases that list individual words, define the words briefly, and tell how the words originated. Some dictionaries, such as the *Oxford English Dictionary,* also show the succession of meanings through a long period of time up to the present day.

8-mm Cartridge—See Microfilm/Microfiche.

Encyclopedias—Multivolume book sets (also available on computers in CD-ROM format) that contain articles arranged alphabetically on a wide variety of topics. They are regularly revised. CD-ROM versions may even be updated daily online. Encyclopedias are available for children (*World Book* and *Compton's*) and adults (*Encyclopaedia Britannica* or *Grolier*). The *Britannica* has both a Micropaedia, consisting of short articles, and a Macropaedia, with longer articles. It is often helpful to start research on an unfamiliar topic with a short article from a basic encyclopedia, such as *World Book,* to get a brief overview of the topic and become familiar with the overall terminology. Some encyclopedias are specific for a subject, such as the *McGraw-Hill Encyclopedia of Science and Technology.*

Fiction—Made-up stories, generally considered to be not true.

Footnotes—Brief listings, usually found at the bottom of a page, of books or articles that the author used in finding information for the book or article. They are helpful in research since they are an excellent source of information on books and articles on related topics. Sometimes notes are found in the back of the book or at the end of each chapter. Works listed in the footnotes are called **citations. See also Bibliography.**

Full Text—The entire text of an article, as opposed to an **abstract** or a **citation**. Online and CD-ROM databases do offer full-text articles. They may also offer abstracts or citations only.

General Encyclopedia—See Encyclopedias.

Hard Copy—Text printed on paper. A magazine article may be found full text on DIALOG or on a CD-ROM, but the words and letters are images on a screen or monitor. Once the article is printed out on paper, it is referred to as being in hard copy. The original magazine itself, published in paper, is also called hard copy.

Hypermedia—A digital linking methodology for digital reference works such as CD-ROMs that make it possible to link various portions of a database referring users to related relevant material (e.g., biographies related to historical events, or literary works related to styles of writing).

Index—A section in the back of a book arranged alphabetically that lists subjects contained in the book. These are usually very specific subjects rather than the more general subjects found in the Table of Contents at the beginning of most nonfiction books. Indexes often refer to collections of other books, such as indexes of magazines or periodicals. Databases are also indexed or serve as indexes to other materials.

Interdisciplinary Assignment—An assignment for students designed to include elements from many courses. For example, history, literature, mathematics, and geography may all be incorporated into an assignment on Shakespeare.

Interlibrary Loan (ILL)—A system that facilitates libraries' borrowing from one another. A user who cannot find a book in the library's computer or catalog can ask the library to borrow it from another library. Users can often identify the book in another library's catalog by a remote electronic search, and some libraries send the book based on an electronic request.

Internet—A worldwide network of communication that can be accessed by a computer with a modem, which connects by telephone line to an Internet provider. The Internet, among a host of other capabilities, can access:
- Library catalogs all over the world to locate books
- List serves that facilitate discussion of many topics
- Current information on many research topics

- Reviews of books and films
- Databases on hundreds of topics
- Reference sources

Keyword, Keyword Searching—Commonly to search by computer program for a word anywhere it occurs in a database. This differs from subject searching, in which specific subject headings have been assigned to the data, and only the subjects may be searched. Keyword searching can be helpful and successful but it can also produce more than is needed—much that may have nothing to do with what the user needs. Some keywords may have no practical result at all, usually because the terms are so common. "History" or "U.S. History" may prove unsuccessful keyword searches because the words are used so frequently.

LAN (Local Area Network)—Computer terminals in the library and within a radius of a mile that are connected together. They may include online public access catalogs, databases, and connections to the Internet. **See also OPAC; Database; Internet.**

Library of Congress Cataloging System—A letter-based system for cataloging and organizing books, it is used by most academic libraries. It signifies major subject divisions with letters. Since there are 26 letters in the alphabet but only 10 major numeric divisions in the Dewey Decimal system, this system has more major divisions than the Dewey system, allowing for a better breakdown of very large collections. Several letters have not yet been assigned to subjects. **See also Dewey Decimal System.**

Macropaedia—The multivolume main portion of the *Encyclopaedia Britannica.*

Magazines—See Periodicals.

Master's in Library Science (MLS)—The degree commonly held by trained librarians. The master's is an advanced degree, completed following a bachelor's degree. The master's requires successful completion of all coursework in the specifics of library operation, including reference service, children's service, cataloging, management, library automation, acquisitions, collection development and management, and readers' advisory services.

Microfilm/Microfiche—Photographing magazines and newspapers and storing the reduced (micro) image on film. Libraries can store many more magazines and newspapers than they possibly could in print, thus making more titles and more years available to library users. They reduce the fire hazard of storing shelves full of magazines and newspapers. They reduce loss of magazines and newspapers to deterioration, theft, or vandalism. Microfilm commonly is produced in three formats: 16-mm roll film, 8-mm roll film stored in plastic cartridges, and microfiche, which is a flat 4" x 6" film card. Microfilm formats are read on special machines with a magnifying lens. These machines are usually equipped with photocopiers, allowing users to take the text home in hard copy. **See also Hard Copy; Periodicals.**

Micropaedia—The two-volume quick reference portion of the *Encyclopaedia Britannica.*

Multimedia—A CD-ROM format that includes text, audio (music, speeches), and visual (usually film clips or photographs).

Noncirculating—See Circulation.

Nonfiction—Publications based on fact or opinion and thus considered to be true, as opposed to made-up stories (fiction), which are considered to be imagined and not true. **See also Fiction.**

Online Databases—Databases stored on computer and accessed over telephone lines through another computer and a modem. When the two computers are connected, they are said to be online. The databases may be business or scientific databases, indexes, magazines or newspapers, books, or just about anything else imaginable as long as it consists of data of some kind stored on a computer. **See also Database.**

OPAC (Online Public Access Catalog)—Computer terminals for public use in the library that contain the library's catalog of books and other materials. In addition they may include several databases on the library's local area network (LAN). These databases may include encyclopedias, dictionaries, a thesaurus, and a magazine index. Selections of which catalog or database to search are usually made through the menu (home) page.

Periodicals—Publications issued periodically by a publisher. Magazines are a particular type of periodical, often published at regular weekly, monthly, or quarterly intervals. Periodicals are often indexed in print, digital, or CD-ROM sources. In many libraries, older back-issue periodicals are available in microformats or on digital full-text databases. Users must first identify the particular issue needed by looking it up in an index. **See also Microfilm/Microfiche.**

Plagiarize—To copy someone else's work or thought exactly, without giving that person credit. Penalties for this type of theft can be severe. The originator of thoughts, words, or work must be credited.

Postcoordinated Searching Method—Database searching that allows a library user to combine terms in the search. **See also Keyword/Keyword Searching.**

Precoordinated Searching Method—Searching that allows only one term to be searched at a time. **See also Subject Searching.**

Predictability—A term suggesting that on finding one item through a catalog or database search, a careful look at that item will suggest others terms to search. Searching those terms will yield other items.

Primary Source—A source created at the time of the event—for example, newspaper articles, soldiers' journals or letters, official army documents, or a general's logbook from the Civil War.

Propaedia—A special volume of the *Encyclopaedia Britannica* that outlines the branches of knowledge.

Public Library—A library supported by tax dollars and available for all to use, usually at no charge. **See also Academic Library; School Library; Special Library.**

Pyramid Style—A style of writing that places the most important information in the first paragraph and then fans out the explanatory information in the following paragraphs.

Reels—Holders for rolls of microfilm.

Reference—The part of the library that contains reference materials that cannot be borrowed from the library because they are frequently consulted by large numbers of library users. It often includes a desk or counter where several librarians work with library users to answer their questions. The reference collection of books is arranged in a subject sequence and marked "R" or "REF" on the spine. In the library catalog or computer they are signified by an R or REF over or in front of the Dewey classification number. This part of the library also contains several computer terminals and microfilm or microfiche readers for searching databases.

Reference (or Information) Desk—The desk in the library from which reference (or information) librarians serve their customers. **See also Reference; Reference Librarians.**

Reference (or Information) Librarians—Librarians who earned the master's of library science degree in graduate school and also hold a bachelor's degree in another subject. They work in the Reference (or Information) Department and have concentrated on learning what materials the library has in its collections, especially the reference sources. They know how to use these sources and where information of specific types is most likely to be found. Their main job is to assist library users in finding the materials and information they are seeking. Reference librarians are experts. **See also Master's in Library Science.**

Reference Sources—A general term used to describe books, databases, and other materials that hold information and have organized it, and provided indexes, so library users can find the information they are looking for.

Roll Film—See Microfilm/Microfiche.

School Library—A library in a school, whether high school, middle or junior high school, or elementary school, that provides reading material for the school's students and supports the coursework offered by the school. **See also Academic Library; Public Library; Special Library.**

See and See Also References—Headings in the card catalog or OPAC referring to other subjects that have more material on the subject. For example, if you looked under the subject "Snakes" you may find some materials, and you may also find a note that says, "See also Reptiles" telling you to look under that other heading for more materials on snakes. "See" references tell you that you have not used the correct heading used by the catalogers. "See also" references tell you that you have used a correct heading, but that other related materials may be found under other headings.

Serendipity—A term referring to the happy occasion when more items (or items closer to what is needed) are found in the catalog or database search than originally expected.

16 mm—See Microfilm/Microfiche.

Special Library—Libraries with focused collections—for example, a library in a business or corporation, a law library, a library in a museum, or a local history library. **See also Academic Library; Public Library; School Library.**

Subject Headings—Subjects selected by the cataloger to match as closely as possible the subject covered by the work being cataloged. They are specific, not general. For example, a book covering the Reconstruction period after the American Civil War would be listed under "United States History 1866–1877" and not under "United States History—Civil War." Subjects elected by catalogers often differ from the "natural language subjects" used by many library users. It is sometimes helpful to look up the subject in the index to a list of subject headings used by catalogers, such as the Library of Congress List of Subject Headings, to find the correct subject heading.

Subject Searching—A method of searching card catalogs and online library catalogs, as well as most other searchable databases, by subject term. In card catalogs the subject catalog and the author/title catalog are sometimes separated. In other libraries author/title and subject cards are interfiled. In either case, subject headings at the top of the card are usually all in capital letters. In online catalogs and databases, a subject term search box is usually provided. The user types in the subject term, and the computer retrieves all the listings using that subject term. **See also Keyword/Keyword Searching; Subject Headings.**

Superintendent of Documents (SuDoc)—Considered the publisher of documents published by the U.S. government. The Superintendent of Documents provides a numbering system for organizing the documents so they can be located. It's sort of a Dewey Decimal system equivalent for government documents. The abbreviated name is "SuDoc Number." Some libraries have special areas where all government documents are collected and organized. Some libraries are either partial or full depositories for government documents, meaning the library has agreed to store the documents, and the government sends them selected (partial depository) or all (full depository) documents. Many libraries collect state documents too.

Table of Contents—A sequential list of chapter headings usually found in the beginning of a book. This list is an excellent guide to the general topics covered in the book. The index found in the rear of the book is a more detailed guide to every name and topic in the book. **See also Indexes.**

URL—Universal (or uniform) resource locator used on the Internet to locate a particular Internet site.

Vertical Files—Rows of tall metal file drawers containing pamphlets, maps, articles, and photographs on a wide variety of subjects. They are usually arranged alphabetically by subject, but sometimes libraries have special vertical files on topics of local interest.

World Wide Web—An Internet resource of information on thousands of topics. **See also Internet.**

Bibliography

American Reference Books Annual. Littleton, CO: Libraries Unlimited, 1970–

Guide to Reference Books. Robert Balay, ed. Chicago: American Library Association, 1996. 11th ed.

Guide to Reference Books for School Media Centers. Christine Gehrt Wynar. Littleton, CO: Libraries Unlimited, 1986. 3d ed.

Guide to Reference Books for School Media Centers. Margaret Irby Nichols. Littleton, CO: Libraries Unlimited, 1992. 4th ed.

Kister's Best Encyclopedias: A Comparative Guide to General and Specialized Encyclopedias. Kenneth F. Kister. Phoenix, AZ: Oryx Press, 1994. 2d ed.

Magazines for Libraries. Bill Katz and Linda Sternberg Katz. New York: R. R. Bowker, 1989. 6th ed.

Public Library Catalog: A Guide to Reference Books and Adult Nonfiction. Juliette Yaakov, ed. New York: H. W. Wilson, 1994. 10th ed. Supp. 1994, 1995.

Reference Books for Children. Carolyn Sue Peterson and Ann D. Fenton. Metuchen, NJ: Scarecrow Press, 1992. 4th ed.

Reference Sources: A Brief Guide. Eleanor A. Swidan. Baltimore, MD: Enoch Pratt Free Library, 1988. 9th ed.

Reference Sources for Small and Medium-Sized Libraries. Jovian P. Lang, ed. Chicago: American Library Association, 1992. 5th ed.

10,000 Ideas for Term Papers, Projects and Reports. Kathryn Lamm. New York: Macmillan, 1995. 4th ed.

Title Index

Subject Index

television, 101, 277–278
tennis, 237–238
term paper guides, 152–153
theater, 102; musical, 102
thesauruses, 145
Thirties (1930s), 278
Time, 37, 41
tobacco, 278
top hits, 100
tornadoes, 278
trade,116
travel, 278
trees, 223, 224
Twenties (1920s), 279

U.S. News and World Report, 38
UMI (University Microfilm Inc.), 44, 47, 49
uniform resource locator, 52
United Nations, 279
United States: atlases, 132; bibliographies, 132; chronologies, 132; Constitution, 134; dictionaries and encyclopedias, 135;   diplomatic history, 134; everyday life, 135; history, 131–138, 279; history general sources, 136; history primary sources, 137; indexes, 132; political history, 136; Revolution, 137–138; statistics, 138
universal resource locator, 52
URL, 52–53, 58

Vermont Life, 42
"Victorian Bibliography," 71
videocassette, 4
Vietnam, 279
Vietnam War, 279
Village Voice, 42
violence, 280
viruses, 166–167
volcanoes, 215, 280
Von Baeyer, Hans, 22

Walker, Janice R., 59
Wall Street Journal, 42, 45
water, 280
weather, 214, 217, 280
Web, 51, 53, 57, 58, 59

Web Crawler, 14
wetlands, 280
whales, 229, 280
What Is the World Made Of?, 20, 26
wife abuse, 280
wildlife, 221, 222, 225
Wired, 42
women: African American, 139; biography, 139, 141, 281; history/issues, 281; in chemistry and physics, 213; in science, 206; in sports, 234–235
Women's Sports and Fitness, 41
word usage, 146
World of the Atom, 26
World War I, 126, 281
World War II, 126–127, 281
World Wide Web, 51–52, 105, 106
Writer's Digest, 42

Yahoo!, 14, 53–57, 72, 105
young adult: department, 5; section, 5

Zen, 197

About the Authors

FRANK FERRO is the Chief of Public Services at the Norwalk, Connecticut Public Library. He has served as a public librarian since 1977 and was head of the Information Department from 1987 to 1997.

NOLAN LUSHINGTON is Associate Professor of Library Science at Southern Connecticut State University. He has worked as a library consultant for over 15 years and has published books on library design.